HANDBOOK OF GARDEN SCIENCE

HANDBOOK OF GARDEN SCIENCE

By

Dr. Shubhrata R. Mishra

Deptt. of Botany
Vikram University
Ujjain (M.P.)
(India)

DPH

DISCOVERY PUBLISHING HOUSE PVT. LTD.
NEW DELHI-110 002

Published by:
Tilak Wasan
DISCOVERY PUBLISHING HOUSE PVT. LTD.
4383/4A, Ansari Road, Darya Ganj
New Delhi-110 002 (India)
Phone : +91-11-23279245, 43596064-65
Fax : +91-11-23253475
E-mail : parul.wasan@gmail.com
discoverypublishinghouse@gmail.com
web : www.discoverypublishinggroup.com

First Edition: **2012**

ISBN: 978-93-5056-008-2

Handbook of Garden Science

Printed at:
Shree Balaji Art Press
Delhi

Preface

Gardening is the practice of growing plants. Ornamental plants are normally grown for their flowers, foliage, overall appearance, or for their dyes. Useful plants are grown for consumption (vegetables, fruits, herbs, and leaf vegetables) or for medicinal use. A gardener is someone who practices gardening.

Gardening ranges in scale from fruit orchards, to long boulevard plantings with one or more different types of shrubs, trees and herbaceous plants, to residential yards including lawns and foundation plantings, to large or small containers grown inside or outside. Gardening may be very specialized, with only one type of plant grown, or involve a large number of different plants in mixed plantings. It involves an active participation in the growing of plants, and tends to be labour intensive, which differentiates it from farming or forestry. Gardening also takes place in non-residential green areas, such as parks, public or semi-public gardens (botanical gardens or zoological gardens), amusement and amusement parks, along transportation corridors, and around tourist attractions and garden hotels. In these situations, a staff of gardeners or groundskeepers maintains the gardens.

Indoor gardening is concerned with the growing of houseplants within a residence or building, in a conservatory, or in a greenhouse. Indoor gardens are sometimes incorporated as part of air-conditioning or heating systems.

Native plant gardening is concerned with the use of native plants with or without the intent of creating wildlife habitat. The goal is to create a garden in harmony with, and adapted to a given area. This type of gardening typically reduces water usage, maintenance, and fertilization costs, while increasing native faunal interest.

Water gardening is concerned with growing plants adapted to pools and ponds. Bog gardens are also considered a type of water garden. These all require special conditions and considerations. A simple water garden may consist solely of a tub containing the water and plant(s). In aquascaping, a garden is created within an aquarium tank.

Container gardening is concerned with growing plants in any type of container either indoors or outdoors. Common containers are pots, hanging baskets, and planters. Container gardening is usually used in atriums and on balconies, patios, and roof tops.

Garden design is considered to be an art in most cultures, distinguished from gardening, which generally means *garden maintenance*. In Japan, Samurai and Zen monks were often required to build decorative gardens or practice related skills like flower arrangement known as *ikebana*. In 18th century Europe, country estates were refashioned by landscape gardeners into formal gardens or landscaped park lands, such as at Versailles, France or Stowe, England. Today, landscape architects and garden designers continue to produce artistically creative designs for private garden spaces.

Author

Contents

1

Introduction

Gardening is the practice of growing plants. Ornamental plants are normally grown for their flowers, foliage, overall appearance, or for their dyes. Useful plants are grown for consumption (vegetables, fruits, herbs, and leaf vegetables) or for medicinal use. A gardener is someone who practices gardening.

Gardening ranges in scale from fruit orchards, to long boulevard plantings with one or more different types of shrubs, trees and herbaceous plants, to residential yards including lawns and foundation plantings, to large or small containers grown inside or outside. Gardening may be very specialized, with only one type of plant grown, or involve a large number of different plants in mixed plantings. It involves an active participation in the growing of plants, and tends to be labour intensive, which differentiates it from farming or forestry.

Residential gardening takes place near the home, in a space referred to as the garden. Although a garden typically is located on the land near a residence, it may also be located on a roof, in an atrium, on a balcony, in a windowbox, or on a patio or vivarium.

Gardening also takes place in non-residential green areas, such as parks, public or semi-public gardens (botanical gardens or zoological gardens), amusement and amusement parks, along transportation corridors, and around tourist attractions and garden hotels. In these situations, a staff of gardeners or groundskeepers maintains the gardens.

Indoor gardening is concerned with the growing of houseplants within a residence or building, in a conservatory, or in a greenhouse. Indoor gardens are sometimes incorporated as part of air conditioning or heating systems.

Native plant gardening is concerned with the use of native plants with or without the intent of creating wildlife habitat. The goal is to create a garden in harmony with, and adapted to a given area. This type of gardening typically reduces water usage, maintenance, and fertilization costs, while increasing native faunal interest.

Water gardening is concerned with growing plants adapted to pools and ponds. Bog gardens are also considered a type of water garden. These all require special conditions and considerations. A simple water garden may consist solely of a tub containing the water and plant(s). In aquascaping, a garden is created within an aquarium tank.

Container gardening is concerned with growing plants in any type of container either indoors or outdoors. Common containers are pots, hanging baskets, and planters. Container gardening is usually used in atriums and on balconies, patios, and roof tops.

Community gardening is a social activity in which an area of land is gardened by a group of people, providing access to fresh produce and plants as well as access to satisfying labour, neighbourhood improvement, sense of community and connection to the environment. Community gardens are typically owned in trust by local governments on non-profits.

Garden sharing partners landowners with gardeners in need of land. These shared gardens, typically front or back yards, are usually used to produce food that is divided between the two parties.

Gardeners

A 'gardener' is any person involved in gardening, arguably the oldest occupation, from the hobbyist in a residential garden, the homeowner supplementing the family food with a small vegetable garden or orchard, to an employee in a plant nursery or the head gardener in a large estate.

The term gardener is also used to describe garden designers and landscape gardeners, who are involved chiefly in the design of gardens, rather than the practical aspects of horticulture.

Gardening Departments and Centres

Gardening departments and centres mainly sell plants, sundries, and garden accessories, but in recent times, many now stock outdoor leisure products as diverse as spas, furniture, and barbecues. Many garden centres now include food halls, and sections for clothing, gifts, pets, and power tools. There are also a number of online garden centres that now deliver direct to customers' doors.

Comparison with Farming

In respect to its food producing purpose, gardening is distinguished from farming chiefly by scale and intent. Farming occurs on a larger scale, and with the production of saleable goods as a major motivation. Gardening is done on a smaller scale, primarily for pleasure and to produce goods for the gardener's own family or community. There is some overlap between the terms, particularly in that some moderate-sized vegetable growing concerns, often called market gardening, can fit in either category.

The key distinction between gardening and farming is essentially one of scale; gardening can be a hobby or an income supplement, but farming is generally understood as a full-time or commercial activity, usually involving more land and quite different practices. One distinction is that gardening is labour-intensive and employs very little infrastructural capital, sometimes no more than a few tools, e.g. a spade, hoe, basket and watering can. By contrast, larger-scale farming often involves irrigation systems, chemical fertilizers and harvesters or at least ladders, e.g. to reach up into fruit trees. However, this distinction is becoming blurred with the increasing use of power tools in even small gardens.

In part because of labour intensity and aesthetic motivations, gardening is very often much more productive per unit of land than farming. In the Soviet Union, half the food supply came from small peasants' garden plots on the huge government-run collective farms, although they were tiny patches of land. Some argue this as evidence of superiority of capitalism, since the peasants were generally able to sell their produce. Others consider it to be evidence of a tragedy of the commons, since the large collective plots were often neglected, or fertilizers or water redirected to the private gardens.

The term precision agriculture is sometimes used to describe gardening using intermediate technology (more than tools, less than harvesters), especially of organic varieties. Gardening is effectively scaled up to feed entire villages of over 100 people from specialized plots. A variant is the community garden which offers plots to urban dwellers; see further in allotment (gardening).

Gardenas as an Art

Garden design is considered to be an art in most cultures, distinguished from gardening, which generally means *garden maintenance*. In Japan, Samurai and Zen monks were often required to build decorative gardens or practice related skills like flower arrangement known as *ikebana*. In 18th century Europe, country estates were refashioned by landscape gardeners into formal gardens or landscaped park lands, such as at Versailles, France or Stowe, England. Today, landscape architects and garden designers continue to produce artistically creative designs for private garden spaces.

Professional landscape designers are certified by the Association of Professional Landscape Designers.

Social Aspects

People can express their political or social views in gardens, intentionally or not. The lawn vs. garden issue is played out in urban planning as the debate over the "land ethic" that is to determine urban land use and whether hyper hygienist bylaws (e.g. weed control) should apply, or whether land should generally be allowed to exist in its natural wild state. In a famous Canadian Charter of Rights case, 'Sandra Bell *vs*. City of Toronto', 1997, the right to cultivate all native species, even most varieties deemed noxious or allergenic, was upheld as part of the right of free expression.

People often surround their house and garden with a hedge. Common hedge plants are privet, hawthorn, beech, yew, leyland cypress, hemlock, arborvitae, barberry, box, holly, oleander, forsythia and lavender. The idea of open gardens without hedges may be distasteful to those who enjoy privacy. This may have an advantage to local wildlife by providing a habitat for birds, animals, and wild plants.

The Slow Food movement has sought in some countries to add an edible school yard and garden classrooms to schools, e.g. in Fergus, Ontario, where these were added to a public school to augment the kitchen classroom. Garden sharing, where urban landowners allow gardeners to grow on their property in exchange for a share of the harvest, is associated with the desire to control the quality of one's food, and reconnect with soil and community.

In US and British usage, the production of ornamental plantings around buildings is called *landscaping*, *landscape maintenance* or *grounds keeping*, while international usage uses the term *gardening* for these same activities.

Garden Pests

A garden pest is generally an insect, plant, or animal that engages in activity that the gardener considers undesirable. It may crowd out desirable plants, disturb soil, eat young seedlings, steal fruit, or otherwise kill plants, hamper their growth, damage their appearance, or reduce the quality of the edible or ornamental portions of the plant.

Because each gardener may have different goals, a garden pest is what the gardener considers a pest. For example, *Tropaeolum speciosum*, while beautiful, can be considered a pest if it seeds and starts to grow where it is not wanted. As the root is well below ground, pulling it up does not remove it: it simply grows again and becomes what may be considered a pest.

As another example, in lawns, moss can become dominant and be impossible to eradicate. In some lawns, lichens, especially very damp lawn lichens such as Peltigera lactucfolia and P. membranacea, can become difficult and be considered pests.

There are many ways to remove unwanted pests from a garden. The techniques vary depending on the pest, the gardener's goals, and the gardener's philosophy. For example, snails may be dealt with through a chemical pesticide, an organic pesticide, hand-picking, barriers, or simply growing snail-resistant plants.

2

Garden

A garden is a planned space, usually outdoors, set aside for the display, cultivation, and enjoyment of plants and other forms of nature. The garden can incorporate both natural and man-made materials. The most common form is known as a residential garden. Western gardens are almost universally based around plants. Zoos, which display wild animals in simulated natural habitats, were formerly called *zoological gardens*.

The etymology of the word refers to enclosure: it is from Middle English *gardin*, from Anglo-French *gardin, jardin*, of Germanic origin; akin to Old High German *gart*, an enclosure. The words *yard, court*, and Latin *hortus* (meaning 'garden', hence horticulture and orchard), are cognates — all referring to an enclosed space.

The term 'garden' in British English refers to an enclosed area of land, usually adjoining a building. This would be referred to as a yard in American English.

Some traditional types of eastern gardens, such as Zen gardens, use plants such as parsley. Xeriscape gardens use local native plants that do not require irrigation or extensive use of other resources while still providing the benefits of a garden environment. Gardens may exhibit structural enhancements, sometimes called follies, including water features such as fountains, ponds (with or without fish), waterfalls or creeks, dry creek beds, statuary, arbors, trellises and more.

Some gardens are for ornamental purposes only, while some gardens also produce food crops, sometimes in separate areas, or sometimes intermixed with the ornamental plants. Food-producing gardens are distinguished from farms by their smaller scale, more labour-intensive methods, and their purpose (enjoyment of a hobby rather than produce for sale). Flower gardens combine plants of different heights, colours, textures, and fragrances to create interest and delight the senses.

Gardening is the activity of growing and maintaining the garden. This work is done by an amateur or professional gardener. A gardener might also work in a non-garden setting, such as a park, a roadside embankment, or other public space. Landscape architecture is a related professional activity with landscape architects tending to specialise in design for public and corporate clients.

Garden design is the creation of plans for layout and planting of gardens and landscapes. Garden design may be done by the garden owner themselves, or by professionals. Most professional garden designers are trained in principles of design and in horticulture, and have an expert knowledge and experience of using plants. Some professional garden designers are also landscape architects, a more formal level of training that usually requires an advanced degree and often a state licence. Elements of garden design include the layout of hard landscape, such as paths, rockeries, walls, water features, sitting areas and decking, as well as the plants themselves, with consideration for their horticultural requirements, their season-to-season appearance, lifespan, growth habit, size, speed of growth, and combinations with other plants and landscape features. Consideration is also given to the maintenance needs of the garden, including the time or funds available for regular maintenance, which can affect the choices of plants regarding speed of growth, spreading or self-seeding of the plants, whether annual or perennial, and bloom-time, and many other characteristics.

The most important consideration in any garden design is, how the garden will be used, followed closely by the desired stylistic genres, and the way the garden space will connect to the home or other structures in the surrounding areas. All of these considerations are subject to the limitations of the budget. Budget limitations can be addressed by a simpler garden style with fewer plants and less costly hardscape materials, seeds rather than sod for lawns, and plants that grow quickly; alternately, garden owners may choose to create their garden over time, area by area.

Elements of a Garden

The elements of a garden consist of the following:

Natural Conditions and Materials

- Soil
- Rocks
- Light conditions
- Wind
- Precipitation
- Air quality
- Pollution

Proximity to Ocean (Salinity)

- Plant materials

Rain from Sky

- Lighting
- Raised beds
- Outdoor art/sculpture, such as Gazebos and Pergolas

  Pool, water garden, or other water elements such as drainage system

Uses for the Garden Space

A garden can have aesthetic, functional, and recreational uses:

- Cooperation with nature

Plant Cultivation

- Observation of nature

Bird and Insect-watching

- Reflection on the changing seasons
- Relaxation
- Family dinners on the terrace
- Children playing in the yard
- Reading and relaxing in the hammock
- Maintaining the flowerbeds
- Pottering in the shed
- Basking in warm sunshine
- Escaping oppressive sunlight and heat
- Growing useful produce
- Flowers to cut and bring inside for indoor beauty
- Fresh herbs and vegetables for cooking

Gardens may feature a particular plant or plant type(s):

- Back garden
- Bog Garden
- Cactus garden
- Fernery
- Flower garden
- Front garden
- Herb garden
- Orangery
- Orchard
- Potager
- Rose garden
- Vegetable garden
- Vineyard
- White garden
- Wildflower garden
- Winter garden

Gardens may feature a particular style or aesthetic:

- Alpine or rock garden
- Bonsai or miniature garden
- Children's Garden
- Chinese garden
- Dutch garden
- English landscape garden
- French formal garden
- Italian garden
- Japanese garden
- Knot garden
- Mughal garden
- Native garden
- Persian garden
- Roman gardens

- Spanish garden
- Terrarium
- Trial garden
- Tropical garden
- Water garden
- Wild garden
- Xeriscaping
- Zen garden

Types of garden:

- Botanical garden
- Butterfly garden
- Butterfly zoo
- Cold frame garden
- Community garden
- Container garden
- Cottage garden
- Cutting garden
- Green house
- Green wall
- Forest garden
- Hanging garden
- Hydroponic garden
- Rain garden
- Raised bed gardening
- Residential garden
- Roof garden
- Sacred garden
- Sensory garden
- Square foot garden
- Vertical garden
- Walled garden
- Windowbox zoological garden

3

Garden Design

'Garden design' is the art and process of designing and creating plans for layout and planting of gardens and landscapes. Garden design may be done by the garden owner themselves, or by professionals of varying levels of experience and expertise. Most professional garden designers are trained in principles of design and in horticulture, and have an expert knowledge and experience of using plants. Some professional garden designers are also landscape architects, a more formal level of training that usually requires an advanced degree and often a state licence. Many amateur gardeners also attain a high level of experience from extensive hours working in their own gardens, through casual study, serious study in Master Gardener Programmes, or by joining gardening clubs. For examples of the latter see 'The Gardeners of America', Men's Garden Clubs of America' and 'National Garden Clubs'. Many gardeners in the United States join the American Horticultural Society.

Garden owners have shown an increasing interest in garden design during the late twentieth century, both as enthusiasts of gardening as a hobby, as well as an expansion in the use of professional garden designers.

Whether a garden is designed by a professional or an amateur, certain principles form the basis of effective garden design, resulting in the creation of gardens to meet the needs, goals and desires of the users or owners of the gardens.

Elements of garden design include the layout of hard landscape, such as paths, walls, water features, sitting areas and decking; as well as the plants themselves, with consideration for their horticultural requirements, their season-to-season appearance, lifespan, growth habit, size, speed of growth, and combinations with other plants and landscape features. Consideration is also given to the maintenance needs of the garden, including the time or funds available for regular maintenance, which can affect the choices of plants regarding speed of growth, spreading or self-seeding of the plants, whether annual or perennial, and bloom-time, and many other characteristics.

The most important consideration in garden design is how the garden will be used, followed closely by the desired stylistic genres, and the way the garden space will connect to the home or other structures in the surrounding areas. All of these considerations are subject to the limitations of the budgetary concerns for the particular project and time. Budget limitations can be addressed by a simpler more basic garden style with fewer plants and less costly hardscape materials, seeds rather than sod for lawns, and plants that grow quickly; alternately, garden owners may choose to create their garden over time, area by area, putting more into each section than could be handled all at once.

The quality of a garden's soil often has a significant influence on the success of the garden. Soil influences the availability of water and nutrients, the activity of beneficial soil organisms, and a wide variety of other factors important to plant growth.

Traditionally, garden soil is improved by amendment, the process of adding beneficial materials to the excavated native subsoil and topsoil. The materials, which may consist of compost, peat, sand, mineral dust, or manure, among others, are mixed with the excavated soil. The amount and type of amendment may depend on the ratio of clay to humus, and on the soil acidity or alkalinity. One source states that, "conditioning the soil thoroughly before planting enables the plants to establish themselves quickly and so play their part in the design."

Recommendations regarding the scope of soil amendment may vary. One rule of thumb suggests that the gardener till and amend an area twice the size high and wide of any plant container.

However, not all gardens are, or should be, amended in this manner. Since "many native plants prefer an impoverished soil, and the closer to their natural habitat they are in the garden, the better". In this case, poor soil is better than a rich soil that has been artificially enriched.

As well, some authorities recommend against the amendment of soil for woody plants.

Boundaries

The look of the garden can be influenced strongly by the boundary impinges. Planting can be used to modify the boundary line or a line between an area of rough grass and smooth, depending on the size of the plot. Introducing internal boundaries, perhaps in the form of hedges or group of shrubs, can help break up a garden.

Hedges vary their colours throughout the seasons dramatically. Hedges, being strong features in a garden, are often used to divide sections of the garden. However, since they use the moisture and nutrient from the garden soil to grow as well as other plants, they may not be a good choice and may bring a negative effect to the other plants.

Besides the boundaries that are made up of plants like the hedges, walls made up of various materials can be built between regions. There are broadly three types of walling material: stone, either random or coursed, brick, and concrete in its various forms. It is good to determine what color, size, and texture will be most appropriate for the garden before actually building the wall.

According to Brookes, fencing can offer an alternative solution, is the walls are too solid for the region of the garden. There are several numbers of fence types that can be used for a garden: animal-proof fence for country situations, peep-proof fences for the suburbs, and urban fences that provide shelter from the winds in exposed roof-top gardens and create internal barriers.

Alternative Surfacing

Usually, a smooth expanse of lawn is often considered essential to a garden. However, a textured surface "made up of loose gravel, small pebbles, or wood chips is much more satisfactory visually" than a smooth surface. According to Brookes, creating a relaxed feel to a garden is often done by loose surfacing made up of bark chips, pebbles, gravels; also, the various textures, shapes, sizes, colors, and materials of many different paving elements can contribute to making a garden plan pattern and texture, if they are mixed successfully.

Planting design requires design judgement combined with a good level of horticultural, ecological and cultural knowledge. It includes two major systems: formal planting design and naturalistic planting design.

The history of planting design is an aspect of the history of gardening and the history of landscape architecture. Planting in ancient gardens was often a mix of herbs for medicinal use, vegetables for consumption and flowers for decoration. Purely aesthetic planting layouts seem to have developed after the renaissance and are clearly shown in late-renaissance paintings and plans. The designs were geometrical and plants were used to form patterns. In the East, naturalistic planting design originated as early as around 200 B.C. in China. In the West, the arrangement of plants in informal groups developed as part of the landscape garden style and was strongly influenced by the picturesque.

A planting plan gives specific instructions, often for a contractor about how the soil is to be prepared, what species are to be planted, what size and spacing is to be used and what maintenance operations are to be carried out under the contract. Owners of private gardens may also use planting plans, not for contractual purposes, as an aid to thinking about a design and as a record of what has been planted. A planting strategy is a long term strategy for the design, establishment and management of different types of vegetation in a landscape or garden.

Planting can be established by directly employed gardeners and horticulturalists or it can be established by a landscape contractor (also known as a landscape gardener). Landscape contractors work to drawings and specifications prepared by garden designers or landscape architects.

Garden Furniture

Garden furniture may range from a *patio set* consisting of a table, four or six chairs and a parasol, through benches, swings, various lighting, to stunning artifacts in brutal concrete or weathered oak. Patio heaters, that run on bottled butane or propane, are often used to enable people to sit outside at night or in cold weather. A picnic table, is used for the purpose of eating a meal outdoors such as in a garden.

The materials used to manufacture modern patio furniture include stones, metals, vinyl, plastics, resins, glass, and treated woods.

Sunlight

While sunlight is not always easily controlled by the gardener, it is an important element of garden design. The amount of available light is a critical factor in determining what plants may be grown. Sunlight will, therefore, have a substantial influence on the character of the garden. For example, a rose garden is generally not successful in full shade, while a garden of hostas may not thrive in hot sun. As another example, a vegetable garden may need to be placed in a sunny location, and if that location is not ideal for the overall garden design goals, the designer may need to change other aspects of the garden.

In some cases, the amount of available sunlight can be influenced by the gardener. The location of trees, other shade plants, garden structures, or, when designing an entire property, even buildings, might be selected or changed based on their influence in increasing or reducing the amount of sunlight provided to various areas of the property.

In other cases, the amount of sunlight is not under the gardener's control. Nearby buildings, plants on other properties, or simply the climate of the local area, may limit the available sunlight. Or, substantial changes in the light conditions of the garden may not be within the gardener's means. In this case, it is important to plan a garden that is compatible with the existing light conditions.

Light regulates three major plant processes: photosynthesis, phototropism, and photoperiodism.

Photosynthesis provides the energy required to produce the energy source of plants.

Phototropism is the effect of light on plant growth that causes the plant to grow toward or away from the light. Photoperiodism is a plant's response or capacity to respond to photoperiod, a recurring cycle of light and dark periods of constant length.

Lighting

Garden lighting can be an important aspect of garden design. In most cases, various types of lighting techniques may be classified and defined by heights: safety lighting, uplighting, and downlighting. Safety lighting is the most practical application. However, it is more important to determine the type of lamps and fittings needed to create the desired effects.

TYPES OF GARDENS

Formal Garden

A formal garden in the Western gardening tradition is a neat and ordered garden laid out in carefully planned geometric and symmetric lines. Lawns and hedges in a formal garden must always be kept neatly clipped. Trees, shrubs, subshrubs and other foliage are carefully arranged, shaped and continually trimmed. A French garden or Garden à la française, is a specific kind of formal garden, laid out in the manner of André Le Nôtre; it is centered on the façade of a building, with radiating avenues and paths of gravel, lawns, parterres and pools (*bassins*) of reflective water enclosed in geometric shapes by stone coping, with fountains and sculpture.

The simplest formal garden would be a box-trimmed hedge lining or enclosing a carefully laid out flowerbed or garden bed of simple geometric shape, such as a knot garden. The most elaborate formal gardens contain pathways, statuary, fountains and beds on differing levels.

The Garden à la française had its origins in sixteenth-century Italian gardens such as Boboli Gardens behind Palazzo Pitti, Florence, laid out by a series of architect-designers for the Grand Duchess Eleanor of Toledo. The formal parterre of clipped evergreens was transferred to France, where some of the earliest formal parterres were those laid out at Anet. Claude Mollet, the founder of a dynasty of nurserymen-designers that lasted deep into the 18th century, introduced the formal parterre.

Features of a formal garden:

- Terrace
- Statuary
- Bosquet
- Sylvan theater
- Pavilion
- Topiary
- Hedge
- Parterre
- Pergola
- Landscaping

Formal gardens were a feature of the stately homes of England from the introduction of the parterre at Wilton House in the 1630s until such geometries were swept away by the naturalistic landscape gardens of the 1730s, but perhaps the best-known example of a formal garden of gravel, stone, water, turf and trees with sculpture is at Versailles, which is actually many different gardens, laid out by André Le Nôtre. In the early eighteenth century, the publication of Dezallier d'Argenville, *La théorie et la pratique du jardinage* (1709) was translated into English and German, and was the central document for the later formal gardens of Continental Europe.

Formal gardening in the French manner was reintroduced at the turn of the twentieth century: Beatrix Farrand's formal gardens at Dumbarton Oaks, Washington DC and Achille Duchêne's restored water parterre at Blenheim Palace are examples of the modern formal garden. New York City's Central Park features a formal garden in the Conservatory Garden at the northern sector.

Cottage Garden

A cottage garden uses an informal design, traditional materials, dense plantings, and a mixture of ornamental and edible plants. Cottage gardens go back many centuries, but their popularity grew in 1870s England in response to the more structured English estate gardens that used formal designs and massed colours of brilliant greenhouse annuals. They are more casual by design, depending on grace and charm rather than grandeur and formal structure.

The earliest cottage gardens were far more practical than their modern descendants — with an emphasis on vegetables and herbs, along with some fruit trees, perhaps a beehive, and even livestock. Flowers were used to fill any spaces in between. Over time, flowers became more dominant. Modern day cottage gardens include countless regional and personal variations of the more traditional English cottage garden.

Residential Garden

A residential or domestic garden, is the most common form of garden and is generally found in proximity to a residence, such as the front or back garden. The front garden may be a formal and semi-public space and so subject to the constraints of convention and law. While typically found in the yard of the residence, a garden may also be established on a roof, in an atrium, on a balcony, in windowboxes, or on a patio. Residential gardens are typically designed at human scale, as they are most often intended for private use. However, the garden of a great house, castle or a large estate may be larger than a public park in a village, and may produce foodstuffs as well.

Residential gardens may feature specialized gardens, such as those for exhibiting one particular type of plant, or special features, such as rockery or water features. They are also used for growing herbs and vegetables and are thus an important element of sustainability.

Kitchen Garden or Potager

The traditional kitchen garden, also known as a potager, is a seasonally used space separate from the rest of the residential garden — the ornamental plants and lawn areas. Most vegetable gardens are still miniature versions of old family farm plots with square or rectangular beds, but the kitchen garden is different not only in its history, but also its design.

The kitchen garden may be a landscape feature that can be the central feature of an ornamental, all-season landscape, but can be little more than a humble vegetable plot. It is a source of herbs, vegetables, fruits, and flowers, but it is also a structured garden space, a design based on repetitive geometric patterns.

The kitchen garden has year-round visual appeal and can incorporate permanent perennials or woody plantings around (or among) the annual plants.

A Shakespeare garden is a themed garden that cultivates plants mentioned in the works of William Shakespeare. In English-speaking countries, particularly the United States, these are often public gardens associated with parks, universities, and Shakespeare festivals. Shakespeare gardens are sites of cultural, educational, and romantic interest and can be locations for outdoor weddings.

Signs near the plants usually provide relevant quotations. A Shakespeare garden usually includes several dozen species, either in herbaceous profusion or in a geometric layout with boxwood dividers. Typical amenities are walkways and benches and a weather-resistant bust of Shakespeare. Shakespeare gardens may accompany reproductions of Elizabethan architecture. Some Shakespeare gardens also grow species typical of the Elizabethan period but not mentioned in Shakespeare's plays or poetry.

Rock Garden

Rock Garden, also known as a rockery or an alpine garden, is a type of garden that features extensive use of rocks or stones, along with plants native to rocky or alpine environments.

Rock garden plants tend to be small, both because many of the species are naturally small, and so as not to cover up the rocks. They may be grown in troughs (containers), or in the ground. The plants will usually be types that prefer well-drained soil and less water.

The usual form of a rock garden is a pile of rocks, large and small, esthetically arranged, and with small gaps between, where the plants will be rooted. Some rock gardens incorporate bonsai.

Some rock gardens are designed and built to look like natural outcrops of bedrock. Stones are aligned to suggest a bedding plane and plants are often used to conceal the joints between the stones. This type of rockery was popular in Victorian times, often designed and built by professional landscape architects. The same approach is sometimes used in modern campus or commercial landscaping, but can also be applied in smaller private gardens.

The Japanese rock garden, in the west often referred to as *Zen garden*, is a special kind of rock garden with hardly any plants. The Rock Garden is a sculpture garden in Chandigarh, India. Spread over an area of forty-acre (160,000 m^2), it is completely built of industrial and home waste and thrown-away items.

Japanese gardens can be found at private homes, in neighbourhood or city parks, and at historical landmarks such as Buddhist temples and old castles. Some of the Japanese gardens most famous in the West, and within Japan as well, are dry gardens or rock gardens, *karesansui*. The tradition of the Tea masters has produced highly refined Japanese gardens of quite another style, evoking rural simplicity. In Japanese culture, garden-making is a high art, intimately related to the linked arts of calligraphy and ink painting. Since the end of the 19th century, Japanese gardens have also been adapted to Western settings. Japanese gardens were developed under the influences of the distinctive and stylized Chinese gardens.

Contemporary Garden

The contemporary style garden has become very popular in the UK in the last 10 years. This is partly due to the increase of modern housing with small gardens as well as the cultural shift towards contemporary design. This style of garden can be defined by the use 'clean' design lines, with focus on hard landscaping materials: stone, hardwood, rendered walls. Planting style is bold but simple with the use of drifts of one or two plants that repeat throughout the design. Grasses are a very popular choice for this style of design. Lighting effects also play an integral role in the modern garden. Subtle lighting effects can be achieved with the use of carefully placed low voltage LED lights incorporated into paving and walls.

4

Botanical Garden

'Botanical gardens' or 'botanic gardens' are generally well-tended parks displaying a wide range of plants labelled with their botanical names. They may contain specialist plant collections such as cacti and succulent plants, herb gardens, plants from particular parts of the world, and so on; there may be greenhouses, again with special collections such as tropical plants, alpine plants or other exotic plants. Visitor services often include garden tours, educational displays, art exhibitions, book rooms, open-air theatrical and musical performances and other entertainment.

Botanical gardens are often run by universities or other scientific research organizations and often have associated herbaria and research programmes in plant taxonomy or some other aspect of botanical science. In principle their role is to maintain documented collections of living plants for the purposes of scientific research, conservation, display and education, although this will depend on the resources available and the special interests pursued at each particular garden.

The origin of modern botanical gardens can be traced to European mediaeval medicinal gardens known as physic gardens, the first of these being founded during the Italian Renaissance in the 16th century. This early concern with medicinal plants changed in the 17th century to an interest in the new plant imports from explorations outside Europe as botany gradually established its independence from medicine. In the 18th century systems of nomenclature and classification were devised by botanists working in the herbaria and universities associated with the gardens, these systems often being displayed in the gardens as educational 'order beds'. With the rapid rise of European imperialism in the late 18th century botanic gardens were established in the tropics and economic botany became a focus with the hub at the Royal Botanic Gardens, Kew, near London.

Over the years botanical gardens, as cultural and scientific organisations, have responded to the interests of botany and horticulture. Nowadays most botanical gardens display a mix of the themes mentioned and more: having a strong connection with the general public there is the opportunity to provide visitors with information relating to the environmental issues being faced at the start of the 21st century, especially those relating to plant conservation and sustainability.

The role of major botanical gardens worldwide has been considered so broadly similar as to fall within textbook definitions. The following definition was produced by staff of the Liberty Hyde Bailey Hortorium of Cornell University in 1976. It covers in some detail the many functions and activities generally associated with botanical gardens.

"A botanical garden is a controlled and staffed institution for the maintenance of a living collection of plants under scientific management for purposes of education and research, together with such libraries, herbaria, laboratories, and museums as are essential to its particular undertakings. Each botanical garden naturally develops its own special fields of interests depending on its personnel, location, extent, available funds, and the terms of its charter. It may include greenhouses, test grounds, an herbarium, an arboretum, and other departments. It maintains a scientific as well as a plant-growing staff, and publication is one of its major modes of expression."

This broad outline is then expanded:

> "The botanic garden maybe an independent institution, a governmental operation, or affiliated to a college or university. If a department of an educational institution, it may be related to a teaching programme. In any case, it exists for scientific ends and is not to be restricted or diverted by other demands. It is not merely a landscaped or ornamental garden, although it may be artistic, nor is it an experiment station or yet a park with labels on the plants. The essential element is the intention of the enterprise, which is the acquisition and dissemination of botanical knowledge."

The 'New Royal Horticultural Society Dictionary of Gardening' (1999) points out that among the various kinds of organisations now known as botanical gardens there are many public gardens with little scientific activity, and it cites a more abbreviated definition that was published by the World Wildlife Fund and IUCN when launching the 'Botanic Gardens Conservation Strategy' in 1989:

> 'A botanic garden is a garden containing scientifically ordered and maintained collections of plants, usually documented and labelled, and open to the public for the purposes of recreation, education and research'.

This has been further reduced by Botanic Gardens Conservation International to the following definition which 'encompasses the spirit of a true botanic garden'.

> 'A botanic garden is an institution holding documented collections of living plants for the purposes of scientific research, conservation, display and education'.

The Botanical Gardens Network

Worldwide there are now about 1800 botanical gardens and arboreta in about 150 countries (mostly in temperate regions) of which about 400 are in Europe, 200 in North America, 150 in Russia. and an increasing number in East Asia. These gardens attract about 150 million visitors a year so it is hardly surprising that many people gained their first exciting introduction to the wonders of the plant world in a botanical garden.

Historically, botanical gardens exchanged plants through the publication of seed lists (these were called Latin: *Index Semina* in the 18th century). This was a means of transferring both plants and information between botanical gardens. This system continues today although the possibility of genetic piracy and the transmission of invasive species has received greater attention in recent times.

The International Association of Botanic Gardens was formed in 1954 as a worldwide organisation affiliated to the International Union of Biological Sciences. More recently coordination has also been provided by Botanic Gardens Conservation International (BGCI) which has the mission "To mobilise botanic gardens and engage partners in securing plant diversity for the well-being of people and the planet". BGCI has over 700 members — mostly botanic gardens — in 118 countries and strongly supports the Global strategy for plant conservation by producing a range resources and publications, and by organizing international conferences and conservation programmes.

Communication also happens regionally. In the United States there is the American Public Gardens Association (formerly the American Association of Botanic Gardens and Arboreta) and in Australasia there is the Botanic Gardens of Australia and New Zealand (BGANZ).

Historical Development

The history of botanical gardens is closely linked to the history of botany itself. When the botanical gardens of the 16th and 17th centuries changed from medicinal gardens to sites displaying beautiful, strange and new (sometimes economically important) plants from distant lands, and further in the 18th century to sites demonstrating the latest plant classification systems devised by botanists working in the associated herbaria, and then to the modern mix of specialist and eclectic gardens serving many interests of horticulture and botany.

Precursors

The idea of 'scientific' gardens used specifically for the study of plants is probably ancient.

Grand Gardens of Ancient History

Substantial gardens set aside for economic use or display, containing at least some plants gained by special collection or military campaigns abroad, are known from ancient Egypt, Assyria, and Mexico. In about 2800 BCE Chinese Emperor Shen Nung sent collectors to distant regions searching for plants with economic or medicinal value. Early mediaeval Islamic Spain had gardens, like that of Ibn Wafid's at Toledo in the 11th century, which have been called 'botanical'. It has also been suggested that the Spanish conquest of Mesoamerica influenced the history of the botanical garden as gardens in Tenochtitlan, Nezahualcoyotl, Chalco and elsewhere greatly impressed the invaders as the Aztecs knew many more medicinal plants than did the classical world of Europe.

Physic Gardens

Botanical gardens, in the modern sense, developed from physic gardens, whose main purpose was to grow herbs for medicinal use. Such gardens have a long history. In Europe, for example, Aristotle (384 BCE - 322 BCE) is said to have had a physic garden in the Lyceum at Athens, which was used for educational purposes and for the study of botany and this was inherited, or possibly set up, by his pupil Theophrastus, the 'Father of Botany'.

Though these ancient gardens shared some of the characteristics of botanical gardens, the forerunners of modern botanical gardens are generally regarded as being the mediaeval monastic physic gardens that originated after the decline of the Roman Empire at the time of Emperor Charlemagne (742-789 CE). These contained a *hortus*, a garden used mostly for vegetables, and another section set aside for specially-labelled medicinal plants and this was called the *herbularis* or *hortus medicus* — more generally known as a physic garden. These gardens were probably given impetus when Charlemagne issued a capitulary of 73 herbs to be used in the physic gardens of his dominions. Many of these were found in British gardens even though they only occurred naturally in continental Europe, demonstrating earlier plant introduction. Certainly the founding of many early botanic gardens was instigated by members of the medical profession.

Sixteenth Century European Gardens

If a botanical garden is defined by its scientific or academic connection then the first true botanical gardens were established with the revival of learning that occurred in the European countries.

Origin in Southern Europe

The botanical gardens of southern Europe were associated with university faculties of medicine and were founded in Northern Italy at Orto botanico di Pisa (1544), Orto botanico di Padova (1545), Orto Botanico di Firenze (1545) and Orto Botanico dell'Università di Bologna (1568). Here the physicians (referred to in English as apothecaries) delivered lectures on the Mediterranean 'simples' or 'officinals' that were being cultivated in the grounds. Student education was no doubt stimulated by the relatively recent advent of printing and the publication of the first herbals. All of these botanical gardens still exist, mostly in their original locations.

Northern Europe

The tradition of these Italian gardens passed into northern Europe where similar gardens were established in the Netherlands (Hortus Botanicus Leiden, 1587; Hortus Botanicus (Amsterdam), 1679), Germany (Alter Botanischer Garten Tübingen, 1535; Leipzig Botanical Garden, 1580; Botanischer Garten Heidelberg, 1597; Herrenhäuser Gärten, Hanover, 1666; Botanical Garden in Berlin, 1672), Switzerland (Botanical Garden Zürich, 1560; Basel, 1589); England (University of Oxford Botanic Garden, 1621; Royal Botanic Garden Edinburgh, 1670; Chelsea Physic Garden, 1673), and in France (Jardin des plantes de Montpellier, 1593; Paris, 1597; Jardin des Plantes, Paris, 1635), Denmark (University of Copenhagen Botanical Garden, 1600); Sweden (Uppsala University, 1655), and also in Spain (Botanical Garden of Valencia(Spanish), 1567).

Seventeenth Century

At the time of the foundation of these first gardens botany had not become a distinct discipline but was simply a descriptive adjunct to medicine. However, it was in the 17th century that botanical gardens began their contribution to a deeper scientific curiosity about plants.

Beginnings of Botanical Science

During the 16th and 17th centuries the first plants were being imported to these major Western European gardens from Eastern Europe and nearby Asia (which provided many bulbs) and these found a place in the new gardens where they could be conveniently studied by the plant experts of the day. For example, Asian introductions were described by Carolus Clusius (1526-1609) who was director, in turn, of the Botanical Garden of the University of Vienna and Hortus Botanicus Leiden. Many plants were being collected from the Near East, especially bulbous plants from Turkey. Clusius laid the foundations of Dutch tulip breeding and the bulb industry, and he helped create one of the earliest formal botanical gardens of Europe at Leyden where his detailed planting lists have made it possible to recreate this garden near its original site. "The *hortus medicus* of Leyden in 1601 was a perfect square divided into quarters for the four continents, but by 1720 however it was a rambling system of beds, struggling to contain the novelties rushing in" and it became better known as the *hortus academicus*. His *Exoticorum libri decem* (1605) is an important survey of exotic plants and animals that is still consulted today. The inclusion of new plant introductions in botanic gardens meant that their scientific role was now widening as botany gradually asserted its independence from medicine.

In the mid to late 17th century the Paris Jardin des Plantes was a centre of interest with the greatest number of new introductions to attract the public. In England the Chelsea Physic Garden was founded in 1673 as the "Garden of the Society of Apothecaries". The Chelsea garden had heated greenhouses and in 1723 appointed Philip Miller (1722-1770) as Head Gardener. He had a wide influence on both botany and horticulture as plants poured into it from around the world. The garden's golden age came in the 18th century, when it became the world's most richly stocked botanical garden. Its seed-exchange programme was established in 1682 and still continues.

With the increase in maritime trade ever more plants were being brought back to Europe as trophies from distant lands and these were triumphantly displayed in the private estates of the wealthy, in commercial nurseries and in the public botanical gardens. Heated conservatories called 'orangeries', such as the one at Kew, became a feature of many botanical gardens. industrial expansion in Europe and North America resulted in new building skills, so plants sensitive to cold were kept over winter in progressively elaborate and expensive heated conservatories and glasshouses.

The Cape, Dutch East Indies

The 18th century was marked by introductions from the Cape of South Africa — including ericas, geraniums, pelargoniums, succulents and proteaceous plants — while the Dutch trade with the Dutch East Indies resulted in a golden era for the Leiden and Amsterdam botanical gardens and a boom in the construction of conservatories.

Royal Botanic Gardens, Kew

The Royal Gardens at Kew were founded in 1760, initially as part of the Royal Garden set aside as a physic garden. William Aiton (1741-1793), the first Curator, was taught by garden chronicler Philip Miller of the Chelsea Physic Garden whose son Charles became first Curator of the original Cambridge Botanic Garden (1762). In 1759 the 'Physick Garden' was planted and by 1767 it was claimed that 'the Exotick Garden is by far the richest in Europe'. Gardens such as the Royal Botanic Gardens, Kew (1759) and Oratava Acclimatization Garden(Spanish), Tenerife (1788) and the Real Jardín Botánico de Madrid (1755) were set up to cultivate new species returned from expeditions to the tropics; they also helped found new tropical botanical gardens. From the 1770s, following the example of the French and Spanish, amateur collectors were supplemented by official horticultural and botanical plant hunters. This was the great era of European, and especially British, imperialism which was 'the means by which ideas, knowledge, styles of economy, politics and goods were given international reach' and justified as the spreading of 'civilization' through 'development' and 'improvement'.

At this time England was importing many woody plants from North America, and the popularity of horticulture had increased enormously encouraged by the horticultural and botanical collecting expeditions overseas fostered by the directorship of Sir William Hooker and his keen interest in economic botany. At the end of the 18th century Kew, under the directorship of Sir Joseph Banks, enjoyed a golden age of plant hunting, sending out collectors to the Southern African Cape, Australia, Chile, China, Ceylon (now Sri Lanka), Brazil and elsewhere, and acting as 'the great botanical exchange house of the British empire'. From its earliest days to the present Kew has in many ways exemplified botanic garden ideals and is respected worldwide for the published work of its scientists, the education of horticultural students, its public programmes, and the scientific underpinning of its horticulture.

Plant Classification

The large number of plants needing description were often listed in garden catalogues and it was at this time that Carl Linnaeus established the system of binomial nomenclature which greatly facilitated the listing process. Names of plants were authenticated by dried plant specimens mounted on card (a *hortus siccus* or garden of dried plants) that were stored in buildings called herbaria, these taxonomic research institutions being frequently associated with the botanical gardens, many of which by then had 'order beds' to display the classification systems being developed by botanists in the gardens' museums and herbaria. Botanical gardens had now become scientific collections as botanists published their descriptions of the new exotic plants, and these were also recorded for posterity in detail by superb botanical illustrations. In this century botanical gardens effectively dropped their medicinal function in favour of scientific and aesthetic priorities and the term 'botanic garden' came to be more closely associated with the herbarium, library (and later laboratories) housed there than with the living collections — on which little research was undertaken.

Nineteenth Century

The late 18th and early 19th centuries were marked by the establishment of tropical botanical gardens as a tool of colonial expansion (for trade and commerce and, secondarily, science) mainly by the British and Dutch, in India, South-east Asia and the Caribbean. This was also the time of Sir Joseph Banks's botanical collections during Captain James Cook's circumnavigations of the planet and his explorations of Oceania which formed the last phase of plant introduction on a grand scale.

Tropical Botanical Gardens

There are currently about 230 tropical botanical gardens with a concentration in southern and south-eastern Asia. The first botanical garden founded in the tropics was the Pamplemousses Botanical Garden in Mauritius, established in 1735 to provide food for ships using the port, but later trialling and distributing many plants of economic importance. This was followed by the West Indies (Botanic Gardens St. Vincent, 1764) and in 1786 by the Acharya Jagadish Chandra Bose

Botanical Garden in Calcutta (now Kolkata), India founded during a period of prosperity when the city was a trading centre for the Dutch East India Company. Other gardens were constructed in Brazil (Jardim Botânico, Rio de Janeiro, 1808), Sri Lanka (Botanical Garden of Peradeniya, 1821 and on a site dating back to 1371), Indonesia (Bogor Botanical Gardens, Kebun Raya Cibodas, 1817), and Singapore (Singapore Botanical Gardens, 1822). These had a profound effect on the economy of the countries, especially in relation to the foods and medicines introduced. The importation of rubber trees to the Singapore Botanic Garden initiated the important rubber industry of the Malay Peninsula. At this time also teak and tea were introduced to India and breadfruit, pepper and starfruit to the Caribbean.

Included in the charter of these gardens was the investigation of the local flora for its economic potential to both the colonists and the local people. Many crop plants were introduced by or through these gardens — often in association with European botanical gardens such as Kew or Amsterdam — and included cloves, tea, coffee, breadfruit, cinchona, sugar, cotton, palm oil and Theobroma cacao (for chocolate). It was during these times that the rubber plant was introduced to Singapore. Especially in the tropics, the larger gardens were frequently associated with a herbarium and museum of economy. The Botanical Garden of Peradeniya had considerable influence on the development of agriculture in Ceylon (now Sri Lanka) where the Para rubber tree (*Hevea brasiliensis*) was introduced from Kew, which had itself imported the plant from South America. Other examples include cotton from the Chelsea Physic Garden to the Province of Georgia in 1732 and tea into India by Calcutta Botanic Garden. The transfer of germplasm between the temperate and tropical botanical gardens was undoubtedly responsible for the range of agricultural crops currently used in several regions of the tropics.

Southern Hemisphere

The first botanical gardens in Australia were founded in the early 19th century (the Royal Botanic Gardens, Sydney, 1816; Royal Tasmanian Botanical Gardens, 1818; the Royal Botanic Gardens, Melbourne, 1845; Adelaide Botanic Gardens, 1854; and Brisbane City Botanic Gardens, 1855) where the tradition of acclimatization and economic exploitation were soon put into practice. To this list can be added major botanical gardens in New Zealand (Dunedin Botanic Gardens, 1863; Christchurch Botanic Gardens, 1863; Wellington Botanic Gardens, 1868) and South Africa (Kirstenbosch National Botanical Garden, 1913 (site dating to 1848).

United States

The first botanical garden in the United States, Bartram's Garden, was founded in 1730 near Philadelphia and in the same year the Linnaean Botanic Garden at Philadelphia itself. In 1859 the Missouri Botanical Garden was founded at St Louis and is now one of the world's leading gardens specializing in tropical plants. This was one of several popular American gardens including Longwood Gardens (1798), Arnold Arboretum (1872), New York Botanical Garden (1891), Huntington Botanical Gardens (1906), Brooklyn Botanic Garden (1910), and Fairchild Tropical Botanic Garden (1938).

Russian Empire and Soviet Union

Russia had more botanical gardens than any other country, with a major garden in every republic, each with many satellite gardens. Better-known gardens are Nikitsky Botanical Garden, Yalta, 1812; Kiev Botanical Gardens, 1939; and Moscow Botanical Garden of Academy of Sciences, 1945.

In all gardens there was a heightened interest in structures including sculptures, pavilion, bandstands, memorials, shadehouses, tea houses and the like.

A large number of civic or municipal botanical gardens were founded in the 19th and 20th centuries. These did not develop scientific facilities or programmes but the horticultural aspects were strong and the plants often labelled. They were botanical gardens in the sense of building up collections of plants and exchanging seeds with other gardens around the world, although their collection policies were determined by those in day-to-day charge of them. They tended to become little more than beautifully-maintained parks and were, indeed, often under general parks administrations.

Community Engagement

The second half of the twentieth century saw increasingly sophisticated educational, visitor service and interpretation services. Botanical gardens started to cater for many interests and their displays reflected this, often including botanical exhibits on themes of evolution, ecology or taxonomy horticultural displays of attractive flowerbeds and herbaceous borders, plants from different parts of the world, special collections of plant groups like bamboos or roses, specialist glasshouse collections such as tropical plants, alpine plants, cacti and orchids, as well as the traditional herb gardens and medicinal plants. Specialized gardens like the Palmengarten in Frankfurt (1869), one of the world's leading orchid and succulent plant collections, have been very popular. There was a renewed interest in gardens of indigenous plants and areas dedicated to natural vegetation.

With decreasing financial support from governments, there was an increase in revenue-raising public entertainment including music, art exhibitions, special botanical exhibitions, theatre and film, this being supplemented by the advent of 'Friends' organizations and the use of volunteer guides.

Plant Conservation

Plant conservation, and the heritage value of exceptional historic landscapes, were treaded with a A growing sense of urgency. Specialist gardens were sometimes given a separate or adjoining site, to display native and indigenous plants.

Plant conservation, and the heritage value of exceptional historic landscapes, were treaded with a A growing sense of urgency. Specialist gardens were sometimes given a separate or adjoining site, to display native and indigenous plants.

In the 1970s gardens became focussed on the plant conservation. The Botanic Gardens Conservation Secretariat was established by the IUCN, and the World Conservation Union in 1987 with the aim of coordinating the plant conservation efforts of botanical gardens around the world. It maintains a database of rare and endangered species in botanical gardens' living collections. Many gardens hold *ex situ* conservation collections that preserve genetic variation. These may be held as: seeds dried and stored at low temperature, or in tissue culture (such as the Kew Millennium Seedbank); as living plants, including those that are of special horticultural, historical or scientific interest (such as those held by the NCCPG in the United Kingdom); or by managing and preserving areas of natural vegetation. Collections are often held and cultivated with the intention of reintroduction to their original habitat. The Center for Plant Conservation at St Louis, Missouri coordinates the conservation of native North American species.

Role and Functions

Many of the functions of botanical gardens have already been dealt with in the sections above, which emphasize the scientific underpinning of botanical gardens with their focus on research, education and conservation. However, as multifaceted organizations all sites have their own special interests. In a remarkable paper on the role of botanical gardens Ferdinand Mueller (1825-1896), the director of the Royal Botanic Gardens Melbourne (1852-1873), stated that "in all cases the objects [of a botanical garden] must be mainly scientific and predominantly instructive". He then detailed many of the objectives that were being pursued by the world's botanical gardens in the middle of the 19th century, when European gardens were at their height. Many of these are listed below to give a sense of the scope of botanical gardens' activities at that time, and the ways in which they differed from parks or what he called 'public pleasure gardens':

- availability of plants for scientific research
- display of plant diversity in form and use
- display of plants of particular regions (including local)
- plants sometimes grown within their particular families
- plants grown for their seed or rarity
- major timber American English (*lumber*) trees
- plants of economic significance
- glasshouse plants of different climates
- all plants accurately labelled
- records kept of plants and their performance
- catalogues of holdings published periodically research facilities utilising the living collections
- studies in plant taxonomy
- examples of different vegetation types
- student education
- a herbarium
- selection and introduction of ornamental and other plants to commerce
- studies of plant chemistry phytochemistry
- report on the effects of plants on livestock
- at least one collector maintained doing field work

Botanical gardens must find a compromise between the need for peace and seclusion, and satisfy the demand for information and visitor services including restaurants, information centres and sales areas that bring with them rubbish, noise and hyperactivity. Attractive landscaping and planting design sometimes compete with scientific interests – with science now often taking second place. Some gardens are now heritage landscapes that are subject to constant demand for new exhibits.

Many gardens now have have plant shops selling flowers, herbs and vegetable seedlings suitable for transplanting; many, like the UBC Botanical Garden and Centre for Plant Research and the Chicago Botanic Garden, have plant breeding programs and introduce new plants to the horticultural trade.

Botanical gardens are still being built, such as the first botanical garden in Oman, which will be one of the largest gardens in the world. Once it is completed and will house the first large scale cloud forest in a huge glasshouse. There has been a remarkable development of botanical gardens in China over recent years including the Hainan Botanical Garden of Tropical Economic Plants South China Botanical Garden at Guangzhou, the Xishuangbanna Botanical Garden of Tropical Plants and the Xiamen Botanic Garden but in developed countries many have closed for lack of financial support, this being especially true of botanical gardens attached to universities.

Botanical gardens have always responded to the interests and values of the day. If a single function were to be chosen from the early literature on botanical gardens it would be their scientific endeavour and, flowing from this, their instructional value. In their formative years botanical gardens were gardens for physicians and botanists but then they progressively became more associated with ornamental horticulture and the needs of the general public. It is by the publications coming out of herbaria and similar facilities that the scientific reputation of a botanical garden is now judged, not by its living collections. The interest in economic plants now has less relevance, and the concern with plant classification systems has all but disappeared, while a fascination with the curious, beautiful and new seems unlikely to diminish.

In recent times the focus has been on creating awareness on danger to ecosystems from human overpopulation and its consequent need for biological and physical resources. Botanical gardens provide an excellent medium for much-needed communication between the world of science and the world at large. Education programmes can help the public develop greater environmental awareness by understanding the meaning and importance of ideas like conservation and sustainability.

5

Kitchen Garden

The traditional kitchen garden, also known as a potager, is a space separate from the rest of the residential garden — the ornamental plants and lawn areas. Most vegetable gardens are still miniature versions of old family farm plots, but the kitchen garden is different not only in its history, but also its design.

The kitchen garden may serve as the central feature of an ornamental, all-season landscape, or it may be little more than a humble vegetable plot. It is a source of herbs, vegetables, fruits, and flowers, but it is often also a structured garden space with a design based on repetitive geometric patterns.

The kitchen garden has year-round visual appeal and can incorporate permanent perennials or woody plantings around (or among) the annuals.

Potager Garden

A potager is a French term for an ornamental vegetable or kitchen garden. Often flowers (edible and non-edible) and herbs are planted with the vegetables to enhance the garden's beauty. The goal is to make the function of providing food aesthetically pleasing.

Plants are chosen as much for their functionality as for their colour and form. Many are trained to grow upward. A well-designed potager can provide food, cut flowers and herbs for the home with very little maintenance. Potagers can disguise their function of providing for a home in a wide array of forms — from the carefree style of the cottage garden to the formality of a knot garden.

Vegetable Garden

A vegetable garden (also known as a vegetable patch or vegetable plot) is a garden that exists to grow vegetables and other plants useful for human consumption, in contrast to a flower garden that exists for aesthetic purposes. It is a small-scale form of vegetable growing. A vegetable garden typically includes a compost heap, and several plots or divided areas of land, intended to grow one or two types of plant in each plot. It is usually located to the rear of a property in the back garden or backyard. Many families have home kitchen and vegetable gardens that they use to produce food. In World War II, many people had a garden called a 'victory garden' which provided food to families and thus freed up resources for the war effort.With worsening economic conditions and increased interest in organic and sustainable living, many people are turning to vegetable gardening as a supplement to their family's diet. Food grown in the backyard consumes little if any fuel for shipping or maintenance, and the grower can be sure of what exactly was used to grow it. Organic horticulture, or organic gardening, has become increasingly popular for the modern home gardener.There are many types of vegetable gardens. The potager, a garden in which vegetables, herbs and flowers are grown together, has become more popular than the more traditional rows or blocks.

Herb Garden

The herb garden is often a separate space in the garden, devoted to growing a specific group of plants known as herbs. These gardens may be informal patches of plants, or they may be carefully designed, even to the point of arranging and clipping the plants to form specific patterns, as in a knot garden.

Herb gardens may be purely functional, or they may include a blend of functional and ornamental plants. The herbs are usually used to flavour food in cooking, though they may also be used in other ways, such as discouraging pests, providing pleasant scents, or serving medicinal purposes (e.g., a physic garden), among others.

A kitchen garden can be created by planting different herbs in pots or containers, with the added benefit of mobility. Although not all herbs thrive in pots or containers, some herbs do better than others. Mint, is an example of herb that is advisable to keep in a container or it will take over the whole garden.

The culinary use of herbs may result in positive medical side-effects. In addition, plants grown within the garden are sometimes specifically targeted to cure common illnesses or maladies such as colds, headaches, or anxiety. During the mediaeval period, monks and nuns developed specialist medical knowledge and grew the necessary herbs in specialist gardens. Now, especially due to the increase in popularity of alternative medicine, this usage is heavily increasing. Making a medicinal garden however, requires a great number of plants, one for each malady.

Borage is commonly grown in herb gardens; its flowers can be used as a garnish.

Some popular culinary herbs in temperate climates are to a large extent still the same as in the mediaeval period.

Examples of herbs used for specific purposes (lists are examples only, and not intended to be complete):

- Annual culinary herbs: basil, dill, summer savory
- Perennial culinary herbs: mint, rosemary, thyme, tarragon
- Herbs used for potpourri: lavender, lemon verbena
- Herbs used for tea: mint, lemon verbena, chamomile, bergamot, Hibiscus sabdariffa (for making karkade).
- Herbs used for other purposes: stevia for sweetening, feverfew for pest control in the garden.

However, herbs often have multiple purposes. For example, mint may be used for cooking, tea, and pest control.

Greenhouse

A greenhouse (also called a glasshouse) is a building where plants are grown.

A greenhouse is a structure with a glass or plastic roof and frequently glass or plastic walls; it heats up because incoming solar radiation from the sun warms plants, soil, and other things inside the building faster than heat can escape the structure. Air warmed by the heat from hot interior surfaces is retained in the building by the roof and wall. These structures range in size from small sheds to very large buildings.

Greenhouses can be divided into glass greenhouses and plastic greenhouses. Plastics mostly used are PEfilm and multiwall sheet in PC or PMMA. Commercial glass greenhouses are often high tech production facilities for vegetables or flowers. The glass greenhouses are filled with equipment like screening installations, heating, cooling, lighting and may be automatically controlled by a computer.

The glass used for a greenhouse works as a barrier to air flow and its effect is to trap energy within the greenhouse, which heats both the plants and the ground inside it. This warms the air near the ground, and this air is prevented from rising and flowing away. This can be demonstrated by opening a small window near the roof of a greenhouse: the temperature drops considerably. This principle is the basis of the autovent automatic cooling system. A miniature greenhouse is known as a cold frame.

Greenhouses protect crops from too much heat or cold, shield plants from dust storms and blizzards, and help to keep out pests. Light and temperature control allows greenhouses to turn inarable land into arable land, thereby improving food production in marginal environments.

Because greenhouses allow certain crops to be grown throughout the year, greenhouses are increasingly important in the food supply of high latitude countries. One of the largest greenhouse complexes in the world is in Almeria, Spain, where greenhouses cover almost 50,000 acres (200 km^2). Sometimes called the sea of plastics.

Greenhouses are often used for growing flowers, vegetables, fruits, and tobacco plants. Bumblebees are the pollinators of choice for most greenhouse pollination, although other types of bees have been used, as well as artificial pollination. Hydroponics can be used in greenhouses as well to make the most use of the interior space.

Besides tobacco, many vegetables and flowers are grown in greenhouses in late winter and early spring, and then transplanted outside as the weather warms. Started plants are usually available for gardeners in farmers' markets at transplanting time. Special greenhouse varieties of certain crops such as tomatoes are generally used for commercial production.

The closed environment of a greenhouse has its own unique requirements, compared with outdoor production. Pests and diseases, and extremes of heat and humidity, have to be controlled, and irrigation is necessary to provide water. Significant inputs of heat and light may be required, particularly with winter production of warm-weather vegetables.

Because the temperature and humidity of greenhouses must be constantly monitored to ensure optimal conditions, a wireless sensor network can be used to gather data remotely. The data is transmitted to a control location and used to control heating, cooling, and irrigation systems.

The idea of growing plants in environmentally controlled areas has existed since Roman times. The Roman emperor Tiberius ate a cucumber-like vegetable daily. The Roman gardeners used artificial methods (similar to the greenhouse system) of growing to have it available for his table every day of the year. Cucumbers were planted in wheeled carts which were put in the sun daily, then taken inside to keep them warm at night. The cucumbers were stored under frames or in cucumber houses glazed with either oiled cloth known as 'specularia' or with sheets of mica, according to the description by Pliny the Elder.

The first modern greenhouses were built in Italy in the thirteenth century to house the exotic plants that explorers brought back from the tropics. They were originally called *giardini botanici* (botanical gardens). The concept of greenhouses soon spread to the Netherlands and then England, along with the plants. Some of these early attempts required enormous amounts of work to close up at night or to winterize. There were serious problems with providing adequate and balanced heat in these early greenhouses.

Charles Lucien Bonaparte, a French botanist, is often credited with building the first practical modern greenhouse in Leiden, Holland to grow medicinal tropical plants.

Originally on the estates of the rich, with the growth of the science of botany greenhouses spread to the universities. The French called their first greenhouses *orangeries*, since they were used to protect orange trees from freezing. As pineapples became popular *pineries*, or pineapple pits, were built. Experimentation with the design of greenhouses continued during the Seventeenth Century in Europe as technology produced better glass and construction techniques improved. The greenhouse at the Palace of Versailles was an example of their size and elaborateness; it was more than 500 feet long, 42 feet wide, and 45 feet high.

In the nineteenth Century the largest greenhouses were built. The conservatory at Kew Gardens in England is a prime example of the Victorian greenhouse. Although intended for both horticultural and non-horticultural exhibition these included London's Crystal Palace, the New York Crystal Palace and Munich's Glaspalast. Joseph Paxton, who had experimented with glass and iron in the creation of large greenhouses as the head gardener at Chatsworth, in Derbyshire, working for the Duke of Devonshire, designed and built the first, London's Crystal Palace. A major architectural achievement in monumental greenhouse building were the Royal Greenhouses of Laeken (1874-1895) for King Leopold II of Belgium.

In Japan, the first greenhouse was built in 1880 by Samuel Cocking, a British merchant who exported herbs.

In the Twentieth Century the geodesic dome was added to the many types of greenhouses. A notable example is the Eden Project, in Cornwall.

Greenhouse structures adapted in the 1960s when wider sheets of polyethylene film became widely available. Hoop houses were made by several companies and were also frequently made by the growers themselves. Constructed of aluminium extrusions, special galvanized steel tubing, or even just lengths of steel or PVC water pipe, construction costs were greatly reduced. This meant many more greenhouses on smaller farms and garden centers. Polyethylene film durability increased greatly when more effective inhibitors were developed and added in the 1970s. These UV inhibitors extended the usable life of the film from one or two years up to 3 and eventually 4 or more years.

Gutter connected greenhouses became more prevalent in the 1980s and 1990s. These greenhouses have two or more bays connected by a common wall, or row of support posts. Heating inputs were reduced as the ratio of floor area to roof area was increased substantially. Gutter connected greenhouses are now commonly used both in production and in situations where plants are grown and sold to the public as well. Gutter connected greenhouses are commonly covered with a double layer of polyethylene film with air blown between to provide increased heating efficiencies, or structured polycarbonate materials.

6

National Park

A 'national park' is a reserve of natural or semi-natural land, declared or owned by a government, set aside for animal safety and/or human recreation and enjoyment, and protected from most development. While ideas for national parks had been suggested previously, what is held to be the first one established was the United States' Yellowstone National Park, established in 1872. An international organization, the International Union for Conservation of Nature (IUCN), and its World Commission on Protected Areas, has defined National Parks as its category II type of protected areas. The largest national park in the world meeting the IUCN definition is the Northeast Greenland National Park, which was established in 1974. According to the IUCN, there are about 7000 national parks worldwide.

In 1969 the IUCN (International Union for the Conservation of Nature and Natural Resources) declared a national park to be a relatively large area with particular defining characteristics. A national park was deemed to be a place, one or several ecosystems are not materially altered by human exploitation and occupation, where plant and animal species, geomorphological sites and habitats are of special scientific, educative and recreative interest or which contain a natural landscape of great beauty.

The highest competent authority of the country has taken steps to prevent or eliminate as soon as possible exploitation or occupation in the whole area and to enforce effectively the respect of ecological, geomorphological or aesthetic features which have led to its establishment.

Visitors are allowed to enter, under special conditions, for inspirational, educative, cultural and recreative purposes.

In 1971 these criteria were further expanded upon leading to more clear and defined benchmarks to evaluate a national park. These include:

- a minimum size of 1,000 hectares within zones in which protection of nature takes precedence;
- statutory legal protection;
- a budget and staff sufficient to provide sufficient effective protection;
- prohibition of exploitation of natural resources (including the development of dams) qualified by such activities as sport, fishing, the need for management, facilities, etc.

While national parks are generally understood to be administered by national governments (hence the name), in Australia national parks are run by State Governments and predate the Federation of Australia.

In 1810, the English poet William Wordsworth described the Lake District as a "sort of national property in which every man has a right and interest who has an eye to perceive and a heart to enjoy".

The painter George Catlin, in his travels through the American West, wrote in 1832 that the Native Americans in the United States might be preserved "by some great protecting policy of government ... in a magnificent park ... A nation's park, containing man and beast, in all the wild and freshness of their nature's beauty!"

Similar ideas were expressed in other countries — in Sweden, for instance, the Finnish-born Baron Adolf Erik Nordenskiöld made such a proposition in 1880. The Scottish-American naturalist John Muir was inspirational in the foundation of national parks, anticipating many ideas of conservationism, environmentalism, and the animal rights movement.

The first effort by any government to set aside such protected lands was in the United States, on April 20, 1832, when President Andrew Jackson signed legislation to set aside four sections of land around what is now Hot Springs, Arkansas to protect the natural, thermal springs and adjoining mountainsides for the future disposal of the US government. It was known as the Hot Springs Reservation. However no legal authority was established and federal control of the area was not clearly established until 1877.

The next effort by any government to set aside such protected lands was, again, in the United States, when President Abraham Lincoln signed an Act of Congress on June 30, 1864, ceding the Yosemite Valley and the Mariposa Grove of Giant Sequoias (later becoming the Yosemite National Park) to the state of California.

> 'The said State shall accept this grant upon the express conditions that the premises shall be held for public use, resort, and recreation; shall be inalienable for all time'.
>
> — *U.S. Congress, 1864*

In 1872, Yellowstone National Park was established as the world's first truly national park. When news of the natural wonders of the Yellowstone were first promulgated, the land was part of a federally governed territory. Unlike Yosemite, there was no state government that could assume stewardship of the land, so the federal government took on direct responsibility for the park, a process formally completed in October 1, 1890 — the official first national park of the United States. It took the combined effort and interest of conservationists, politicians and especially businesses — namely, the Northern Pacific Railroad, whose route through Montana would greatly benefit by the creation of this new tourist attraction — to ensure the passage of that landmark enabling legislation by the United States Congress to create Yellowstone National Park. Theodore Roosevelt, already an active campaigner and so influential as good stump speakers were highly necessary in the pre-telecommunications era, was highly influential in convincing fellow Republicans and big business to back the bill.

The 'dean of western writers', American Pulitzer prize-winning author Wallace Stegner, has written that national parks are 'America's best idea,' — a departure from the royal preserves that Old World sovereigns enjoyed for themselves – inherently democratic, open to all, "they reflect us at our best, not our worst'. Even with the creation of Yellowstone, Yosemite, and nearly 37 other national parks and monuments, another 44 years passed before an agency was created in the United States to administer these units in a comprehensive way — the U.S. National Park Service (NPS). Businessman Stephen Mather and his journalist partner Robert Sterling Yard pushed hardest for the creation of the NPS, writing then-Secretary of the Interior Franklin Knight Lane about such a need and spearheading a large publicity campaign for their movement. Lane invited Mather to come to Washington, DC to work with him to draft and see passage of the NPS Organic Act, which was approved by Congress and signed into law on August 25, 1916. Of the 392 sites managed by the National Park Service of the United States, only 58 carry the designation of National Park.

Following the idea established in Yellowstone there soon followed parks in other nations. In Australia, the Royal National Park was established just south of Sydney in 1879. Rocky Mountain National Park became Canada's first national park in 1885. New Zealand had its first national park in 1887. In Europe the first national parks were a set of nine parks in Sweden in 1909; Europe has some 370 national parks as of this writing. Africa's first national park was established in 1925 when Albert I of Belgium designated an area of what is now Democratic Republic of Congo centred around the Virunga Mountains as the Albert National Park (since renamed Virunga National Park). In 1926, the government of South Africa designated Kruger National Park as the nation's first national park. After World War II, national parks were founded all over the world. The Vanoise National Park in the Alps was the first French national park, created in 1963 after public mobilization against a touristic project.

In 1872, Yellowstone National Park was established as the world's first truly national park. When news of the natural wonders of the Yellowstone were first promulgated, the land was part of a federally governed territory. Unlike Yosemite, there was no state government that could assume stewardship of the land, so the federal government took on direct responsibility for the park, a process formally completed in October 1, 1890 — the official first national park of the United States. It took the combined effort and interest of conservationists, politicians and especially businesses — namely, the Northern Pacific Railroad, whose route through Montana would greatly benefit by the creation of this new tourist attraction — to ensure the passage of that landmark enabling legislation by the United States Congress to create Yellowstone National Park. Theodore Roosevelt, already an active campaigner and so influential as good stump speakers were highly necessary in the pre-telecommunications era, was highly influential in convincing fellow Republicans and big business to back the bill.

The 'dean of western writers', American Pulitzer prize-winning author Wallace Stegner, has written that national parks are 'America's best idea,' — a departure from the royal preserves that Old World sovereigns enjoyed for themselves — inherently democratic, open to all, 'they reflect us at our best, not our worst'. Even with the creation of Yellowstone, Yosemite, and nearly 37 other national parks and monuments, another 44 years passed before an agency was created in the United States to administer these units in a comprehensive way — the U.S. National Park Service (NPS). Businessman Stephen Mather and his journalist partner Robert Sterling Yard pushed hardest for the creation of the NPS, writing then-Secretary of the Interior Franklin Knight Lane about such a need and spearheading a large publicity campaign for their movement. Lane invited Mather to come to Washington, DC to work with him to draft and see passage of the NPS Organic Act, which was approved by Congress and signed into law on August 25, 1916. Of the 392 sites managed by the National Park Service of the United States, only 58 carry the designation of National Park.

Following the idea established in Yellowstone there soon followed parks in other nations. In Australia, the Royal National Park was established just south of Sydney in 1879. Rocky Mountain National Park became Canada's first national park in 1885. New Zealand had its first national park in 1887. In Europe the first national parks were a set of nine parks in Sweden in 1909; Europe has some 370 national parks as of this writing. Africa's first national park was established in 1925 when Albert I of Belgium designated an area of what is now Democratic Republic of Congo centred around the Virunga Mountains as the Albert National Park (since renamed Virunga National Park). In 1926, the government of South Africa designated Kruger National Park as the nation's first national park. After World War II, national parks were founded all over the world. The Vanoise National Park in the Alps was the first French national park, created in 1963 after public mobilization against a touristic project.

Park

A park is a protected area, in its natural or semi-natural state, or planted, and set aside for human recreation and enjoyment, or for the protection of wildlife or natural habitats. It may consist of rocks, soil, water, flora and fauna and grass areas.

Wilderness parks are intact and undeveloped areas used mainly by wild species. Many parks are legally protected by law.

Protected wilderness zones are required for some wild species to survive. Some protected parks focus mainly on the survival of a few threatened species, such as gorillas or chimpanzees.

National Parks

A national park is a reserve of land, usually, but not always declared and owned by a national government, protected from most human development and pollution. National parks are a protected area of IUCN category II. The largest national park in the world is the Northeast Greenland National Park, which was established in 1974.

In the United States the concept of preserving landscapes for the pleasure of the people was established on June 30, 1864, when President Abraham Lincoln signed the bill creating the Yosemite Grant. A policy of preservation, rather than co-usage as in the National Forests, where grazing, farming and logging are licensed, was implemented four decades later during the presidential administration of Teddy Roosevelt, and Yosemite became a national park. Tourism and, later, recreation were the intended purposes of the lands Roosevelt set aside in the system. John Muir was instrumental in this effort.

These parks were termed national parks and today are looked after by the U.S. National Park Service. U.S. state governments have also set aside land to preserve for the enjoyment of the public. There are also national parks in many other countries.

Sub-national Parks

In Federal systems, many parks are managed by the local levels of government, rather than by the central government. In the United States these are called state parks and in Canada provincial or terriorial parks, except in Quebec where they are known as National Parks.

A park is an area of open space provided for recreational use, usually owned and maintained by a local government. Parks commonly resemble savannas or open woodlands, the types of landscape that human beings find most relaxing. Grass is typically kept short to discourage insect pests and to allow for the enjoyment of picnics and sporting activities. Trees are chosen for their beauty and to provide shade.

The world's first public park is claimed to be the City Park, Budapest, Hungary, which was property of the Batthyány family. In 1808 an Imperial law converted it to the English style. Some years later the Count Batthyány ordered that it should be established as a public park. The second public park in the world is the Peel Park, Salford, England opened on 22 August 1846 Another possible claimant for status as the world's first public park is Boston Common, set aside in 1634, whose first recreational promenade, Tremont Mall, dates from 1728. True park status for the entire common seems to have emerged no later than 1830, when the grazing of cows was ended and renaming the Common as Washington Park was proposed (renaming the bordering Sentry Street to Park Street in 1808 already acknowledged the reality).

Parks can be divided into active and passive recreation. Active recreation is that which require intensive development and often involves cooperative or team activity, including playgrounds, ball fields and skateparks. Passive recreation is that which emphasizes the open-space aspect of a park and which involves a low level of development, including picnic areas and trails. Organized football matches take place in parks.

Many smaller *neighborhood parks* are receiving increased attention and valuation as significant community assets and places of refuge in heavily populated urban areas. Neighborhood groups around the world are joining together to support local parks that have suffered from urban decay and government neglect.

A linear park is a park that has a much greater length than width. A typical example of a linear park is a section of a former railway that has been converted into a park (i.e. the tracks removed, vegetation allowed to grow back). Parks are sometimes made out of oddly shaped areas of land, much like the vacant lots that often become city neighborhood parks.

Country Parks

In some countries, especially the United Kingdom, *country parks* are areas designated for recreation, and managed by local authorities. They are often located near urban populations, but they provide recreational facilities typical of the countryside rather than the town.

Private Parks

Private parks are owned by individuals or businesses and are used at the discretion of the owner. There are a few types of private parks, and some which once were privately maintained and used have now been made open to the public.

Hunting parks were originally areas maintained as open space where residences, industry and farming were not allowed, often originally so that nobility might have a place to hunt . These were known for instance, as deer parks (deer being originally a term meaning any wild animal). Many country houses in Great Britain and Ireland still have parks of this sort, which since the 18th century have often been landscaped for aesthetic effect. They are usually a mixture of open grassland with scattered trees and sections of woodland, and are often enclosed by a high wall. The area immediately around the house is the garden. In some cases this will also feature sweeping lawns and scattered trees; the basic difference between a country house's park and its garden is that the park is grazed by animals, but they are excluded from the garden.

The term park is also used in reference to industrial areas, often termed industrial parks. Some technology research areas are also called research parks. Small environmental areas, often part of urban renewal plans, are called pocket parks. The word park may also be used in community names, such as Oak Park or College Park. Sometimes the active recreational aspect may be expressed in the extreme of naming an amusement park, usually privately owned. A car park is an area of land or a building in which cars are parked.

An amusement park, or theme park is a generic term for a collection of rides and other entertainment attractions assembled for the purpose of entertainment.

Grass

Grasses, or more technically graminoids, are monocotyledonous, usually herbaceous plants with narrow leaves growing from the base. They include the 'true grasses', of the Poaceae (or Gramineae) family, as well as the sedges (Cyperaceae) and the rushes (Juncaceae). The true grasses include cereals, bamboo and the grasses of lawns (turf) and grassland. Sedges include many wild marsh and grassland plants, and some cultivated ones such as water chestnut (Eleocharis dulcis) and papyrus sedge (Cyperus papyrus). Uses for graminoids include food (as grain, sprouted grain, shoots or rhizomes), drink (beer, whisky), pasture for livestock, thatch, paper, fuel, insulation, construction, sports turf, basket weaving and many others.

Graminoids are among the most versatile life forms. They became widespread toward the end of the Cretaceous period, and fossilized dinosaur dung (coprolites) have been found containing phytoliths of a variety of grasses that include the ancestors of rice and bamboo. Grasses have adapted to conditions in lush rain forests, dry deserts, cold mountains and even intertidal habitats, and are now the most widespread plant type; grass is a valuable source of food and energy for all sorts of wildlife and organics.

Graminoids are the dominant vegetation in many habitats, including grassland, salt-marsh, reedswamp and steppes. They also occur as a smaller part of the vegetation in almost every other terrestrial habitat.

There are some 3,500 species of graminoids.

Many types of animals eat grass as their main source of food, and are called graminivores — these include cattle, sheep, horses, rabbits and many invertebrates, such as grasshoppers and the caterpillars of many brown butterflies. Grasses are also eaten by omnivorous or even occasionally by primarily carnivorous animals.

In the study of ecological communities, herbaceous plants are divided into graminoids and forbs, which are herbaceous dicotyledons, mostly with broad leaves.

Agriculture

Plants of this type have always been important to humans. They have been grown as food for domesticated animals for up to 10,000 years. (See grass fed beef.) They have been used for paper-making since 2400 BC or before. Now they provide the majority of food crops, and have many other uses, such as feeding animals, and for lawns. There are many minor uses, and grasses are familiar to most human cultures.

Lawns

In some places, particularly in suburban areas throughout the world, the maintenance of a grass lawn is a sign of a homeowner's responsibility to the overall appearance of their neighborhood. One work credits lawn maintenance to '. . . the desire for upward mobility and its manifestation in the lawn. As Virginia Jenkins, author of *The Lawn*, put it quite bluntly, 'Upper middle-class Americans emulated aristocratic society with their own small, semi-rural estates.' In general, the lawn was one of the primary selling points of these new suburban homes, as it shifted social class designations from the equity and ubiquity of urban homes connected to the streets with the upper-middle class designation of a 'healthy' green space and the status symbol that is the front lawn'.

Many municipalities and homeowner's associations have rules which require lawns to be maintained to certain specifications, sanctioning those who allow the grass to grow too long. In communities with drought problems, watering of lawns may be restricted to certain times of day or days of the week. Some people have allergies to grass.

Grass is important in many sports, notably with those played on fields such as American football, Association football, baseball, cricket, and rugby. In some sports facilities, including indoor domes and places where maintenance of a grass field would be difficult, grass may be replaced with artificial turf, a synthetic grass-like substitute. Sports such as golf, tennis and cricket are particularly dependent on the quality of the grass on which the sport is played.

Cricket

The gray area is the cricket pitch currently in use. Parallel to it are other pitches in various states of preparation which could be used in other matches.

In cricket, the pitch is the strip of carefully mowed and rolled grass where the bowler bowls. In the days leading up to the match it is repeatedly mowed and rolled to produce a very hard, flat surface for the ball to bounce off. The quality of the preparation can have a considerable influence on the game; a relatively grassy pitch will favour bowlers and a hard and dryer pitch, with less grass remaining, will typically favour batsmen (at least initially). As the grass dries out and is damaged over the course of the match the pitch's characteristics will change, resulting in batting on the first day of a test match being vastly different to batting on the same pitch after 5 days of play.

Golf

Golf is very dependent on a quality grass surface. Grass on golf courses is kept in three distinct conditions: that of the *rough*, the *fairway*, and the *putting green*. Grass on the fairway is short and even, allowing the player to cleanly strike the ball. Playing from the rough is a disadvantage because the grass is generally much longer, which may affect the flight of the ball. Grass on the putting green is the shortest and most even, ideally allowing the ball to roll smoothly over the surface. An entire industry revolves around the development and marketing of grasses for golf courses.

Tennis

In tennis, grass is grown on very hard-packed soil, and bounce may vary depending on the grass's health, how recently it has been mowed, and the wear and tear of recent play. The surface is softer than hard courts and clay (other tennis surfaces), so the ball bounces lower, and players must reach the ball faster resulting in a different style of play which may suit some players more than others. The most famous grass tennis court in the world is Centre Court at Wimbledon located in England, home of the Wimbledon Championship. This is considered the most expensive lawn in the world.

Fiction

Grass plays a central role in two important science fiction catastrophe novels from the 1940s and 1950s, Ward Moore's *Greener Than You Think*, in which the world is slowly taken over by unstoppable Bermuda Grass, and John Christopher's *The Death of Grass*, in which a plague that kills off all forms of grass threatens the survival of the human species.

Wilderness

Wilderness or wildland is a natural environment on Earth that has not been significantly modified by human activity. It may also be defined as: "The most intact, undisturbed wild natural areas left on our planet — those last truly wild places that humans do not control and have not developed with roads, pipelines or other industrial infrastructure." Wilderness areas can be found in preserves, estates, farms, conservation preserves, ranches, National Forests, National Parks and even in urban areas along rivers, gulches or otherwise undeveloped areas. These areas are considered important for the survival of certain species, biodiversity, ecological studies, conservation, solitude, and recreation. Wilderness is deeply valued for cultural, spiritual, moral, and aesthetic reasons. Some nature writers believe wilderness areas are vital for the human spirit and creativity. They may also preserve historic genetic traits and that they provide habitat for wild flora and fauna that may be difficult to recreate in zoos, arboretums or laboratories.

The word wilderness derives from the notion of 'wildness' — in other words, that which is not controllable by humans. The word's etymology is from the Old English *wildeornes*, which in turn derives from *wildeor* meaning wild beast (wild + deor = beast, deer) (The Collins English Dictionary, 2000). From this point of view, it is the wildness of a place that makes it a wilderness. The mere presence or activity of people does not disqualify an area from being 'wilderness'. Many ecosystems that are, or have been, inhabited or influenced by activities of people may still be considered 'wild'. This way of looking at wilderness includes areas within which natural processes operate without human interference.

The Wild Foundation states that wilderness areas have two dimensions: they must be biologically intact and legally protected. The World Conservation Union (IUCN) classifies wilderness at two levels, Ia (Strict Nature Preserves) and Ib (Wilderness areas). Most scientists and conservationists agree that no place on earth is completely untouched by humanity, either due to past occupation by indigenous people, or through global processes such as climate change. Activities on the margins of specific wilderness areas, such as fire suppression and the interruption of animal migration also affect the interior of wildernesses.

Especially in wealthier, industrialized nations, it has a specific legal meaning as well: as land where development is prohibited by law. Many nations have designated wilderness, including Australia, Canada, New Zealand, South Africa and the United States. Many new parks are currently being planned and legally passed by various Parliaments and Legislatures at the urging of dedicated individuals around the globe who believe that "in the end, dedicated, inspired people empowered by effective legislation will ensure that the spirit and services of wilderness will thrive and permeate our society, preserving a world that we are proud to hand over to those who come after us."

Looked at through the lens of the visual arts, nature and wildness have been important subjects in various epochs of world history. An early tradition of landscape art occurred in the Tang Dynasty (618-907). The tradition of representing nature as it is became one of the aims of Chinese painting and was a significant influence in Asian art. Artists in the tradition of Shan shui (lit. mountain-water-picture), learned to depict mountains and rivers 'from the perspective of nature as a whole and on the basis of their understanding of the laws of nature . . . as if seen through the eyes of a bird'. In the 13th century, Shih Erh Chi recommended avoiding painting 'scenes lacking any places made inaccessible by nature'.

The idea of wilderness having intrinsic value emerged in the Western world in the 1800s. British artists John Constable and JMW Turner turned their attention to capturing the beauty of the natural world in their paintings. Prior to that, paintings had been primarily of religious scenes or of human beings. William Wordsworth's poetry described the wonder of the natural world, which had formerly been viewed as a threatening place. Increasingly the valuing of nature became an aspect of Western culture.

Over the course of the 19th century wilderness became to be viewed not as a place to fear but a place to enjoy and protect, hence came the conservation movement in the latter half of the 19th century. Rivers were rafted and mountains were climbed solely for the sake of recreation, not to determine their geographical contexture. This was a profound shift in wilderness thought. It reached a pinnacle in the US in the 1960s with the passage of the Wilderness Act of 1964, that allowed for parts of U.S. National Forests to be designated as 'wilderness preserves'.

The 21st century has seen another slight shift in wilderness thought and theory. It is now understood that simply drawing lines around a piece of land and declaring it a wilderness does not necessarily make it a wilderness. All landscapes are intricately connected and what happens outside a wilderness certainly affects what happens inside it. For example, pollution from Los Angeles and the California Central Valley smog up Kern Canyon and Sequoia National Park. The national park has miles of 'wilderness' but the air is filled with pollution from the valley. This then brings us to the paradox of what a wilderness really is, which is precisely the issue in 21st century wilderness thought.

For most of human history, the greater part of the Earth's terrain was wilderness, and human attention was concentrated in settled areas. The first known laws to protect parts of nature date back to the Babylonian Empire and Chinese Empire. Ashoka, the Great Mauryan King, defined the first laws in the world to protect flora and fauna in Edicts of Ashoka around 3rd Century B.C. In the Middle Ages, the Kings of England initiated one of the world's first conscious efforts to protect natural areas. They were motivated by a desire to be able to hunt wild animals in private hunting preserves rather than a desire to protect wilderness. Nevertheless, in order to have animals to hunt they would have to protect wildlife from subsistence hunting and the land from villagers gathering firewood. Similar measures were introduced in other European countries.

Early in the 19th century, Wordsworth and other romanticists in the U.K., concerned about 'the excesses of industrialization and urbanization', called for a return to natural environments. This movement achieved some gains in protecting sensitive ecosystems, but a more successful form of environmentalism emerged in Germany by the mid 19th century. 'Scientific Conservation', as it was called, advocated "the efficient utilization of natural resources through the application of science and technology'. Concepts of forest management based on the German approach were applied in other parts of the world, but with varying degrees of success.

By the latter 19th century it had become clear that in many countries wild areas had either disappeared or were in danger of disappearing. This realisation gave rise to the conservation movement in the USA, partly through the efforts of writers and activists such as John Burroughs and John Muir, and politicians such as U.S. President Teddy Roosevelt.

The creation of National Parks, beginning in the 19th century, preserved some especially attractive and notable areas, but the pursuits of commerce, lifestyle, and recreation combined with increases in human population have continued to result in human modification of relatively untouched areas. Such human activity often negatively impacts native flora and fauna. As such, to better protect critical habitats and preserve low-impact recreational opportunities, legal concepts of 'wilderness' were established in many countries, beginning with the United States.

The first National Park was Yellowstone, established in 1872 . The creation of this and other parks showed a growing appreciation of wild nature, but also an economic reality. The railways wanted to entice people to travel west. The world's second national park, the Royal National Park, was established in 1879. just 25-km to the south of Sydney, Australia.

This U.S. concept of national parks soon caught on in Canada, which created Banff National Park in the 1880s, at the same time as the transcontinental Canadian Pacific Railway was being built. Parks such as Banff and Yellowstone gained favor as the railroads advertised travel to 'the great wild spaces' of North America. When outdoorsman Teddy Roosevelt became president of the United States, he began to enlarge the U.S. National Parks system, and established the National Forest system.

By the 1920s, travel across North America by train to experience the "wilderness" (often viewing it only through windows) had become wildly popular. This led to the commercialization of some of Canada's National Parks with the building of great hotels such as the Banff Springs Hotel and Chateau Lake Louise.

Two opposing factions had emerged within the environmental movement by the early 20th century: the conservationists and the preservationists. The conservationists (such as Gifford Pinchot) focussed on the proper use of nature, whereas the preservationists sought the protection of nature from use. Put another way, conservation sought to regulate human use while preservation sought to eliminate human impact altogether.

The idea of protecting nature for nature's sake began to gain more recognition in the 1930s with American writers like Aldo Leopold, calling for a 'land ethic' and urging wilderness protection. It had become increasingly clear that wild spaces were disappearing rapidly and that decisive action was needed to save them.

Global conservation became an issue at the time of the dissolution of the British Empire in Africa in the late 1940s. The British established great wildlife preserves there. As before, this interest in conservation had an economic motive: in this case, big game hunting. Nevertheless, this led to growing recognition in the 1950s and the early 1960s of the need to protect large spaces for wildlife conservation worldwide. The World Wildlife Fund (WWF), founded in 1961, grew to be one of the largest conservation organizations in the world.

Preservation again came to the fore in the 1960s with the publication of Rachel Carson's Silent Spring in 1962, which was the genesis of the modern environmental movement. Major environmental groups such as the Sierra Club shifted from protesting to working with politicians to influence environmental policy.

Nevertheless, initiatives for wilderness conservation continue to increase. There are a growing number of projects to protect tropical rainforests through conservation initiatives. There are also large-scale projects to conserve wilderness regions, such as Canada's Boreal Forest Conservation Framework. The Framework calls for conservation of fifty per cent of the 6,000,000 square kilometres of boreal forest in Canada's north. In addition to the World Wildlife Fund, organizations such as The WILD Foundation, The Nature Conservancy, Conservation International, The Wilderness Society (United States) and many others are active in such conservation efforts.

In the United States, a Wilderness Area is an area of federal land set aside by an act of Congress. Human activities in wilderness areas are restricted to scientific study and non-mechanized recreation; horses are permitted but mechanized vehicles and equipment, such as cars and bicycles, are not.

The Great Swamp of New Jersey, donated for federal protection by concerned residents, was designated as the first wilderness refuge in the United States — winter scene in March, 2008.

The United States was the first country to officially designate land as 'wilderness' through the Wilderness Act of 1964. Wilderness designation helps preserve the natural state of the land and protects flora and fauna by prohibiting development and providing for non-mechanized recreation only. The first wilderness refuge designation was for the Great Swamp in New Jersey. Properties in the swamp had been acquired by residents of the area who donated it to the federal government as a park for perpetual protection. Today the refuge amounts to 7,600 acres (31 km^2) that are within thirty miles of Manhattan.

Wilderness designations are granted by an Act of Congress for Federal land that retains a 'primeval character' and that has no human habitation or development. Approximately 100 million acres (400,000 km^2) are designated as wilderness in the United States. This accounts for 4.71 per cent of the total land of the country; however, 54 per cent of wilderness is in Alaska, although recreation and development in Alaskan wilderness is often less restrictive, and only 2.58 per cent of the lower continental United States is designated as wilderness.

At the forefront of the international wilderness movement has been The wild Foundation, its founder Dr. Ian Player and its network of sister and partner organizations around the globe. The pioneer World Wilderness Congress in 1977 introduced the wilderness concept as an issue of international importance, and began the process of defining the term in biological and social contexts. Today, this work is continued by many international groups who still look to the World Wilderness Congress as the international venue for wilderness and to The wild Foundation network for wilderness tools and action. The wild Foundation also publishes the standard references for wilderness professionals and others involved in the issues: Wilderness Management: Stewardship and Protection of Resources and Values (3rd Edition 2002; 4th Edition in press), the International Journal of Wilderness, A Handbook on International Wilderness Law and Policy (2008) and Protecting Wild Nature on Native Lands (2008) are the backbone of information and management tools for international wilderness issues.

The Wilderness Task Force within the World Commission on Protected Areas (WTF/WCPA) of the International Union for the Conservation of Nature (IUCN) plays a critical role in defining legal and management guidelines for wilderness at the international level and is also a clearing-house for information on wilderness issues. The IUCN Protected Areas Classification System, defines wilderness as "A large area of unmodified or slightly modified land, and/or sea retaining its natural character and influence, without permanent or significant habitation, which is protected and managed so as to preserve its natural condition (Category 1b)." The WILD Foundation founded the WTF/WCPA in 2002 and remains co-chair.

According to a major study, Wilderness: Earth's Last Wild Places, carried out by Conservation International, 46 per cent of the world's land mass is wilderness. For purposes of this report, 'wilderness' was defined as an area that "has 70 per cent or more of its original vegetation intact, covers at least 10,000 square kilometers (3,861 square miles) and must have fewer than five people per square kilometer." However, an IUCN/UNEP report published in 2003, found that only 10.9 per cent of the world's land mass is currently a Category 1 Protected Area, that is, either a *strict nature reserve* (5.5%) or protected wilderness (5.4%). Such areas remain relatively untouched by humans. Of course, there are large tracts of lands in National Parks and other protected areas that would also qualify as wilderness. However, many protected areas have some degree of human modification or activity, so a definitive estimate of true wilderness is difficult.

The Wildlife Conservation Society generated a human footprint using a number of indicators, the absence of which indicate wildness: human population density, human access via roads and rivers, human infrastructure for agriculture and settlements and the presence of industrial power (lights visible from space). The society estimates that 26 per cent of the Earth's land mass falls into the category of 'Last of the wild'. The wildest regions of the world include the tundra, the taiga, the Amazonian rain forest, the Tibetan Plateau, the Australian outback and deserts such as the Sahara, and the Gobi.

It should be noted that the percentage of land area designated 'wilderness' does not reflect 'quality' of remaining wilderness, part of which is barren areas with low biodiversity. Of the last natural wilderness areas, the taiga — which is mostly wilderness — represents 11% of the total land mass in the Northern Hemisphere. Tropical rainforest represent a further 7 per cent of the world's land base Estimates of the Earth's remaining wilderness underscore the rate at which these lands are being developed, with dramatic declines in biodiversity as a consequence.

The American concept of wilderness has been criticized by some nature writers. For example, William Cronon writes that what he calls a wilderness ethic or cult may 'teach us to be dismissive or even contemptuous of such humble places and experiences', and that 'wilderness tends to privilege some parts of nature at the expense of others', using as an example 'the mighty canyon more inspiring than the humble marsh'. This is most clearly visible with the fact that nearly all U.S. National Parks preserve spectacular canyons and mountains, and it was not until the 1940s that a swamp became a national park — the Everglades. In the mid-1900s national parks started to protect biodiversity, not simply attractive scenery.

Cronon also believes the passion to save wilderness 'poses a serious threat to responsible environmentalism' and writes that it allows people to 'give ourselves permission to evade responsibility for the lives we actually lead ... to the extent that we live in an urban-industrial civilization" but at the same time pretend to ourselves that our real home is in the wilderness'.

Michael Pollan has argued that the wilderness ethic leads people to dismiss areas whose wildness is less than absolute. In his book Second Nature, Pollan writes that "once a landscape is no longer 'virgin' it is typically written off as fallen, lost to nature, irredeemable." Another challenge to the conventional notion of wilderness comes from Robert Winkler in his book, Going Wild: Adventures with Birds in the Suburban Wilderness. 'On walks in the unpeopled parts of the suburbs', Winkler writes, 'I've witnessed the same wild creatures, struggles for survival, and natural beauty that we associate with true wilderness'.

7

Succulent Plant

Succulent plants, also known as succulents or fat plants, are water-retaining plants adapted to arid climate or soil conditions. Succulent plants store water in their leaves, stems and/or roots. Geophytes survive unfavourable periods by dying back to underground storage organs (tuberous roots, corms, bulbs, and rhizomes). They can be regarded as succulents. Some plants are succulent geophytes. The storage of water often gives succulent plants a more swollen or fleshy appearance than other plants, also known as succulence. In addition to succulence, succulent plants variously have other water-saving features. These may include:

- Crassulacean acid metabolism (CAM) to minimize water loss;
- Absent, reduced, or cylindrical to spherical leaves;
- reduction in the number of stomata;
- stems, rather than leaves, as the main site of photosynthesis;
- a compact, reduced, cushion-like, columnar or spherical growth form;
- ribs enabling rapid increases in plant volume and decreasing surface area exposed to the sun;
- a waxy, hairy or spiny outer surface to create a humid microhabitat around the plant which reduces air movement near the surface of the plant, thereby reducing water loss;
- roots very near the surface of the soil, so they are able to take up moisture from very small showers or even from heavy dew;

- ability to remain plump and full of water even with high internal temperatures (e.g. 52° Celsius);
- a very impervious outer cuticle (skin);
- they contain mucilaginous substances which retain water strongly.

Many succulents come from the dry areas of the tropics and subtropics, such as steppes, semi-desert and desert. High temperatures and low precipitation force plants to collect and store water in order to survive long dry periods. Succulents also occur as epiphytes, as such they have limited or no contact with the ground, and are dependent on their ability to store water. Succulents also occur as inhabitants of sea coasts, or salt pans which are exposed to high levels of dissolved minerals.

The best known succulents are cacti (family: Cactaceae). Virtually all cacti are succulents, but not all succulents are cacti.

Families and Genera

Plant families and genera in which succulent species occur are listed below:

- **Agavaceae**: Agave, Beschorneria, Chlorophytum, Furcraea, Hesperaloe, Hesperoyucca, Yucca
- **Aizoaceae**: Aizoanthemum, Aizoon, Galenia, Sesuvium, Tetragonia, Trianthema, Zaleya
- **Mesembryanthemoideae** (syn. Mesembryanthemaceae Subfamily)

  Acrodon, Aethephyllum, Aloinopsis, Amoebophyllum (non-current), Amphibolia, Antegibbaeum, Antimima, Apatesia, Aptenia, Arenifera, Argyroderma, Aridaria, Aspazoma, Astridia, Bergeranthus, Berrisfordia (non-current), Bijlia, Braunsia, Brianhuntlia, Brownanthus, Calamophyllum, Carpanthia, Carpobrotus, Carruanthus, Eberlanzia, Ebracteola, Ectotropis (non-current), Enarganthe, Erepsia, Esterhuysenia, Eurystigma (non-current), Faucaria, Fenestraria, Frithia, Gibbaeum, Glottiphyllum, Halenbergia (non-current), Hallianthus, Hameria, Hartmanthus, Hereroa, Herrea (non-current), Herreanthus (now Conophytum), Hydrodea (non-current), Hymenogyne, Ihlenfeldtia, Imitaria (non-current), Jacobsenia, Jensenbotrya, Jordaaniella, Juttadinteria, Kensitia (non-current), Khadia, Lampranthus, Lapidaria, Leipoldtia, Lithops, Machairophyllum, Malephora, Marlothistela, Maughaniella (non-current), Mesembryanthemum, Mestoklama, Meyerophytum, Micropterum (non-current), Mimetophytum (non-current), Mitrophyllum, Monilaria, Mossia, Muiria, Namaquanthus, Namibia,

Nanathus, Nelia, Neohenricia, Neorhine (non-current), Nycteranthus (non-current), Octopoma, Odontophorus, Oophytum, Ophthalmophyllum (non-current), Orthopterum, Oscularia, Ottosonderia, Pherelobus (non-current), Phiambolia, Phyllobolus, Platythyra (non-current), Pleiospilos, Polymita, Prenia, Psammophora, Psicaulon, Rabiea, Rhinephyllum, Rhombophyllum, Ruschia, Ruschianthemum (non-current), Ruschianthus, Ruschiella, Saphesia, Sarozona,Sceletium, Schlecteranthus, Schwantesia, Scopologena, Semnanthe (now Erepsia), Skiatophytum, Smicrostigma, Sphalmanthus (non-current), Stayneria, Stoeberia, Stomatium, Synaptophyllum, Tanquana, Titanopsis, Trichodiadema, Vanheerea, Vanzijlia, Viokia, Wooleya, Zeuktophyllum

- **Amaranthaceae**: Arthraerua
- **Amaryllidaceae** (geophytes): Ammocharis, Apodolirion, Boophone, Brunsvigia, Crinum, Crossyne, Cryptostephanus, Cyrtanthus, Gethyllis, Habranthus, Haemanthus, Hessea, Nerine, Pancratium, Rauhia, Scadoxus, Strumaria, Zephyranthes
- **Anacardiaceae**: Operculicaria, Pachycormus
- **Apiaceae**: Steganotaenia
- **Apocynaceae**: Adenium, Mandevilla, Pachypodium, Plumeria
- **Asclepiadoideae** (syn. Asclepiadaceae Subfamily)

  Absolmsia, Asclepias, Australluma, Aspidoglossum, Aspidonepsis, Baynesia, Brachy-stelma, Caralluma, Ceropegia, Chlorocyathus, Cibirhiza, Cordylogyne, Cynanchum, Dischidia, Dischidiopsis, Duvalia, Duvaliandra, Echidnopsis Edithcolea, Eustegia, Fanninia, Fockea, Glossostelma, Hoodia, Hoya, Huernia, Huerniopsis, Ischnolepis, Larryleachia, Lavrania, Marsdenia, Matelea, Miraglossum, Notechidnopsis, Odontostelma, Ophionella, Orbea, Orbeanthus, Pachycarpus, Parapodium, Pectinaria, Periglossum, Petopentia, Piaranthus, Pseudolithos, Quaqua, Raphionacme (geophyte), Rhytidocaulon, Riocreuxia, Sarcorrhiza, Sarcostemma, Schizoglossum, Schlechterella, Stapelia, Stapelianthus, Stapeliopsis, Stathmostelma, Stenostelma, Stomatostemma, Tavaresia, Trachycalymma, Tridentea, Tromotriche, Tylophora, White-sloanea, Woodia, Xysmalobium
- **Araceae**: Zamioculcas
- **Araliaceae**: Cussonia
- **Asparagaceae**: Myrsiphyllum (now Asparagus)

- **Asphodelaceae**: Aloe (succulents and succulent geophytes), Astroloba, x Astroworthia, Bulbine (succulent geophytes, succulents, and geophytes), Bulbinella (geophyte), Chortolirion (succulent geophytes), Gasteria, Haworthia, Poellnitzia, Trachyandra (succulent geophytes and succulents)
- **Asteraceae**: Arctotheca, Baeriopsis, Cadiscus, Chrysanthemoides, Coulterella, Crassocephalum, Didelta, Emilia, Eremothamnus, Gymnodiscus, Gynura, Hillardiella (geophyte), Lopholaena, Monoculus, Nidorella, Osteospermum, Othonna (succulents and succulent geophytes), Phaneroglossa, Poecilolepis, Polyachyrus, Pteronia, Senecio, Solanecio,Tripteris
- **Balsaminaceae**: Impatiens
- **Basellaceae**: Anredera, Basella
- **Begoniaceae**: Begonia
- **Bombacaceae**: Adansonia, Cavanillesia, Ceiba, Pseudobombax
- **Boraginaceae**: Heliotropium
- **Brassicaceae**: Heliophila, Lepidium
- **Bromeliaceae**: Abromeitiella
- **Burseraceae**: Boswellia, Bursera, Commiphora
- **Cactaceae**: Acanthocalycium, Acanthocereus, Ariocarpus, Armatocereus, Arrojadoa, Arthrocereus, Astrophytum, Austrocactus, Aztekium, Bergerocactus, Blossfeldia, Brachycereus, Browningia, Brasilicereus, Calymmanthium, Carnegiea, Cephalocereus, Cephalocleistocactus, Cereus, Cintia, Cipocereus, Cleistocactus, Coleocephalocereus, Copiapoa, Corryocactus, Coryphantha, Dendrocereus, Denmoza, Discocactus, Disocactus, Echinocactus, Echinocereus, Echinopsis, Epiphyllum, Epithelantha, Eriosyce, Escobaria, Escontria, Espostoa, Espostoopsis, Eulychnia, Facheiroa, Ferocactus, Frailea, Geohintonia, Gymnocalycium, Haageocereus, Harrisia, Hatiora, Hylocereus, Jasminocereus, Lasiocereus, Leocereus, Lepismium, Leptocereus, Leuchtenbergia, Lophophora, Maihuenia, Malacocarpus, Mammillaria, Mammilloydia, Matucana, Melocactus, Micranthocereus, Mila, Monvillea, Myrtillocactus, Neobuxbaumia, Neolloydia, Neoraimondia, Neowerdermannia, Obregonia, Opuntia, Oreocereus, Oroya, Ortegocactus, Pachycereus, Parodia, Pediocactus, Pelecyphora, Peniocereus, Pereskia, Pereskiopsis, Pilosocereus, Polaskia, Praecereus, Pseudoacanthocereus, Pseudorhipsalis, Pterocactus, Pygmaeocereus, Quiabentia, Rauhocereus, Rebutia, Rhipsalis,

Samaipaticereus, Schlumbergera, Sclerocactus, Selenicereus, Stenocactus, Stenocereus, Stephanocereus, Stetsonia, Strombocactus, Tacinga, Thelocactus, Turbinicarpus, Uebelmannia, Weberbauerocereus, Weberocereus, Yungasocereus

- **Campanulaceae**: Brighamia
- **Capparidaceae**: Maerua
- **Caricaceae**: Carica, Jacarathia
- **Chenopodiaceae** Atriplex, Chenopodium, Dissocarpus, Einadia, Enchylaena, Eremophea, Halopeplis, Maireana, Malacocera, Neobassia, Osteocarpum, Rhagodia, Roycea, Halosarcia, Salicornia, Salsola, Sarcocornia, Sclerochlamys, Sclerolaena, Sueda, Tecticornia, Threlkeldia
- **Cochlospermaceae Commelinaceae**: Aneilema, Callisia, Cyanotis, Tradescantia, Tripogandra
- **Convolvulaceae**: Ipomea, Merremia, Stictocardia, Turbina
- **Crassulaceae**: Adromischus, Aeonium, Afrovivella, Aichryson, Bryophyllum, Cotyledon, Crassula, Cremnophila, Cremnosedum, Dudleya, Echeveria, Graptopetalum, Hylotelephium, Hypagophytum, Kalanchoe, Lenophyllum, Meterostachys, Monanthes, Orostachys, Pachyphytum, Perrierosedum, Phedimus, Pistorinia, Prometheum, Pseudosedum, Rhodiola, Rosularia, Sedella, Sedum, Sempervivum, Sinocrassula, Thompsonella, Tacitus, Tylecodon, Umbilicus, Villadia
- **Cucurbitaceae**: Acanthosicyos, Apodanthera, Brandegea, Cephalopentandra, Ceratosanthes, Citrullus, Coccinia, Corallocarpus, Cucumella, Cucumis, Cucurbita, Cyclantheropsis, Dactyliandra, Dendrosicyos, Doyera, Eureindra, Fevillea, Gerrandanthus, Gynostemma, Halosicyos, Ibervilla, Kedostris, Lagenaria, Marah, Momordica, Neoalsomitra, Odosicyos, Parasicyos, Syrigia, Telfairia, Trochomeria, Trochomeriopsis, Tumamoca, Xerosicyos, Zehneria, Zygosicyos
- **Didiereaceae**: Alluaudia, Alluaudiopsis, Decaria, Didierea
- **Dioscoreaceae**: Dioscorea (geophytic succulent)
- **Doryanthaceae**: Doryanthes
- **Ericaceae**: Sphyrospermum
- **Eriospermaceae**: Eriospermum (geophyte)
- **Euphorbiaceae**: Cnidoscolus, Euphorbia, Jatropha, Monadenium, Pedilanthus, Synadenium

- **Fabaceae**: Delonix, Dolichos, Erythrina, Lotononis, Neorautanenia, Pachyrhizus, Tylosema
- **Fouquieriaceae**: Fouquieria
- **Geraniaceae**: Monsonia, Pelargonium (succulents and geophytes), Sarcocaulon
- **Gesneriaceae**: Aeschynanthus, Alsobia, Chirita, Codonanthe, Columnea, Nematanthus, Sinningia, Streptocarpus
- **Hyacinthaceae** (geophytes, a few succulent geophytes): Albuca, Bowiea, Daubenya, Dipcadi, Drimia, Drimiopsis, Eucomis, Hyacinthus, Lachenalia, Ledebouria, Litanthus, Massonia, Merwilla, Namophila, Ornithogalum, Polyxena, Pseudogaltonia, Pseudoprospero, Resnova, Rhadamanthus, Rhodocodon, Schizobasis, Schizocarphus, Spetaea, Urginea, Veltheimia, Whiteheadia
- **Hypoxidaceae** (geophytes): Empodium, Hypoxis, Pauridia, Saniella, Spiloxene
- **Icacinaceae**: Pyrenacantha (geophyte)
- **Iridaceae** (geophytes): Babiana, Chasmanthe, Crocosmia, Devia, Dierama, Dietes, Duthiastrum, Ferraria, Freesia, Geissorhiza, Gladiolus, Hesperantha, Ixia, Lapeirousia, Melasphaerula, Micranthus, Moraea, Pillansia, Radinosiphon, Romulea, Sparaxis, Syringodea, Thereianthus, Tritonia, Tritoniopsis, Watsonia, Xenoscapa
- **Lamiaceae**: Aeollanthus, Dauphinea, Perrierastrum, Plectranthus, Rotheca, Solenostemon, Tetradenia, Thorncroftia
- **Lentibulariaceae Loasaceae**: Schismocarpus
- **Loranthaceae**: Actinanthella, Agelanthus, Erianthemum, Helixanthera, Moquiniella, Oncocalyx, Pedistylis, Plicosepalus, Septulina, Tapinanthus, Vanwykia
- **Melastomataceae**: Medinilla
- **Meliaceae**: Entandrophragma
- **Menispermaceae**: Chasmanthera, Stephania, Tinospora
- **Molluginaceae**: Hypertelis
- **Moraceae**: Dorstenia, Ficus
- **Moringaceae**: Moringa
- **Nolanaceae**: Nolana
- **Nolinaceae**: Beaucarnea, Calibanus, Dasylirion, Nolina

- **Orchidaceae**: subfamily Epidendroideae Phalaenopsis
- **Orchidaceae** (succulents) Acampe, Aerangis, Ansellia, Bolusiella, Bulbophyllum, Calanthe, Cyrtorchis, Oberonia, Polystachya, Tridactyle, Vanilla (succulent geophytes) Eulophia, Liparis, Oeceoclades (geophytes) Acroliphia, Bartholina, Bonatea, Brachycorythis, Brownleea, Centrostigma, Ceratandra, Corycium, Cynorkis, Didymoplexis, Disa, Disperis, Dracomonticola, Eulophia, Evotella, Gastrodia, Habernaria, Holothrix, Huttonaea, Neobolusia, Nervilia, Plicosepalus, Pachites, Platycoryne
- **Oxalidaceae** (geophytes): Oxalis
- **Passifloraceae**: Adenia
- **Pedaliaceae**: Holubia, Pterodiscus, Sesamothamnus, Uncarina
- **Phyllanthaceae**: Phyllanthus
- **Phytolaccaceae**: Phytolacca
- **Piperaceae**: Peperomia
- **Poaceae**: Dregeochloa
- **Portulacaceae**: Amphipetalum, Anacampseros, Avonia, Calyptrotheca, Ceraria, Cistanthe, Calandrinia, Dendroportulaca, Grahamia, Lewisia, Parakeelya (this name is not accepted by the Australian State and National Herbaria) Portulaca, Portulacaria, Schreiteria, Talinella, Talinum
- **Rubiaceae**: Anthorrhiza, Anthospermum, Hydnophythum, Hydrophylax, Myrmecodia, Myrmephythum, Phylohydrax, Squamellaria
- **Ruscaceae**: Cordyline, Dracaena, Sansevieria
- **Sapindaceae**: Erythrophysa
- **Saxifragaceae**
- **Sterculiaceae**: Brachychiton, Sterculia
- **Urticaceae**: Laportea, Obetia, Pilea, Pouzolzia, Sarcopilea
- **Viscaceae**: Viscum
- **Vitaceae**: Cissus, Cyphostemma
- **Xanthorrhoeaceae**: Xanthorrhoea
- **Zygophyllaceae**: Augea, Seetzenia, Zygophyllum

For some families, most members are succulent; for example the Cactaceae, Agavaceae, Aizoaceae, and Crassulaceae.

8

Community Gardening

A community garden is a single piece of land gardened collectively by a group of people.

Community gardens provide access to fresh produce and plants as well as access to satisfying labor, neighbourhood improvement, sense of community and connection to the environment. They are publicly functioning in terms of ownership, access, and management as well as typically owned in trust by local governments or non-profits. A community garden brings your community closer.

A city's community gardens can be as diverse as its communities of gardeners. Some choose to solely grow flowers, others are nurtured communally and their bounty shared, some have individual plots for personal use, while others are equipped with raised beds for disabled gardeners.

Community gardens encourage an urban community's food security, allowing citizens to grow their own food or for others to donate what they have grown The gardens also combat two forms of alienation that plague modern urban life, by bringing urban gardeners closer in touch with the source of their food, and by breaking down isolation by creating a social community. It has also been found that active communities experience less crime and vandalism.

Unlike public parks, whether community gardens are open to the general public is dependent upon the lease agreements with the management body of the park and the community garden membership.

Open or closed gate policies vary from garden to garden. There is no 'off the shelf model' of a community garden, however; they provide a green space in urban areas, along with opportunities for social gatherings, beautification, education and recreation. However, in a key difference, community gardens are managed and maintained with the active participation of the gardeners themselves, rather than tended only by a professional staff. A second difference is food production: Unlike parks, where plantings are ornamental (or more recently ecological), community gardens often encourage food production by providing gardeners a place to grow vegetables and other crops. To facilitate this, a community garden may be divided into individual plots or tended in a communal fashion, depending on the size and quality of a garden and the members involved.

As discussed below, 'community garden' is the term favoured in the United States and Canada, with a strong presence in Australia and New Zealand as well. The best source and clearinghouse on community gardening information in North America is a coalition of community gardening groups — The American Community Gardening Association.

Community gardens vary widely throughout the world. In North America, community gardens range from familiar 'victory garden' areas where people grow small plots of vegetables, to large 'greening' projects to preserve natural areas, to tiny street beautification planters on urban street corners. In the UK and the rest of Europe, closely related 'allotment gardens' can have dozens of plots, each measuring hundreds of square metres and rented by the same family for generations. In the developing world, commonly held land for small gardens is a familiar part of the landscape, even in urban areas, where they may function as mini-truck farms.

For all their diversity, however, most community gardens share at least four elements in common:

- land (or a place to grow something);
- plantings;
- gardeners; and
- some sort of organizing arrangements.

Land for a community garden can be publicly or privately held. One strong tradition in American community gardening in urban areas is cleaning up abandoned vacant lots and turning them into productive gardens. Alternatively, community gardens can be seen as a health or recreational amenity and included in public parks, similar to ball fields or playgrounds. Historically, community gardens have also served to provide food during wartime or periods of economic depression. Access to land and security of land tenure remains a major challenge for community gardeners and their supporters throughout the world, since in most cases the gardeners themselves do not own or control the land directly.

Some gardens are grown collectively, with everyone working together; others are split into clearly divided plots, each managed by a different gardener (or group or family). Many community gardens have both 'common areas' with shared upkeep and individual/family plots.

Two national surveys sponsored by the American Community Gardening Association in the late 1980s and mid-1990s, and other research, strongly support the observation that there is no 'standard' community garden plot size, at least in the United States and Canada. Individual plot sizes vary widely depending on many factors, including location, land available for gardening, demand, physical and time limitations of the gardeners, among others. As a general rule, North American community garden plots tend to be smaller than European allotments. 6m × 6m (20 ft × 20 ft) is one common plot size (larger gardens in parks); 3m × 3m (10 ft × 10 ft) or 3m × 4.5 m (10 ft × 15 ft) is another (inner city gardens on small lots).

While food production is central to many community and allotment gardens, not all have vegetables as a main focus. Restoration of natural areas and native plant gardens are also popular, as are 'art' gardens. Many gardens have several different planting elements, and combine plots with such projects as small orchards, herbs and butterfly gardens. Individual plots can become 'virtual' backyards, each highly diverse, creating a 'quilt' of flowers, vegetables and folk art.

Gardeners may form a grassroots group to initiate the garden, such as the Green Guerrillas of New York City, or a garden may be organized 'top down' by a municipal agency. The community gardening movement in North American prides itself on being inclusive, diverse, pro-democracy, and supportive of community involvement. Gardeners may be of any cultural background, young or old, new gardeners or seasoned growers, rich or poor. A garden may have only a few people active, or hundreds.

Finally, all community gardens have a structure. The organization depends in part on whether the garden is 'top down' or 'grassroots'. There are many different organizational models in use for community gardens. Some elect boards in a democratic fashion, while others can be run by appointed officials. Some are managed by non-profit organizations, such as a community gardening association, a church, or other land-owner; others by a city's recreation or parks department, a school or University. In most cases, gardeners are expected to pay annual dues to help with garden upkeep, and the organization must manage these fees. The tasks in a community garden are endless — keeping up the area's appearance, mulching paths, recruiting new members, reminding members to tend plots when they get weedy, fund raising, the list goes on... Sensible rules and an 'operations manual' are both invaluable tools, and ideas for both are available at ACGA and other sites.

United Kingdom

In the United Kingdom, community gardening is generally distinct from allotment gardening, though the distinction is sometimes blurred. Allotments are generally plots of land rented to individuals for their cultivation by local authorities or other public bodies — the upkeep of the land is usually the responsibility of the individual plot owners. Allotments tend (but not invariably) to be situated around the outskirts of built-up areas. Use of allotment areas as open space or play areas is generally discouraged. However, there are an increasing number of community-managed allotments, which may include allotment plots and a community garden area.

The community garden movement is of more recent provenance than allotment gardening, with many such gardens built on patches of derelict land, waste ground or land owned by the local authority or a private landlord that is not being used for any purpose. A community garden in the United Kingdom tends to be situated in a built-up area and is typically run by people from the local community as an independent, non-profit organisation (though this may be wholly or partly funded by public money).

It is also likely to perform a dual function as an open space or play area (in which role it may also be known as a 'city park') and — while it may offer plots to individual cultivators — the organisation that administers the garden will normally have a great deal of the responsibility for its planting, landscaping and upkeep. An example inner-city garden of this sort is Islington's Culpeper Community Garden, or Camden's Phoenix Garden.

Some of the larger community gardens act as a hub for the community, offering not just a pleasant green space, but also facilities for education and training. There are estimated to be more than 1,000 community-managed gardens in the UK.

The Federation of City Farms and Community Gardens (a registered charity) is a membership organisation that supports, promotes and represents community-run gardens in the UK.

Spain

Most older Spaniards grew up in the countryside and moved to the city to find work. Strong family ties often keep them from retiring to the countryside, and so urban community gardens are in great demand. Potlucks and paellas are common, as well as regular meetings to manage the affairs of the garden.

United States and Canada

In Canada and the United States, 'community gardening' encompasses a wide variety of approaches. Some influential community gardens, such as the Clinton Street garden in the middle of Manhattan in New York City, and the Peralta garden in Berkeley, California, inspired by architect and community garden visionary Karl Linn, are gathering places for neighbours and showcases for art and ecological awareness, with food production cherished but seen as one part of a much larger vision. Other gardens resemble European 'allotment' gardens, with plots where individuals and families can grow vegetables and flowers, including a number (for instance, in Minneapolis and Ann Arbor, Michigan) which began as 'Victory Gardens' during World War II. Even such 'food' gardens are very different, however — for instance, plot sizes range widely from as small as 1.5m × 1.5m (5 ft × 5 ft) in some inner city gardens and art gardens, such as the Dovetail Garden in Charlotte, North Carolina, to relatively large plots of 15m × 15m (50 ft × 50 ft) such as those at Hilton Head, South Carolina.

Some community gardens, in contrast, are devoted entirely to creating ecological green space or habitat, still others to growing flowers, and others to education or providing access to gardening to those who otherwise could not have a garden, such as the elderly, recent immigrants or the homeless — for example, the Community Garden for the Homeless, also in Charlotte, not far away from the very different Dovetail Garden. Some gardens are worked as community farms with no individual plots at all, shading into becoming urban farms.

In short, the key word to describe the United States is 'diversity'.

That said, a majority of gardens in a majority of community gardening programmes are collections of individual garden plots, frequently between 3m × 3m (10′ × 10′) and 6m × 6m (20′ × 20′). This holds true whether they are sponsored by public agencies such as Park and Recreation Districts (Portland, Oregon; Toronto, Canada), city departments (Seattle, Washington — perhaps the model community gardening programme in the US), large non-profits, or (most commonly) a coalition of different entities and groups, Whether the garden is run as a co-op by the gardeners themselves (still common in New York, Boston and other East Coast cities) or managed by a public or non-profit agency, plot holders typically are asked to pay a modest fee each year and to abide by a set of rules. Many gardens encourage activities such as work days, fundraisers, and social gatherings. Community garden organizers typically say that 'growing community' is as important as growing vegetables, or, as the American Community Gardening Association (ACGA) puts it: "In community gardening, 'community' comes first."

Equally important, according to ACGA, is encouraging political involvement. As storied New York community gardener Adam Honigman puts it: "Community gardening is 50 per cent gardening and 100 per cent local political organizing." Community gardens are more than a meeting ground — they are also a training ground for political empowerment. In a sense, as Karl Linn pointed out, they are the 21st Century version of the New England village green, common space that brings people together and inspires shared action.

ACGA, a non-profit coalition founded in 1979, is the primary advocacy group for community gardening in the US and Canada. After many years of being hosted by the community garden support programme Philadelphia Green in Philadelphia, Pennsylvania, ACGA is now based at the Franklin Park Conservatory in Columbus, Ohio.

Although community gardening exists across northern North America, it remains strongest in the Northeast, where literally thousands of community gardens grow in New York City, Philadelphia and Boston. It is also strong along the West Coast, especially in British Columbia, and in Midwestern centers such as Chicago and Minneapolis.

The European history of community gardening in the US dates back to the early 1700s, when Moravians created a community garden as part of the community of Bethabara, near modern Winston-Salem, North Carolina — a garden still active and open for visitors today! First Nations peoples also gardened with a community approach (Buffalo Bird Woman's Garden paints a picture of gardens among the Hidatsa), likely for generations before the arrival of waves of immigrants.

Academic study of American community gardening by T.J. Bassett and more recently Laura Lawson ('City Bountiful') suggests that the community gardening 'movement' is best described as a series of distinct phases each with contrasting ideologies and purposes, even though all resulted in people creating gardens on public or abandoned land. The latest phase began with the alternative politics and culture and dawning ecological activism of the late 1960s.

From the mid-1970s through the early 1990s, community gardening in a select number of major American cities enjoyed Federal financial support, though many programmes struggled to find funding. The loss of the Federal programme increased the challenge of finding funding to support programmes. Funding remains a key challenge, along with secure land tenure for garden sites, finding insurance, and helping gardeners develop ways to work together smoothly.

Community gardening in the United States overlaps to some extent with the related but distinct movement to encourage local food production, local farmers' markets and community supported agriculture farms (CSAs). Leases and rules prevent some, though not all, community gardeners from selling their produce commercially, although their gardens may donate fresh fruits and vegetables to local food pantries, cooperatives, and homeless members of their community. However, community gardens offer ideal sites for local farmers markets, and gardeners often seek farmers to provide space-intensive crops such as corn or potatoes. They also can hire farmers to provide services such as plowing and providing mulch and manure. In turn, small farmers can reach a wider audience and consumer base by drawing on community gardeners and their contacts. Although the two approaches are distinct, both can be effective ways to produce local food in urban areas, safeguard green space, and contribute to food security.

In an interesting variant on the practice of reclaiming bombed-out areas for community gardens (also practiced during WWII in the ghettos of Eastern Europe), in American inner-cities, community groups have reclaimed abandoned or junked lots for garden plots. In these cases, groups have subsequently leased from a municipality that claims the property or claimed squatter's rights or a right to subsistence not currently recognized by the legal system. Two notable cases include the gardens of Manhattan's lower Eastside and the South Central Farm of Los Angeles, California. A lasting legacy of the New York gardens is 'guerrilla gardening', perfected by NYC's legendary 'Green Guerrillas', founded by Liz Christy. In contrast, The South Central Farm was recently bulldozed in Los Angeles.

ACGA provides resources to assist anyone wishing to start a community garden or find a garden near their home, as well as training classes in community gardening organizing and management. They also offer a website, a newsletter, an email listserv and a magazine. ACGA's most recent survey suggests that the total number of community gardens around the US alone is over 5000.

Boston, Massachusetts

In the city of Boston, Massachusetts there are a variety of local and non-profit organizations which own, promote and manage approximately 180 community gardens throughout the city. These organizations include the Boston Natural Areas Network (BNAN), Boston Nature Center of the Massachusetts Audubon Society, Boston Parks and Recreation Department, Boston Urban Gardeners (BUG), MA Department of Conservation and Recreation, Dorchester Gardenlands Preserve, ReVision House, and the South End Lower Roxbury Open Space Land Trust.

In 2002, the volunteer-run Boston Community Garden Council was formed as a means of facilitating communication and cooperation between these organizations along with individual gardeners in Boston.

San Francisco, California

In San Francisco, community gardens are available through various public and private entities. Most community gardens in San Francisco are available through its Recreation and Park Department, which manages over 35 community gardens on City property. These are allotment gardens whereby individuals or groups volunteer to be assigned garden plots. Garden members within their respective gardens democratically organize themselves to set bylaws that are consistent with City policy. These gardeners often self-impose garden dues as a membership requirement to cover common expenses. To standardize the development and management of its community gardens, the Recreation and Park Commission adopted its Community Garden Policy in 2006.

Though not plot-based, the City's Department of Public Works supports communal-style gardening on City property whereby community groups participate in the development and maintenance of public gardens. No one person is responsible for any portion of the site. One group, a community-based and resident-led volunteer group in an underserved neighborhood called Bayview Hunters Point, has created an enclosed food-producing garden on City-owned land, as well as developed many residential urban farms around privately owned homes. This group, the Quesada Gardens Initiative, is one of many organizations in the San Francisco Bay Area working at the nexus of environmental justice, health and wellness and food security, and community-building.

All of the community gardens of San Francisco are listed on the San Francisco Garden Resource Organization web site with detailed directions and garden pictures of some of the gardens.

Seattle, Washington

The Seattle P-Patch programme for community garden plots began in the early 70s during an economic downturn known locally as the 'Boeing Bust' which had resulted in many people without work or money. Darlyn Rundberg Del Boca, a University of Washington student, saw an opportunity to promote children's gardening with a focus on growing for the local Neighbours in Need food bank programme, and with the help of a Seattle Councilmember obtained permission to use part of the Picardo family's truck garden in northeast Seattle with the City of Seattle renting the land for the cost of its real estate taxes. The first garden consisted of a large central garden plot planted by children from the nearby elementary school and their parents; families who volunteered to help were offered smaller individual plots around the perimeter of the central plot. The City subsequently purchased the Picardo farm, and the programme of renting individual garden plots arising from the first efforts was named 'P-Patch' in honour of the Picardo family's contribution. The P-Patch programme continued to grow and currently consists of 1900 plots in 68 locations with a total of 23 acres of land, with additions planned each year, and the tradition of growing for local food banks resulted in 12.3 tons of food donated in 2008.

Salt Lake City, Utah

In Salt Lake City, community gardens are available through the non-profit organization Wasatch Community Gardens. On May 16, 2009 Wasatch Community Gardens, in collaborated with The Redevelopment Agency of Salt Lake City (RAD), launched the first People's Portable Garden in Salt Lake City. The garden is designed to stimulate growth and revitalize different areas of the city. Salt Lake City put $48,000 into the People's Portable Garden on 900 South. The People's Portable Garden is located at 900 S 200 W, Salt Lake City.

9

Allotment (Gardening)

Allotment gardens are characterised by a concentration in one place of a few or up to several hundreds of land parcels that are assigned to individuals or families. In allotment gardens, the parcels are cultivated individually, contrary to other community garden types where the entire area is tended collectively by a group of people. The individual size of a parcel ranges between 50 and 400 square meters, and often the plots include a shed for tools and shelter. The individual gardeners are organised in an allotment association which leases the land from the owner who may be a public, private or ecclesiastical entity, provided that it is only used for gardening (i.e. growing vegetables, fruits and flowers), but not for residential purposes. The gardeners have to pay a small membership fee to the association, and have to abide by the corresponding constitution and by-laws. However, the membership entitles them to certain democratic rights.

Socio-cultural and Economic Functions of Allotment Gardens

The *Office International du Coin de Terre et des Jardins Familiaux*, a Luxembourg-based organization representing three million European allotment gardeners since 1926, describes the socio-cultural and economic functions of allotment gardens as follows:

- for the *community* a better quality of urban life through the reduction of noise, the binding of dust, the establishment of open green spaces in densely populated areas;
- for the *environment* the conservation of biotopes and the creation of linked biotopes;

- for *families* a meaningful leisure activity and the personal experience of sowing, growing, cultivating and harvesting healthy vegetables amidst high-rise buildings and the concrete jungle;
- for *children and adolescents* a place to play, communicate and to discover nature and its wonders;
- for *working people* relaxation from the stress of work;
- for the *unemployed* the feeling of being useful and not excluded as well as a supply of fresh vegetables at minimum cost;
- for *immigrant families* a possibility of communication and better integration in their host country;
- for *disabled persons* a place enabling them to participate in social life, to establish contacts and overcome loneliness;
- for *senior citizens* a place of communication with persons having the same interests as well as an opportunity of self-fulfillment during the period of retirement.

ALLOTMENT GARDENS IN DIFFERENT COUNTRIES

Czechoslovakia

Allotment gardening used to be widely popular in Czechoslovakia under the communist regime. It gave people from suburban prefab apartment blocks 'paneláky' a chance to escape from a city chaos, pollution and concrete architecture.

Denmark

In 1778 land was laid out outside the fortifications of Fredericia for allotment gardens and according to a 1828 circular from the royal chancellery allotment gardens were established in several towns.

Private initiative formed the first Danish allotment association in Aalborg in 1884 and in Copenhagen an association named 'Arbejdernes Værn' (lit. 'The Worker's Protection') founded the first allotment gardens of the Danish Capital in 1891. Since then allotment gardens has spread to most Danish towns.

In 1904 there were about 20.000 allotment gardens in Denmark. 6.000 of them were in Copenhagen. During the interwar years the number of allotment gardens grew rapidly. In 2001 the number of allotment gardens was estimated to about 62.120.

In 1908 twenty allotment associations in Copenhagen formed the Allotment Garden Union which in 1914 was expanded to cover all of Denmark. The Allotment Garden Federation was founded to negotiate more favourable deals with the state and the municipalities from which the allotments associations rented the land. Today the federation represent roughly 400 allotment associations in 75 municipalities.

The Danish tradition for allotment gardens later spread to the other Scandinavian countries; first Sweden, then Norway and Finland.

Today most allotment gardens are on land owned by the municipality which rents the land to an allotment association. The association in turn gives each member a plot of land. To preserve allotment gardens as something that is available for all kinds of people the membership charge is set significantly below what a market price would be. Since allotments are often placed on attractive plots of land, this has led to huge waiting lists for membership in many allotment associations.

Although the main purpose of the allotment is gardening, most allotment gardens have a pavilion built in them. These pavilions can range in size from an old rebuilt railway car to a small summer house. Many people grow so fond of their allotment gardens that they live there the entire summer. In most cases, however, members are not allowed to live there the entire year.

In Danish culture the allotment garden has become a symbol of blue-collar culture. Both as a positive image of a more simple life closer to nature, with time to spend with the family and friendly neighbours to have a chat and a beer with, but also as a negative image of intolerant flag-waving whites keeping to themselves inside their small hedged kingdoms. However despite these negative stereotypes the garden idyll of the allotment still attracts people living in the city, regardless of class.

Finland

The first allotment garden was established 1916 in Tampere. Nowadays there are about 50 allotment gardens all around Finland. Those gardens have 5000 allotmenteers. Allotment gardens are very desired and prices are quite high.

Germany

The history of the allotment gardens in Germany is closely connected with the period of industrialization and urbanization in Europe during the 19th century when a large number of people migrated from the rural areas to the cities to find employment and a better life. Very often, these families were living under extremely poor conditions suffering from inappropriate housing, malnutrition and other forms of social neglect. To improve their overall situation and to allow them to grow their own food, the city administrations, the churches or their employers provided open spaces for garden purposes. These were initially called the 'gardens of the poor' and were later termed as 'allotment gardens'.

The idea of organised allotment gardening reached a first peak after 1864, when the so-called 'Schreber Movement' started in the city of Leipzig in Saxony. A public initiative decided to lease areas within the city, with the purpose to make it possible for children to play in a healthy environment, and in harmony with nature. Later on, these areas included actual gardens for children, but soon adults tended towards taking over and cultivating these gardens. This kind of gardening type rapidly gained popularity not only in Germany, but also in other European countries, such as Austria and Switzerland. The aspect of food security provided by allotment gardens became particularly evident during World Wars I and II. The socio-economic situation was very miserable, particularly as regards the nutritional status of urban residents. Many cities were isolated from their rural hinterlands and agricultural products did not reach the city markets anymore or were sold at very high prices at the black markets. Consequently, food production within the city, especially fruit and vegetable production in home gardens and allotment gardens, became essential for survival (*Berliners cultivate vegetables by the ruins of the Reichstag in June 1946*). The importance of allotment gardens for food security was so obvious that in 1919, one year after the end of World War I, the first legislation for allotment gardening in Germany was passed. The so-called 'Small Garden and Small-Rent Land Law', provided security in land tenure and fixed leasing fees. In 1983, this law was amended by the 'Federal Allotment Gardens Act' *(Bundeskleingartengesetz)*. Today, there are still about 1.4 million allotment gardens in Germany covering an area of 470 km^2. Nevertheless, the importance of allotment gardening in Germany has shifted over the years. While in times of crisis and widespread poverty (from 1850 to 1950), allotment gardening was a part time job, and its main importance was to enhance food security and improve food supply, its present functions have to be seen under a different point of view. In times of busy working days and the hectic urban atmosphere, allotment gardens have turned into recreational areas and locations for social gatherings. As green oases within oceans of asphalt and cement, they are substantially contributing to the conservation of nature within cities. What was previously a part time job is nowadays considered as a hobby where the hectic schedule of the day becomes a distant memory, while digging the flowerbeds and getting a little soil under the fingernails. It appears young families are also rediscovering gardens as a place where children can grow up within a more natural environment.

Netherlands

The first allotment gardens in the Netherlands were founded in 1838. In the 19th century, cities started allotment gardens for working class families. Around the first world war, the users of the gardens started demanding that the gardens would be governed by the members. In 1928 the allotment garden societies founded the national level 'het Algemeen Verbond van Volkstuindersverenigingen in Nederland (AVVN)'. Until the 1950's, the gardens were primarily used for vegetable production, since then there has been a shift to recreational use. Depending on the city and society, small sheds, greenhouses or small garden houses are allowed. In some cases, permanent habitation is allowed during summertime. The Netherlands has 240.000 allotments.

Philippines

In 2003, the first allotment garden of the Philippines was established in Cagayan de Oro City, Northern Mindanao as part of a European Union funded project. Meanwhile, with the assistance of the German Embassy in Manila and several private donors from Germany, this number has grown to five self-sustaining gardens located in different urban areas of the city, enabling a total of 55 urban poor families the legal access to land for food production. Further four allotment gardens, two of them within the premises of public elementary schools are presently being set up for additional 36 families using the Asset Based Community Development approach. (*Health Promoting Schools, Ecological Sanitation and School Gardens in Mindanao*) Some of the gardeners belong to the poorest in the city, the garbage pickers of the city's landfill site . Aside of different vegetables, the gardeners grow also herbs and tropical fruits. In some gardens, small animals are kept and fish ponds are maintained to avail the gardeners of additional protein sources for the daily dietary needs. Each allotment garden has a compost heap where biodegradable wastes from the garden as well as from the neighbouring households are converted into organic fertilizer, thus contributing to the integrated solid waste management programme of the city. Further, all gardens are equipped with so-called urine-diverting ecological sanitation toilets similar to practices in Danish allotment gardens described by Bregnhøj et al.

Sweden

In 1895, the first allotment garden of Sweden was established in Malmö, followed by Stockholm in 1904. The local authorities were inspired by Anna Lindhagen, a social-democratic leader and a woman in the upper ranks of society, who visited allotment gardens in Copenhagen and was delighted by them. In her first book on the topic devoted to the usefulness of allotment gardens she wrote:

> 'For the family, the plot of land is a uniting bond, where all family members can meet in shared work and leisure. The family father, tired with the cramped space at home, may rejoice in taking care of his family in the open air, and feel responsible if the little plot of earth bestows a very special interest upon life'.

Anna Lindhagen is said to have met Lenin when he passed through Stockholm from the exile in Switzerland on their return trip to Russia after the February Revolution in 1917 . She invited him to the allotment gardens of "Barnangen" to show all its benefits. However, she did not win his approval. Lenin was totally unresponsive to this kind of activity. To poke in the soil was to prepare the ground for political laziness in the class struggle. The workers should not be occupied with gardening, they should rather devote themselves to the proletarian revolution.

The Swedish Federation of Leisure Gardening was founded in 1921 and represents today more than 26000 allotment and leisure gardeners. The members are organised in about 275 local societies all over Sweden. The land is usually rented from the local authorities.

United States

Several so called 'community gardens' have been founded in the United States. Many of these began as 'victory gardens' in World War II, and evolved into community gardens. Plots in these gardens are often rented out by the city, starting at plots of just 5ft × 5ft, (1.52 m × 1.52 m). Due to the green movement many new gardens are being erected.

United Kingdom

A 1732 engraving of Birmingham, England shows the town encircled by allotments, some of which still exist to this day. St Ann's Allotments in Nottingham, created in the 1830s, are currently regarded as the oldest allotments site in England, as well as the largest site of Victorian gardens in the world. Following the Inclosure Acts and the Commons Act 1876 the land available for personal cultivation by the poor was greatly diminished. To fulfil the need for land allotment legislation was included. The law was first fully codified in the Small Holdings and Allotments Act 1908, it was modified by the Allotments Act 1922 and subsequent Allotments Acts up until 1950.

Under the acts a local authority is required to maintain an 'adequate provision' of land, usually a large allotment field which can then be subdivided into allotment gardens for individual residents at a low rent. Allotment sizes are often quoted in square rods, although the use of the rod has been illegal for trade purposes since 1965 and unit prices must by law be quoted in pounds per square metre. The rent is set at what a person 'may reasonably be expected to pay' (1950), in 1997 the average rent for a 10 square rods (approx. 250 m^2) plot was £22 a year. Each plot cannot exceed 40 square rods (1000 m^2) and must be used for the production of fruit or vegetables for consumption by the plot-holder and their family (1922), or of flowers for use by the plot-holder and their family. The exact size and quality of the plots is not defined. The council has a duty to provide sufficient allotments to meet demand. The total income from allotments was £2.61 million and total expenditure was £8.44 million in 1997.

The total number of plots has varied greatly over time. In the 19th and early 20th century, the allotment system supplied much of the fresh vegetables eaten by the poor. In 1873 there were 244,268 plots and by 1918 there were around 1,500,000 plots. While numbers fell in the 1920s and 1930s, following an increase to 1,400,000 during World War II there were still around 1,117,000 plots in 1948. This number has been in decline since then, falling to 600,000 by the late 1960s. The Thorpe Inquiry of 1969 investigated the decline and put the causes as the decline in available land, increasing prosperity and the growth of other leisure activities.

Increased interest in 'green' issues from the 1970s revived interest in allotment gardening, whilst the National Society of Allotment and Leisure Gardeners (NSALG), and the Scottish Allotments and Gardens Society (SAGS) in Scotland, continued to campaign on the behalf of allotment users. However, the rate of decline was only slowed, falling from 530,000 plots in 1970 to 497,000 in 1977, although there was a substantial waiting list. By 1980 the surge in interest was over, and by 1997 the number of plots had fallen to around 265,000, with waiting lists of 13,000 and 44,000 vacant plots. In 2008 The Guardian reported that 330 000 people held an allotment, whilst 100,000 were on waiting lists. The keeping of an allotment is colloquially referred to as allotmenteering. This term has not yet been officially recognised, but is widely used among tenants of allotments, including Gardeners World presenter, Joe Swift.

In 2006, a report commissioned by the London Assembly identified that whilst demand was at an all time high across the capital, the pressures caused by high density building was further decreasing the amount of allotment land. The issue was given further publicity when The Guardian newspaper reported on the community campaign against the potential impact of the development for the 2012 Summer Olympics on the future of the century-old Manor Garden Allotments. In March, 2008, Geoff Stokes, secretary of the NSALG, claimed that Councils are failing in their duty to provide allotments. "They sold off land when demand was not so high. This will go on because developers are now building houses with much smaller gardens." The Local Government Association has issued guidance asking councils to consider requiring developers to set land aside to make up for the shortfalls in allotment plots.

Against the falling trend of land set aside for allotments is an increasing awareness of the need for cities to counter issues of food security and climate change through greater self-sufficiency. This drive to expand allotmenteering is also a response to food price inflation, a need to reduce food miles and surplus provision of land in post-industrial towns and cities in the developed world. It finds some inspiration in the urban agriculture response of Cuba to the United States embargo against Cuba in 1962. Some of these themes were taken up in a recent urban agriculture project in Middlesbrough in the Tees Valley.

Albert Einstein spent the summers of the early 1920s in his allotment garden in the 'Kolonie Bocksfelde' in Berlin-Spandau, which he used to call his 'Spandau Castle'. According to contemporaries, Einstein was fully integrated in the community and a frequent guest in the garden restaurant of the Feuerherd brothers. However, he did not fully comply with the expectations of the allotment garden association as regards proper weeding as a note from the local authority (Bezirksamt Spandau) dated September 12, 1922 addressed to 'Herrn Professor Einstein' shows:

> "You are presently leasing allotment 2 at the Burgunderweg in Boxfelde. Said allotment has not been managed since a long time, weeds have spread all over the whole parcel and have soared. The fence is not in order, and the whole allotment makes an unaesthetic impression. We have to assume that you are no longer interested in leasing the parcel, and we will give it away to someone else, unless you object prior to the 25th of this month, and the allotment is put in order until that date. Please take care of the removal of this nuisance, and give us further notice."

Einstein stated in his reply that he is willing to comply with the demands in the coming spring, 'since we are very interested to keep the parcel'. It is not known how many more years Einstein stayed in Bocksfelde before he transferred his summer residence to Caputh near Potsdam in 1929.

10

Roof Garden

A 'roof garden' is any garden on the roof of a building. Besides the decorative benefit, roof plantings may provide food, temperature control, hydrological benefits, architectural enhancement, habitats or corridors for wildlife, and recreational opportunities.

Humans have grown plants atop structures since antiquity. The ziggurats of ancient Mesopotamia (4th millennium BC-600 BC) had plantings of trees and shrubs on above ground terraces. An example in Roman times was the Villa of the Mysteries in Pompeii, which had an elevated terrace where plants were grown. A roof garden has also been discovered around an audience hall in Roman-Byzantine Caesarea. The mediaeval Egyptian city of Fustat had a number of high-rise buildings that Nasir Khusraw in the early 11th century described as rising up to 14 stories, with roof gardens on the top storey complete with ox-drawn water wheels for irrigating them.

Environmental Impact

Roof gardens are most often found in urban environments. Plants have the ability to reduce the overall heat absorption of the building which then reduces energy consumption. "The primary cause of heat build-up in cities is insolation, the absorption of solar radiation by roads and buildings in the city and the storage of this heat in the building material and its subsequent re-radiation. Plant surfaces however, as a result of transpiration, do not rise more than 4-5 °C above the ambient and are sometimes cooler." This then translates into a cooling of the environment between 3.6 and 11.3 degrees Celsius (6.5 and 20.3 °F), depending on the area on earth (in hotter areas, the environmental temperature will cool more). The study was performed by the University of Cardiff.

A study at the National Research Council of Canada showed the differences between roofs with gardens and roofs without gardens against temperature. The study shows temperature effects on different layers of each roof at different times of the day. Roof gardens are obviously very beneficial in reducing the effects of temperature against roofs without gardens. "If widely adopted, rooftop gardens could reduce the urban heat island, which would decrease smog episodes, problems associated with heat stress and further lower energy consumption."

Aside for rooftop gardens providing resistance to thermal radiation, rooftop gardens are also beneficial in reducing rain run off. A roof garden can delay run off; reduce the rate and volume of run off. "As cities grow, permeable substrates are replaced by impervious structures such as buildings and paved roads. Storm water run-off and combined sewage overflow events are now major problems for many cities in North America. A key solution is to reduce peak flow by delaying (e.g., control flow drain on roofs) or retaining run-off (e.g., rain detention basins). Rooftop gardens can delay peak flow and retain the run-off for later use by the plants."

Urban Agriculture

"In an accessible rooftop garden, space becomes available for localized small-scale urban agriculture, a source of local food production. An urban garden can supplement the diets of the community it feeds with fresh produce and provide a tangible tie to food production." At Trent University, there is currently a working rooftop garden which provides food to the student café and local citizens.

Available gardening areas in cities are often seriously lacking, which is likely the key impetus for many roof gardens. The garden may be on the roof of an autonomous building which takes care of its own water and waste. Hydroponics and other alternative methods can expand the possibilities of roof top gardening by reducing, for example, the need for soil or its tremendous weight. Plantings in containers are used extensively in roof top gardens. Planting in containers prevents added stress to the roof's waterproofing. One high-profile example of a building with a roof garden is Chicago City Hall.

For those who live in small apartments with little space, square foot gardening, or (when even less space is available) living walls (vertical gardening) can be a solution. These use much less space than traditional gardening (square foot gardening uses 20 per cent of the space of conventional rows; ten times more produce can be generated from vertical gardens). These also encourage environmentally responsible practices, eliminating tilling, reducing or eliminating pesticides, and weeding, and encouraging the recycling of wastes through composting.

Importance to Urban Planning

Becoming green is a high priority for urban planners. The environmental and aesthetic benefits to cities is the prime motivation. It was calculated that "the temperature in Tokyo could be lowered by 0.11-0.84 °C if 50 per cent of all available rooftop space were planted with greenery. This would lead to a savings of approximately 100 million yen per day in the city's electricity bill."

Singapore is very active in green urban development. "Roof gardens present possibilities for carrying the notions of nature and open space further in tall building development." When surveyed, 80 per cent of Singapore residents voted for more roof gardens to be implemented in the city's plans. Recreational reasons, such as leisure and relaxation, beautifying the environment, and greenery and nature, received the most amount of votes.

Roof Garden *vs.* Green Roof

A roof garden is actually very different from a green roof, although the two terms are often and incorrectly used interchangeably. A roof garden is an area that is generally used for recreation, entertaining, and as an additional outdoor living space for the building's residents. It may include planters, plants, dining and lounging furniture, outdoor structures such as pergolas and sheds, and automated irrigation and lighting systems. A roof garden reestablishes the relationship between man and nature that can be lost in urban environments.

It is different from a green roof in that the considerations are primarily of an aesthetic or recreational nature, whereas a green roof is usually constructed to cover a large area in the most economical and efficient means possible with an emphasis towards improving the insulation or improving the overall energy efficiency of cooling and heating costs within a building.

The panels that comprise a green roof are generally no more than a few inches up to a foot in depth, since weight is an important factor when covering an entire roof surface. The plants that go into a green roof are usually sedum or other shallow-rooted plants that will tolerate the hot, dry, windy conditions that prevail on most rooftop gardens. With a green roof, "the plants layer can shield off as much as 87 per cent of solar radiation while a bare roof receives 100 per cent direct exposure".

The planters on a roof garden, on the other hand, can generally range anywhere from 6 in up to 3 ft (0.15 to 0.9 m) in depth, depending on the weight-bearing capacity of the roof, and would be placed more for aesthetic purposes. These planters can hold a range of ornamental plants, anything from trees, shrubs, vines, or an assortment of flowers. Since the planters on a roof garden are placed in random fashion, it would much less likely to provide the environmental and energy benefits of a green roof.

The related idea of a living machine is based on the most basic cycle of gardening: using wastes (organic waste and sewage), appropriately broken down, usually in some specialized container, on the soil, and harvesting food which, when processed, generates biodegradable waste, and when eaten, generates sewage. In most of the world, this kind of very tight closed loop gardening is used, despite certain health risks if necessary precautions are not taken. Composting human or pet waste should achieve thermophilic conditions and age for at least a year before being used.

Composting itself is a safe process which, when composed of a variety of different materials, is one of the best forms of fertilization available.

11

Zoological Garden

A zoological garden, zoological park, menagerie, or zoo is a facility in which animals are confined within enclosures, displayed to the public, and in which they may also be bred.

The term zoological garden refers to zoology, the study of animals, a term deriving from the Greek (*zoon* — 'animal') and (*lógos* — 'study'). The abbreviation 'zoo' was first used of the *London Zoological Gardens*, which opened for scientific study in 1828 and to the public in 1847. The number of major animal collections open to the public around the world now exceeds 1,000, around 80 per cent of them in cities.

London Zoo, launched in 1828, first called itself a menagerie or 'zoological garden', short for 'Gardens and Menagerie of the Zoological Society of London'. The abbreviation 'zoo' first appeared in print in the UK around 1847, when it was used for the Clifton Zoo, but it was not until some twenty years later that the shortened form became popular in the song 'Walking in the Zoo on Sunday' by music-hall artist Alfred Vance. The term 'zoological park' was used for more expansive facilities in Washington, D.C., and the Bronx in New York, which opened in 1891 and 1899 respectively.

Relatively new terms for zoos coined in the late twentieth century are 'conservation park' or 'biopark'. Adopting a new name is a strategy used by some zoo professionals to distance their institutions from the stereotypical and nowadays criticized zoo concept of the nineteenth century. The term 'biopark' was first coined and developed by the National Zoo, Washington, D.C. in the late 1980s. In 1993, the *New York*

Zoological Society changed its name to the Wildlife Conservation Society and rebranded the zoos under its jurisdiction as 'wildlife conservation parks'.

Ancient World

The predecessor of the zoological garden is the menagerie, which has a long history from the ancient world to modern times. In the second century BCE, the Chinese Empress Tanki had a 'house of deer' built, and King Wen of Zhou kept a 1,500-acre zoo called *Ling-Yu,* or the Garden of Intelligence. Other well-known collectors of animals included King Solomon of the Kingdom of Israel and Judah, Kings Semirami and Ashurbanipal of Assyria, and King Nebuchadrezzar of Babylonia. By the fourth century BCE, zoos existed in most of the Greek city states; Alexander the Great is known to have sent animals that he found on his military expeditions back to Greece. The Roman emperors kept private collections of animals for study or for use in the arena, the latter faring notoriously poorly. The 19th-century historian W.E.H. Lecky wrote of the Roman games, first held in 366 BCE.

At one time, a bear and a bull, chained together, rolled in fierce combat across the sand ... Four hundred bears were killed in a single day under Caligula ... Under Nero, four hundred tigers fought with bulls and elephants. In a single day, at the dedication of the Colosseum by Titus, five thousand animals perished. Under Trajan ... lions, tigers, elephants, rhinoceroses, hippopotami, giraffes, bulls, stags, even crocodiles and serpents were employed to give novelty to the spectacle.

Henry I of England kept a collection of animals at his palace in Woodstock, which reportedly included lions, leopards, and camels. The most prominent collection in mediaeval England was in the Tower of London, created as early as 1204 by King John I. Henry III received a wedding gift in 1235 of three leopards from Frederick II, Holy Roman Emperor, and in 1264, the animals were moved to the Bulwark, renamed the Lion Tower, near the main western entrance of the Tower. It was opened to the public during the reign of Elizabeth I in the 16th century. During the 18th century, the price of admission was three half-pence, or the supply of a cat or dog for feeding to the lions. The animals were moved to the London Zoo when it opened.

The oldest existing zoo, the Vienna Zoo in Austria, evolved from the Imperial Menagerie at the Schönbrunn Palace in Vienna, an aristocratic menagerie founded in 1752 by the Habsburg monarchy, which was opened to the public in 1765. In 1775, a zoo was founded in Madrid, and in 1795, the zoo inside the *Jardin des Plantes* in Paris was founded by Jacques-Henri Bernardin, with animals from the royal menagerie at Versailles, primarily for scientific research and education. The Zoological Society of London, founded in 1826 by Stamford Raffles, adopted the idea of the Paris zoo when they established the London Zoo in Regent's Park in 1828, which opened to paying visitors in 1847. The first zoological garden in Australia was Melbourne Zoo in 1860. In the same year, Central Park Zoo, the first public zoo in the United States, opened in New York, although in 1859, the Philadelphia Zoological Society had made an effort to establish a zoo, but delayed opening it until 1874 because of the American Civil War.

In 1907, the German entrepreneur Carl Hagenbeck founded the Tierpark Hagenbeck in Stellingen, now a quarter of Hamburg. It is known for being the first zoo to use open enclosures surrounded by moats, rather than barred cages, to better approximate animals' natural environments.

When ecology emerged as a matter of public interest in the 1970s, a few zoos began to consider making conservation their central role, with Gerald Durrell of the Jersey Zoo, George Rabb of Brookfield Zoo, and William Conway of the Bronx Zoo (Wildlife Conservation Society) leading the discussion. From then on, zoo professionals became increasingly aware of the need to engage themselves in conservation programmes, and the American Zoo Association soon said that conservation was its highest priority. Because they wanted to stress conservation issues, many large zoos stopped the practice of having animals perform tricks for visitors. The Detroit Zoo, for example, stopped its elephant show in 1969, and its chimpanzee show in 1983, acknowledging that the trainers had probably abused the animals to get them to perform.

Human beings were sometimes displayed in cages along with non-human animals, supposedly to illustrate the differences between people of European and non-European origin. In September 1906, William Hornaday, director of the Bronx Zoo in New York — with the agreement of Madison Grant, head of the New York Zoological Society — had Ota Benga, a Congolese pygmy, displayed in a cage with the chimpanzees, then with an orangutan named Dohong, and a parrot. The exhibit was intended as an example of the 'missing link' between the orangutan and white man. It triggered protests from the city's clergymen, but the public reportedly flocked to see it.

Human beings were also displayed in cages during the 1931 Paris Colonial Exposition, and as late as 1958 in a 'Congolese village' display at Expo '58 in Brussels.

Zoo animals usually live in enclosures that attempt to replicate their natural habitats, for the benefit of the animals and the visitors. They may have special buildings for nocturnal animals, with dim white or red lighting used during the day, so the animals will be active when visitors are there, and brighter lights at night to help them sleep. Special climate conditions are created for animals living in radical environments, such as penguins. Special enclosures for birds, insects, reptiles, fish, and other aquatic life forms have also been developed. Some zoos have walk-through exhibits where visitors enter enclosures of non-aggressive species, such as lemurs, marmosets, birds, lizards, and turtles. Visitors are asked to keep to paths and avoid showing or eating foods that the animals might snatch.

Some zoos keep fewer animals in larger, outdoor enclosures, confining them with moats and fences, rather than in cages. Safari parks, also known as zoo parks and lion farms, allow visitors to drive through them and come in close contact with the animals. The first of this kind of zoo was Whipsnade Park in Bedfordshire, England, opened by the Zoological Society of London in 1931, and covering 600 acres (2.4 km^2). Since the early 1970s, a 1,800-acre (7 km^2) park in the San Pasqual Valley near San Diego has featured the San Diego Wild Animal Park, run by the Zoological Society of San Diego. One of two state-supported zoo parks in North Carolina is the 535-acre North Carolina Zoo in Asheboro. The 500-acre Werribee Open Range Zoo in Melbourne, Australia, displays animals living in a savannah.

Public Aquaria

The first public aquarium was opened in London Zoo in 1853. This was followed by the opening of public aquaria in Europe (for example, Paris 1859, Hamburg 1864, Berlin 1869, Brighton 1872) and the United States (Boston 1859, Washington 1873, San Francisco Woodward's Garden 1873, New York Battery Park 1896). In 2005 the non-profit Georgia Aquarium with more than 8 million US gallons (30,000 m^3; 30,000,000 litres) of marine and fresh water, and more than 100,000 animals of 500 different species opened in Atlanta, Georgia. The aquarium's specimens include whale sharks and beluga whales.

Roadside Zoos

Roadside zoos are found throughout North America, particularly in remote locations. They are small, unregulated, for-profit zoos, often intended to attract visitors to some other facility, such as a gas station. The animals may be trained to perform tricks, and visitors are able to get closer to them than in larger zoos. Since they are unregulated, roadside zoos are notorious for instances of neglect and cruelty.

A petting zoo, also called children's farms or children's zoos, features a combination of domestic animals and wild species that are docile enough to touch and feed. To ensure the animals' health, the food is supplied by the zoo, either from vending machines or a kiosk nearby.

Animal Theme Parks

An animal theme park is a combination of an amusement park and a zoo, mainly for entertaining and commercial purposes. Marine mammal parks such as Sea World and Marineland are more elaborate dolphinariums keeping whales, and containing additional entertainment attractions. Another kind of animal theme park contains more entertainment and amusement elements than the classical zoo, such as a stage shows, roller coasters, and mythical creatures. Some examples are Busch Gardens Tampa Bay in Tampa, Florida, Disney's Animal Kingdom in Orlando, Florida, Flamingo Land in North Yorkshire, England and Six Flags Discovery Kingdom in Vallejo, California.

In a modern zoo, about five animals are bred in captivity for every 20 animals on display. When they arrive at the zoo, the animals are placed in quarantine, and slowly acclimatized to enclosures which seek to mimic their natural environment. For example, some species of penguins may require refrigerated enclosures. Guidelines on necessary care for such animals is published in the *International Zoo Year Book*.

Conservation and Research

The position of most modern zoos in Australasia, Europe, and North America, particularly those with scientific societies, is that they display wild animals primarily for the conservation of endangered species, as well as for research purposes and education, and secondarily for the entertainment of visitors, an argument disputed by critics. The Zoological Society of London states in its charter that its aim is "the advancement of Zoology and Animal Physiology and the introduction of new and curious subjects of the Animal Kingdom." It maintains two research institutes, the Nuffield Institute of Comparative Medicine and the Wellcome Institute of Comparative Physiology. In the U.S., the Penrose Research Laboratory of the Philadelphia Zoo focuses on the study of comparative pathology. The World Association of Zoos and Aquariums produced its first conservation strategy in 1993, and in November 2004, it adopted a new strategy that sets out the aims and mission of zoological gardens of the twenty-first century.

The breeding of endangered species is coordinated by cooperative breeding programmes containing international studbooks and coordinators, who evaluate the roles of individual animals and institutions from a global or regional perspective, and there are regional programmes all over the world for the conservation of endangered species.

The animal rights organization, People for the Ethical Treatment of Animals (PETA), argues against the position of the zoos that their main purpose is to undertake research and aid in conservation, alleging that most zoo research is geared toward finding new ways to breed and maintain animals in captivity. Andrew Linzey, director of the Oxford Centre for Animal Ethics, argues that zoos make a 'minuscule contribution to conservation'.

Surplus Animals

Because for every animal caught in the wild, several more are killed in the process, the breeding of animals within zoos is encouraged Eric Baratay and Elisabeth Hardouin-Fugier of the Université Jean-Moulin, Lyon, say that the overall 'stock turnover' of animals is one-fifth to one-fourth over the course of a year—with three-quarters of apes dying in captivity within the first twenty months. They say that the high mortality rate is the reason for the 'massive scale of importations'.

The downside to breeding the animals in captivity is that thousands of them are placed on 'surplus lists' each year, and sold to circuses, animal merchants, auctions, pet owners, and game farms. The *San Jose Mercury News* conducted a two-year study that suggested of the 19,361 mammals who left accredited zoos in the U.S. between 1992 and 1998, 7,420 (38 per cent) went to dealers, auctions, hunting ranches, unaccredited zoos and individuals, and game farms.

Zoos have advertised surplus animals in the *Animal Finders' Guide*, a newsletter in which the owners of hunting ranches post notices of sales and auctions. Matthew Scully writes that many hunters prefer killing animals from zoos because they make better-looking trophies; the mane of a zoo lion will tend to be cleaner than that of a wild one. In one case, a zoo owner named William Hampton was found to have been buying animals and systematically slaughtering them in order to sell their skins, heads, and pelts as trophies.

Animals who breed frequently, such as deer, tiger, and lions may be killed for their meat; Nuremberg zoo's deputy director, Helmut Mägdefrau, has said, 'If we cannot find good homes for the animals, we kill them and use them as feed'. Other animals may be sold to smaller zoos with poor conditions. PETA cites the example of Edith, a chimpanzee found in a concrete pit in a roadside zoo called the Amarillo

Wildlife Refuge in Texas. She had been born in the Saint Louis Zoo, but had been sold just after her third birthday, and for the next 37 years was passed around five other facilities before landing in the roadside zoo.

It was alleged in March 2008 that hundreds of the Berlin Zoo's 23,000 animals are missing, amid allegations that they have been slaughtered, and that some tigers and leopards were sent to China to make drugs for traditional Chinese medicine. Claudia Hämmerling, a Green Party politician, said she had evidence that four Asian black bears and a hippopotamus were taken from Berlin to go to a new home, but were transported instead to Wortel in Belgium, which *The Guardian* reports has no zoo, but does have a slaughterhouse. The zoo's director, Bernhard Blaszkiewitz, replied that the allegations were 'untruths, half-truths and lies'.

The condition of the animals varies widely, especially in zoos in countries with little or no regulations. The majority of the large non-profit and scientifically oriented institutions are working to improve their animal enclosures, although constraints like size and expense make it difficult to create ideal captive environments for some species, such as dolphins and whales.

Some critics argue that animals who live in zoos are treated as voyeuristic objects rather than living creatures, and are often driven to insanity in the transition from being free and wild to incarcerated and dependent on humans for survival.

A four-decade Oxford University study found that polar bears, lions, tigers, and cheetahs show the most evidence of stress in captivity. A PETA investigation of zoos in the U.S. found that several bear species were engaging in neurotic, stereotypical behaviour, including pacing, walking in circles, and swaying or rolling their heads. The Badaltearing Safari Park in China keeps a pair of moon bears in cages so small that they are unable to turn around. The *Daily Mail* reported in January 2008 that one of them appeared to have gone insane and spends its time shaking its head and banging into the sides of the cage.

In the Badaltearing Safari Park in China, zoo visitors can throw live goats into the lions' enclosure and watch them being eaten, or can purchase live chickens tied to bamboo rods for the equivalent of £2 to dangle into lion pens. Visitors can drive through the lion's compound on buses with specially designed chutes leading into the enclosure into which they can push live chickens. In the Xiongsen Bear and Tiger Mountain Village near Guilin in south-east China, live cows and pigs are thrown to tigers to amuse visitors.

In Qingdao zoo, near Beijing, visitors engage in 'tortoise baiting', where tortoises are kept inside small rooms with elastic bands round their necks, so that they are unable to retract their heads. Visitors then throw coins at them. If you hit one of them on the head and make a wish, it will be fulfilled, the story goes.

REGULATION OF ZOOS

United States of America

In the United States, any public animal exhibit must be licensed and inspected by the United States Department of Agriculture, United States Environmental Protection Agency, Drug Enforcement Agency, Occupational Safety and Health Administration, and others. Depending on the animals they exhibit, the activities of zoos are regulated by laws including the Endangered Species Act, the Animal Welfare Act, the Migratory Bird Treaty Act of 1918 and others. Additionally, zoos in North America may choose to pursue accreditation by the Association of Zoos and Aquariums (AZA). To achieve accreditation, a zoo must pass an application and inspection process and meet or exceed the AZA's standards for animal health and welfare, fundraising, zoo staffing, and involvement in global conservation efforts. Inspection is performed by three experts (typically one veterinarian, one expert in animal care, and one expert in zoo management and operations) and then reviewed by a panel of twelve experts before accreditation is awarded. This accreditation process is repeated once every five years. The AZA estimates that there are approximately 2,400 animal exhibits operating under USDA licence as of February 2007; fewer than 10 per cent are accredited.

Europe

In April 1999, the European Union introduced a directive to strengthen the conservation role of zoos, making it a statutory requirement that they participate in conservation and education, and requiring all member states to set up systems for their licensing and inspection. Zoos are regulated in the UK by the Zoo Licensing Act of 1981, which came into force in 1984. A zoo is defined as any "establishment where wild animals are kept for exhibition ... to which members of the public have access, with or without charge for admission, seven or more days in any period of twelve consecutive months," excluding circuses and pet shops. The Act requires that all zoos be inspected and licenced, and that animals kept in enclosures are provided with a suitable environment in which they can express most normal behaviour.

12

Green Wall

A green wall is a wall, either free-standing or part of a building, that is partially or completely covered with vegetation and, in some cases, soil or an inorganic growing medium. The vegetation for a green façade is always attached on outside walls; with living walls this is also usually the case, although some living walls can also be green walls for interior use. For living walls there are many methods including attaching to the air return of the building to help with air filtration. They are also referred to as living walls, biowalls, or vertical gardens.

There are two main categories of green walls: green façades and living walls. Green façades are made up of climbing plants either growing directly on a wall or, more recently, specially designed supporting structures. The plant shoot system grows up the side of the building while being rooted to the ground. In a living wall the modular panels are often made of polypropylene plastic containers, geotextiles, irrigation systems, a growing medium and vegetation.

Living walls can be further broken down into passive and active systems.'Active living walls' are a new, concept in which the living wall is integrated into a building's air circulation system. Active living walls are based upon the sciences of biofiltration and phytoremediation. According to a study done at the University of Waterloo, 'Living walls with biofilters increase the capacity of air filtration'. The Active Living Wall harnesses nature's cleansing power by drawing air through the root system of the wall. Beneficial microbes actively degrade the pollutants in the air before returning the new, fresh air back to the buildings interior. Passive living walls do not have any means of moving the air into the root system where most of the degradation of pollutants occur. The impact of passive systems on air quality are scientifically questionable.

Some active walls are kept behind glass to ensure more predictable airflow than can be achieved with inactive walls, which have no mechanized air circulation. Instead, they are kept open to promote as much free air circulation as possible. Green walls are found most often in urban environments where the plants reduce overall temperatures of the building which in turn reduces energy consumption. "The primary cause of heat build-up in cities is insolation, the absorption of solar radiation by roads and buildings in the city and the storage of this heat in the building material and its subsequent re-radiation. Plant surfaces however, as a result of transpiration, do not rise more than 4-5 °C above the ambient and are sometimes cooler."

Living walls may also be a means for water reuse. The plants may purify slightly polluted water (such as greywater) by absorbing the dissolved nutrients. Bacteria mineralize the organic components to make them available to the plants.

Living walls are particularly suitable for cities, as they allow good use of available vertical surface areas. They are also suitable in arid areas, as the circulating water on a vertical wall is less likely to evaporate than in horizontal gardens.

The living wall could also function for urban agriculture or urban gardening. It may be built as a work of art for its beauty. It is sometimes built indoors to help cure sick building syndrome.

Green Façades

Some popular plants (for temperate climates) include:

- Actinidia
- Akebia quinata/trifoliata
- Aristolochia
- Campsis
- Celastrus
- Clematis
- Cotoneaster
- Euonymus fortunei
- Hedera
- Humulus lupulus

Hydrangea petiolaris Lonicera Parthenocissus tricuspidata/ quinquefolia/inserta Vitis berlandieri/riparia *Polygonum auberti Pyracantha Wisteria.*

Leaf

In botany, a leaf is an above-ground plant organ specialized for photosynthesis. For this purpose, a leaf is typically flat (laminar) and thin. There is continued debate about whether the flatness of leaves evolved to expose the chloroplasts to more light or to increase the absorption of carbon dioxide. In either case, the adaption was made at the expense of water loss. In the Devonian period, when carbon dioxide concentration was at several times its present value, plants did not have leaves or flat stems. Many bryophytes have flat, photosynthetic organs, but these are not true leaves. Neither are the microphylls of lycophytes. The leaves of ferns, gymnosperms, and angiosperms are variously referred to as macrophyll, megaphylls, or euphylls.

Leaves are also the sites in most plants where transpiration and guttation take place. Leaves can store food and water, and are modified in some plants for other purposes. The comparable structures of ferns are correctly referred to as fronds. Furthermore, leaves are prominent in the human diet as leaf vegetables.

A structurally complete leaf of an angiosperm consists of a petiole (leaf stem), a *lamina* (leaf blade), and stipules (small processes located to either side of the base of the petiole). The petiole attaches to the stem at a point called the 'leaf axil'. Not every species produces leaves with all of the aforementioned structural components. In certain species, paired stipules are not obvious or are absent altogether. A petiole may be absent, or the blade may not be laminar (flattened). The tremendous variety shown in leaf structure (anatomy) from species to species is presented in detail below under Leaf morphology. Periodically (*i.e.* seasonally, during the autumn), deciduous trees shed their leaves. These leaves then decompose into the soil.

A leaf is considered a plant organ and typically consists of the following tissues:

- An epidermis that covers the upper and lower surfaces;
- An interior *chlorenchyma* called the mesophyll.

The epidermis is the outer layer of cells covering the leaf. It forms the boundary separating the plant's inner cells from the external world. The epidermis serves several functions: protection against water loss, regulation of gas exchange, secretion of metabolic compounds, and (in some species) absorption of water. Most leaves show dorsoventral anatomy: the upper (adaxial) and lower (abaxial) surfaces have somewhat different construction and may serve different functions.

The epidermis is usually transparent (epidermal cells lack chloroplasts) and coated on the outer side with a waxy cuticle that prevents water loss. The cuticle is in some cases thinner on the lower epidermis than on the upper epidermis, and is thicker on leaves from dry climates as compared with those from wet climates.

The epidermis tissue includes several differentiated cell types: epidermal cells, guard cells, subsidiary cells, and epidermal hairs (trichomes). The epidermal cells are the most numerous, largest, and least specialized. These are typically more elongated in the leaves of monocots than in those of dicots.

The epidermis is covered with pores called *stomata*, part of a stoma complex consisting of a pore surrounded on each side by chloroplast-containing guard cells, and two to four subsidiary cells that lack chloroplasts. The stoma complex regulates the exchange of gases and water vapour between the outside air and the interior of the leaf. Typically, the stomata are more numerous over the abaxial (lower) epidermis than the adaxial (upper) epidermis.

Mesophyll

Most of the interior of the leaf between the upper and lower layers of epidermis is a *parenchyma* (ground tissue) or *chlorenchyma* tissue called the mesophyll (Greek for 'middle leaf'). This assimilation tissue is the primary location of photosynthesis in the plant. The products of photosynthesis are called 'assimilates'.

In ferns and most flowering plants the mesophyll is divided into two layers:

- An upper palisade layer of tightly packed, vertically elongated cells, one to two cells thick, directly beneath the adaxial epidermis. Its cells contain many more chloroplasts than the spongy layer. These long cylindrical cells are regularly arranged in one to five rows. Cylindrical cells, with the *chloroplasts* close to the walls of the cell, can take optimal advantage of light. The slight separation of the cells provides maximum absorption of carbon dioxide. This separation must be minimal to afford capillary action for water distribution. In order to adapt to their different environment (such as sun or shade), plants had to adapt this structure to obtain optimal result. Sun leaves have a multi-layered palisade layer, while shade leaves or older leaves closer to the soil, are single-layered between the spongy layer cells.

- These two different layers of the mesophyll are absent in many aquatic and marsh plants. Even an epidermis and a mesophyll may be lacking. Instead for their gaseous exchanges they use a homogeneous aerenchyma (thin-walled cells separated by large gas-filled spaces). Their stomata are situated at the upper surface.

Leaves are normally green in color, which comes from chlorophyll found in plastids in the chlorenchyma cells. Plants that lack chlorophyll cannot photosynthesize.

Leaves in temperate, boreal, and seasonally dry zones may be seasonally deciduous (falling off or dying for the inclement season). This mechanism to shed leaves is called abscission. After the leaf is shed, a leaf scar develops on the twig. In cold autumns they sometimes change color, and turn yellow, bright orange or red as various accessory pigments (carotenoids and xanthophylls) are revealed when the tree responds to cold and reduced sunlight by curtailing chlorophyll production. Red anthocyanin pigments are now thought to be produced in the leaf as it dies, possibly to mask the yellow hue left when the chlorophyll is lost - yellow leaves appear to attract herbivores such as aphids.

Veins

The veins are the vascular tissue of the leaf and are located in the spongy layer of the mesophyll. They are typical examples of pattern formation through ramification. The pattern of the veins is called venation.

The veins are made up of:

- **Xylem:** tubes that brings water and minerals from the roots into the leaf;
- **Phloem:** tubes that usually move sap, with dissolved sucrose, produced by photosynthesis in the leaf, out of the leaf.

The xylem typically lies over the phloem. Both are embedded in a dense parenchyma tissue, called 'pith', with usually some structural collenchyma tissue present.

External leaf characteristics (such as shape, margin, hairs, etc.) are important for identifying plant species, and botanists have developed a rich terminology for describing leaf characteristics. These structures are a part of what makes leaves determinant; they grow and achieve a specific pattern and shape, then stop. Other plant parts like stems or roots are non-determinant, and will usually continue to grow as long as they have the resources to do so.

Classification of leaves can occur through many different designative schema, and the type of leaf is usually characteristic of a species, although some species produce more than one type of leaf. The longest type of leaf is a leaf from palm trees, measuring at nine feet long.

Spongy Cells

Beneath the palisade layer is the spongy layer. The cells of the spongy layer are more rounded and not so tightly packed. There are large intercellular air spaces. These cells contain fewer chloroplasts than those of the palisade layer.

The pores or *stomata* of the epidermis open into substomatal chambers, connecting to air spaces.

Basic Leaf Types

- Leaves of the White Spruce (Picea glauca) are needle-shaped and their arrangement is spiral.
- Ferns have fronds.
- Conifer leaves are typically needle-, awl-, or scale-shaped
- Angiosperm (flowering plant) leaves: the standard form includes stipules, a petiole, and a lamina
- Lycophytes have microphyll leaves.
- Sheath leaves (type found in most grasses).
- Other specialized leaves (such as those of *Nepenthes*)

Arrangement on the Stem

Different terms are usually used to describe leaf placement (phyllotaxis):

- **Alternate:** Leaf attachments are singular at nodes, and leaves alternate direction, to a greater or lesser degree, along the stem.
- **Opposite:** Leaf attachments are paired at each node; decussate if, as typical, each successive pair is rotated 90° progressing along the stem; or distichous if not rotated, but two-ranked (in the same geometric flat-plane).
- **Whorled:** Three or more leaves attach at each point or node on the stem. As with opposite leaves, successive whorls may or may not be decussate, rotated by half the angle between the leaves in the whorl (i.e., successive whorls of three rotated 60°, whorls of four rotated 45°, etc). Opposite leaves may appear whorled near the tip of the stem.

❖ **Rosulate:** Leaves form a rosette.

As a *stem* grows, leaves tend to appear arranged around the stem in a way that optimizes yield of light. In essence, leaves form a helix pattern centred around the stem, either clockwise or counterclockwise, with (depending upon the species) the same angle of divergence. There is a regularity in these angles and they follow the numbers in a Fibonacci sequence: 1/2, 2/3, 3/5, 5/8, 8/13, 13/21, 21/34, 34/55, 55/89. This series tends to a limit close to 360° × 34/89 = 137.52 or 137° 30′, an angle known mathematically as the golden angle. In the series, the numerator indicates the number of complete turns or 'gyres' until a leaf arrives at the initial position. The denominator indicates the number of leaves in the arrangement. This can be demonstrated by the following:

❖ alternate leaves have an angle of 180° (or 1/2)

❖ 120° (or 1/3): three leaves in one circle

❖ 144° (or 2/5): five leaves in two gyres

❖ 135° (or 3/8): eight leaves in three gyres

Two basic forms of leaves can be described considering the way the blade is divided. A simple leaf has an undivided blade. However, the leaf shape may be formed of lobes, but the gaps between lobes do not reach to the main vein. A compound leaf has a fully subdivided blade, each leaflet of the blade separated along a main or secondary vein. Because each leaflet can appear to be a simple leaf, it is important to recognize where the petiole occurs to identify a compound leaf. Compound leaves are a characteristic of some families of higher plants, such as the Fabaceae. The middle vein of a compound leaf or a frond, when it is present, is called a rachis.

Palmately compound leaves have the leaflets radiating from the end of the petiole, like fingers off the palm of a hand, e.g. *Cannabis* (hemp) and *Aesculus* (buckeyes).

Pinnately compound leaves have the leaflets arranged along the main or mid-vein.

Odd pinnate: with a terminal leaflet, e.g *Fraxinus* (ash).

Even pinnate: lacking a terminal leaflet, e.g. *Swietenia* (mahogany).

Bipinnately compound leaves are twice divided: the leaflets are arranged along a secondary vein that is one of several branching off the rachis. Each leaflet is called a 'pinnule'. The pinnules on one secondary vein are called 'pinna'; e.g. *Albizia* (silk tree).

Trifoliate (or *trifoliolate*): a pinnate leaf with just three leaflets, e.g. *Trifolium* (clover), *Laburnum* (laburnum).

Pinnatifid: pinnately dissected to the central vein, but with the leaflets not entirely separate, e.g. *Polypodium*, some *sorbus* (whitebeams). In pinnately veined leaves the central vein in known as the *midrib*.

Petiolated leaves have a petiole. Sessile leaves do not: the blade attaches directly to the stem. In clasping or decurrent leaves, the blade partially or wholly surrounds the stem, often giving the impression that the shoot grows through the leaf. When this is actually the case, the leaves are called 'perfoliate', such as in *Claytonia perfoliata*. In peltate leaves, the petiole attaches to the blade inside from the blade margin.

In some *Acacia* species, such as the Koa Tree (*Acacia koa*), the petioles are expanded or broadened and function like leaf blades; these are called phyllodes. There may or may not be normal pinnate leaves at the tip of the phyllode.

A stipule, present on the leaves of many dicotyledons, is an appendage on each side at the base of the petiole resembling a small leaf. Stipules may be lasting and not be shed (a stipulate leaf, such as in roses and beans), or be shed as the leaf expands, leaving a stipule scar on the twig (an exstipulate leaf).

The situation, arrangement, and structure of the stipules is called the 'stipulation'.

- free
- *adnate:* fused to the petiole base
- *ochreate:* provided with ochrea, or sheath-formed stipules, e.g. rhubarb
- encircling the petiole base
- *interpetiolar:* between the petioles of two opposite leaves
- *intrapetiolar:* between the petiole and the subtending stem

Venation (Arrangement of the Veins)

There are two subtypes of venation, namely, *craspedodromous*, where the major veins stretch up to the margin of the leaf, and *camptodromous*, when major veins extend close to the margin, but bend before they intersect with the margin.

Feather-veined, reticulate -- the veins arise pinnately from a single mid-vein and subdivide into veinlets. These, in turn, form a complicated network. This type of venation is typical for (but by no means limited to) dicotyledons.

Pinnate-netted, penniribbed, penninerved, penniveined; the leaf has usually one main vein (called the mid-vein), with veinlets, smaller veins branching off laterally, usually somewhat parallel to each other; eg *Malus* (apples).

Three main veins branch at the base of the lamina and run essentially parallel subsequently, as in *Ceanothus*. A similar pattern (with 3-7 veins) is especially conspicuous in Melastomataceae.

Palmate-netted, palmate-veined, fan-veined; several main veins diverge from near the leaf base where the petiole attaches, and radiate toward the edge of the leaf; e.g. most *Acer* (maples).

Parallel-veined, parallel-ribbed, parallel-nerved, penniparallel — veins run parallel for the length of the leaf, from the base to the apex. Commissural veins (small veins) connect the major parallel veins. Typical for most monocotyledons, such as grasses.

Dichotomous — There are no dominant bundles, with the veins forking regularly by pairs; found in *Ginkgo* and some pteridophytes.

Note that although it is the more complex pattern, branching veins appear to be plesiomorphic and in some form were present in ancient seed plants as long as 250 million years ago. A pseudo-reticulate venation that is actually a highly modified penniparallel one is an autapomorphy of some Melanthiaceae which are monocots, e.g. *Paris quadrifolia* (True-lover's Knot).

Morphology Changes within a Single Plant

Homoblasty — Characteristic in which a plant has small changes in leaf size, shape, and growth habit between juvenile and adult stages.

Heteroblasty — Characteristic in which a plant has marked changes in leaf size, shape, and growth habit between juvenile and adult stages.

Margins (Edge)

The leaf margin is characteristic for a genus and aids in determining the species.

- *ciliate:* fringed with hairs
- *crenate:* wavy-toothed; dentate with rounded teeth, such as *Fagus* (beech)
- *crenulate:* finely or shallowly crenate
- *coarse-toothed:* with large teeth
- *glandular toothed:* with teeth that bear glands.
- *denticulate:* finely toothed

- *doubly toothed:* each tooth bearing smaller teeth, such as *Ulmus* (elm)
- *entire:* even; with a smooth margin; without toothing
- *lobate:* indented, with the indentations not reaching to the center, such as many *Quercus* (oaks)
- *palmately lobed:* indented with the indentations reaching to the center, such as *Humulus* (hop).
- *serrate:* saw-toothed with asymmetrical teeth pointing forward, such as *Urtica* (nettle)
- *serrulate:* finely serrate
- *sinuate:* with deep, wave-like indentations; coarsely crenate, such as many *Rumex* (docks)
- *spiny:* with stiff, sharp points, such as some *Ilex* (hollies) and *Cirsium* (thistles)

Tip of the Leaf

Leaves showing various morphologies. Clockwise from upper left: tripartite lobation, elliptic with serrulate margin, peltate with palmate venation, acuminate odd-pinnate (center), pinnatisect, lobed, elliptic with entire margin.

- *acuminate:* long-pointed, prolonged into a narrow, tapering point in a concave manner
- *acute:* ending in a sharp, but not prolonged point
- *cuspidate:* with a sharp, elongated, rigid tip; tipped with a cusp
- *emarginate:* indented, with a shallow notch at the tip
- *mucronate:* abruptly tipped with a small short point, as a continuation of the midrib; tipped with a mucro
- *mucronulate:* mucronate, but with a smaller spine
- *obcordate:* inversely heart-shaped, deeply notched at the top
- *obtuse:* rounded or blunt
- *truncate:* ending abruptly with a flat end, that looks cut off

Base of the Leaf

- *acuminate:* coming to a sharp, narrow, prolonged point
- ***acute:*** coming to a sharp, but not prolonged point
- *auriculate:* ear-shaped
- *cordate:* heart-shaped with the notch towards the stalk

- *cuneate:* wedge-shaped
- *hastate:* shaped like an halberd and with the basal lobes pointing outward
- *oblique:* slanting
- *reniform:* kidney-shaped but rounder and broader than long
- *rounded:* curving shape
- *sagittate:* shaped like an arrowhead and with the acute basal lobes pointing downward
- *truncate:* ending abruptly with a flat end, that looks cut off

Surface of the Leaf

The surface of a leaf can be described by several botanical terms:

- *farinose:* bearing farina; mealy, covered with a waxy, whitish powder
- *glabrous:* smooth, not hairy
- *glaucous:* with a whitish bloom; covered with a very fine, bluish-white powder
- *glutinous:* sticky, viscid
- *papillate*, or *papillose:* bearing papillae (minute, nipple-shaped protuberances)
- *pubescent:* covered with erect hairs (especially soft and short ones)
- *punctate:* marked with dots; dotted with depressions or with translucent glands or colored dots
- *rugose:* deeply wrinkled; with veins clearly visible
- *scurfy:* covered with tiny, broad scalelike particles
- *tuberculate:* covered with tubercles; covered with warty prominences
- *verrucose:* warted, with warty outgrowths
- *viscid*, or *viscous:* covered with thick, sticky secretions

Hairiness (Trichomes)

'Hairs' on plants are properly called trichomes. Leaves can show several degrees of hairiness. The meaning of several of the following terms can overlap.

- *arachnoid*, or *arachnose:* with many fine, entangled hairs giving a cobwebby appearance
- *barbellate:* with finely barbed hairs (barbellae)
- *bearded:* with long, stiff hairs

- *bristly:* with stiff hair-like prickles
- *canescent:* hoary with dense grayish-white pubescence
- *ciliate:* marginally fringed with short hairs (cilia)
- *ciliolate:* minutely ciliate
- *floccose:* with flocks of soft, woolly hairs, which tend to rub off
- *glabrous:* no hairs of any kind present
- *glandular:* with a gland at the tip of the hair
- *hirsute:* with rather rough or stiff hairs
- *hispid:* with rigid, bristly hairs
- *hispidulous:* minutely hispid
- *hoary:* with a fine, close grayish-white pubescence
- *lanate*, or *lanose:* with woolly hairs
- *pilose:* with soft, clearly separated hairs
- *puberulent*, or *puberulous:* with fine, minute hairs
- *pubescent:* with soft, short and erect hairs
- *scabrous*, or *scabrid:* rough to the touch
- *sericeous:* silky appearance through fine, straight and appressed (lying close and flat) hairs
- *silky:* with adpressed, soft and straight pubescence
- *stellate*, or *stelliform:* with star-shaped hairs
- *strigose:* with appressed, sharp, straight and stiff hairs
- *tomentose:* densely pubescent with matted, soft white woolly hairs
- *cano-tomentose:* between canescent and tomentose
- *felted-tomentose:* woolly and matted with curly hairs
- *villous:* with long and soft hairs, usually curved
- *woolly: with long, soft and tortuous or matted hairs*

In the course of evolution, leaves have adapted to different environments in the following ways:

- A certain surface structure avoids moistening by rain and contamination
- Sliced leaves reduce wind resistance
- Hairs on the leaf surface trap humidity in dry climates and create a large boundary layer thereby reducing water loss

- Waxy leaf surfaces reduce water loss
- Large surface area of leaf provides large area for sunlight and provides shade for plant to minimize heating and reduce water loss
- In more or less opaque or buried in the soil leaves, translucent windows filter the light before the photosynthesis takes place at the inner leaf surfaces (e.g. *Fenestraria*)
- Succulent leaves store water and organic acids for use in CAM photosynthesis
- Aromatic oils, poisons or pheromones produced by leaf borne glands deter herbivores (e.g. eucalypts)

Inclusions of crystalline minerals deter herbivores (e.g. silica in grasses. A transformation into petals attracts pollinators. A transformation into spines protects the plants (*e.g.* cacti). A transformation into insect traps helps feeding the plants (carnivorous plants). A transformation into bulbs helps storing food and water (*e.g.* onions). A transformation into tendrils allows the plant to climb (*e.g.* peas). A transformation into bracts and pseudanthia (*false flowers*) replaces normal flower structures if the true flowers are extremely reduced (*e.g.* Spurges).

Although not as nutritious as other organs such as fruit, leaves provide a food source for many organisms. Animals which eat leaves are known as folivores. The leaf is one of the most vital parts of the plant, and plants have evolved protection against folivores such as tannins, chemicals which hinder the digestion of proteins and have an unpleasant taste.

Some animals have cryptic adaptations to avoid their own predators. For example, some caterpillars will create a small home in the leaf by folding it over themselves, while other herbivores and their prey mimic the appearance of the leaf. Some insects, such as the katydid, take this even further, moving from side to side much like a leaf does in the wind.

13

Rain Garden

A rain garden is a planted depression that allows rainwater runoff from impervious urban areas like roofs, driveways, walkways, and compacted lawn areas the opportunity to be absorbed. This reduces rain runoff by allowing stormwater to soak into the ground (as opposed to flowing into storm drains and surface waters which causes erosion, water pollution, flooding, and diminished groundwater). Rain gardens can cut down on the amount of pollution reaching creeks and streams by up to 30 per cent.

Native plants are recommended for rain gardens because they generally don't require fertilizer and are more tolerant of one's local climate, soil, and water conditions. The plants — a selection of wetland edge vegetation, such as wildflowers, sedges, rushes, ferns, shrubs and small trees — take up excess water flowing into the rain garden. Water filters through soil layers before entering the groundwater system. Root systems enhance infiltration, moisture redistribution, and diverse microbial populations involved in biofiltration. Also, through the process of transpiration, rain garden plants return water vapour into the atmosphere. A more wide-ranging definition covers all the possible elements that can be used to capture, channel, divert, and make the most of the natural rain and snow that falls on a property. The whole garden can become a rain garden, and all of the individual elements that we deal with in detail are either components of it, or are small-scale rain gardens in themselves.

In developed areas, the natural depressions are filled in. The surface of the ground is levelled or paved, and water is directed into storm drains. This causes several problems. First of all, streams that are fed by storm drains are subjected to sudden surges of water each time it rains, which contributes to erosion and flooding. Also, the water is warmer than the groundwater that normally feeds a stream, which upsets the delicate system. Warmer water cannot hold as much dissolved oxygen (DO). Many fish and other creatures in streams are unable to live in an environment with fluctuating temperatures. Finally, a wide variety of pollutants spill or settle on land surfaces between rain events. The initial rinse from each runoff event can wash this accumulation directly into streams and ponds.

Excess water from an expanding area or increasing development density is cumulative. Flooding results from ever smaller events requiring upgrades of drainage infrastructure. Areas compacted by heavy equipment during past construction activities remain less permeable long after vegetation is reintroduced. Both groundwater recharge and subsurface flow paths are disrupted. Strategies to retain water and soil at their source can slow this harmful cascade.

Rain gardens may be located near a drain pipe from a building's roof (with or without rain barrels), although if there's a basement, a French drain may be used to direct the rainwater to a location farther from the building. Normally, a rain garden — or a series of rain gardens – is the endpoint of drainage, but sometimes it can be designed as a pass-through system where water will percolate through a series of gravel layers and be captured by a drain under the gravel and carried to a storm water system. Rapid pass-through systems reduce peak discharge and extend hydraulic lag time of the discharge — reversing urbanization's major hydraulic impact. However, rapidly drained systems do not achieve pollution removal rates that more slowly percolating rain gardens do.

Runoff volumes from impervious surfaces in many urban cities make green roofs necessary to reduce peak volumes to magnitudes that areas available for rain gardens can handle. While some rain garden wash through is acceptable from heavy storms that dilute pollution, depression focussed recharge of contaminated runoff is avoided by proper rain garden design. The simplest fail safe for handling polluted runoff is for a garden with one inlet not to accept more volume than it can handle, and not pond to sufficient depth to push water into the water table faster than required for adequate biofiltration.

Rain gardens are beneficial for many reasons: improve water quality by filtering run-off, provide localized flood control, aesthetically pleasing, and provide interesting planting opportunities. They also encourage wildlife and biodiversity, tie together buildings and their surrounding environments in attractive and environmentally advantageous ways, and provide significant partial solutions to important environmental problems that affect us all.

A rain garden provides a way to use and optimize any rain that falls, reducing or avoiding the need for irrigation. They allow a household or building to deal with excessive rainwater runoff without burdening the public storm water systems. Rain gardens differ from retention basins, in that the water will infiltrate the ground within a day or two. This creates the advantage that the rain garden does not allow mosquitoes to breed.

The first rain gardens were created to mimic the natural water retention areas that occurred naturally before development of an area. The rain gardens for residential use were developed in 1990 in Prince George's County, Maryland, when Dick Brinker, a developer building a new housing subdivision had the idea to replace the traditional best management practices (BMP) pond with a bioretention area. He approached Larry Coffman, the county's Associate Director for Programmes and Planning in the Department of Environmental Resources, with the idea. The result was the extensive use of rain gardens in Somerset, a residential subdivision which has a 300-400 ft^2 rain garden on each house's property. This system proved to be highly cost-effective. Instead of a system of curbs, sidewalks, and gutters, which would have cost nearly $400,000, the planted drainage swales cost $100,000 to install. This was also much more cost effective than building BMP ponds that could handle 2-, 10-, and 100-year storm events. Flow monitoring done in later years showed that the rain gardens have resulted in a 75-80 per cent reduction in stormwater runoff during a regular rainfall event.

This is also referred to as Low Impact Development (LID), and is cited by the EPA on their website as a success on the Stormwater Case Studies section of their website. This webpage has many links to information on Prince George's County's literature on implementing LID in a community.

Some *de facto* rain gardens predate their recognition by professionals as a significant LID tool. Any shallow garden depression implemented to capture and retain rain water within the garden so as to drain adjacent land without running off a property is at conception a rain garden — particularly if vegetation is maintained with recognition of its role in this function. Vegetated roadside swales, now promoted as 'bioswales', remain the conventional drainage system in many parts of the world from long before extensive networks of cement sewers became the conventional engineering practice in the USA.

What is globally new about such technology is the emerging rigour of increasingly quantitative understanding of how such tools may make sustainable development possible. This is as true for wealthy developed communities retrofitting bioretention into built stormwater management systems, as for developing communities seeking a faster and more sustainable development path.

A rain garden requires an area where water can collect and infiltrate, and plants to maintain infiltration rates, diverse microbe communities, and water holding capacity. Transpiration by growing plants accelerates soil drying between storms. This includes any plant extending roots to the garden area.

Simply adjusting the landscape so that downspouts and paved surfaces drain into existing gardens may be all that is needed because the soil has been well loosened and plants are well established. However, many plants don't tolerate saturated roots for long and often more water runs off one's roof than people realize. Often the required location and storage capacity of the garden area must be determined first. Rain garden plants are then selected to match the situation, not the other way around.

Soil and Drainage

When an area's soils are not permeable enough to allow water to drain and filter properly, the soil should be replaced. This mixture should typically containing 60 per cent sand, 20 per cent compost, and 20 per cent topsoil. Deep plant roots also create additional channels for storm water to filter into the ground. Sometimes a drywell with a series of gravel layers near the lowest spot in the rain garden will help facilitate percolation. However, a drywell placed at the lowest spot can become clogged with silt prematurely turning the garden into an infiltration basin defeating its purpose. Depression focussed recharge of polluted water into wells poses a serious threat and should be avoided. Similarly plans to install a rain garden near a septic system should be reviewed by a qualified engineer. The more polluted the water, the longer it must be retained in the soil for purification. This is often achieved by installing several smaller rain garden basins with soil deeper than the seasonal high watertable. In some cases lined bioretention cells with subsurface drainage are used to retain smaller amounts of water and filter larger amounts without letting water percolate as quickly.

Rain gardens are at times confused with bioswales. Swales slope to a destination, while rain gardens do not; however, a bioswale may end with a rain garden. Drainage ditches may be handled like bioswales and even include rain gardens in series, saving time and money on maintenance. Part of a garden that nearly always has standing water is a water garden, wetland, or pond, and not a rain garden. Using the proper terminology ensures that the proper methods are used to achieve the desired results.

Plant Selection

Plants selected for use in a rain garden should tolerate both saturated and dry soil. Using native plants is generally encouraged. This way the rain garden may contribute to urban habitats for native butterflies, birds, and beneficial insects.

Well planned plantings require minimal maintenance to survive, and are compatible with adjacent land use. Trees under power lines, or that up-heave sidewalks when soils become moist, or whose roots seek out and clog drainage tiles can cause expensive damage.

Trees generally contribute most when located close enough to tap moisture in the rain garden depression, yet do not excessively shade the garden. That said, shading open surface waters can reduce excessive heating of habitat. Plants tolerate inundation by warm water for less time because heat drives out dissolved oxygen, thus a plant tolerant of early spring flooding may not survive summer inundation.

Melbourne Water's database of Water Sensitive Urban Design projects, including 57 case studies relating to rain gardens/bioretention systems. Melbourne Water is the Victorian State Government agency responsible for managing Melbourne's water supply catchments.

Water by Design is a capacity building program that supports the uptake of Water Sensitive Urban Design, including rain gardens, in South East Queensland. It was established by the South East Queensland Healthy Waterways Partnership in 2005, as an integral component of the SEQ Healthy Waterways Strategy.

The Sydney Metropolitan Catchment Management Authority's (CMA) Water Sensitive Urban Design (WSUD) Program increases the abilities and resources of individuals and organisations responsible for implementing WSUD; facilitates the exchange of information and embedding of WSUD in policy, practices and on-ground works. Case studies cover projects relating to planning and policy; industrial, greenfield an infill/brownfield sites; roadway retrofits; and educational and capacity building projects.

Kingston City Council, in Southern metropolitan Melbourne have designed and constructed a over 130 rain gardens as part of its Water Sensitive Urban Design projects since 2001.

Stringy Bark Creek rain garden project in Mt Evelyn, Victoria is part of a research program co-ordinated by The University of Melbourne and Monash University. It is putting into practice new approaches to stormwater management, that focus on improving the health of creeks and rivers.

United States of America

Maplewood, Minnesota has implemented a policy of encouraging residents to install rain gardens. Many neighborhoods had swales added to each property, but installation of a garden at the swale was voluntary. The project was a partnership between the City of Maplewood, University of Minnesota Department of Landscape Architecture, and the Ramsey Washington Metro Watershed District. A focus group was held with residents and published so that other communities could use it as a resource when planning their own rain garden projects.

In Seattle, a prototype project, used to develop a plan for the entire city, was constructed in 2003. Called *SEA Street,* for Street Edge Alternatives, it was a drastic facelift of a residential street. The street was changed for a typical linear path to a gentle curve, narrowed, with large rain gardens placed along most of the length of the street. The street has 11 per cent less impervious surface than a regular street. There are 100 evergreen trees and 1100 shrubs along this 3-block stretch of road, and a 2-year study found that the amount of stormwater which leaves the street has been reduced by 98 per cent.

10,000 Rain Gardens is a public initiative in the Kansas City, Missouri metro area. Property owners are encouraged to create rain gardens, with an eventual goal of 10,000 individual gardens. Mayor Kay Barnes took the unconventional advice of Lynn Hinkle to bring widespread use of rain gardens to offset the increasing demand on the city's stormwater infrastructure.

The West Michigan Environmental Action Council has established Rain Gardens of West Michigan as an outreach water quality programme. Also in Michigan, the Southeastern Oakland County Water Authority has published a pamphlet to encourage residents to add a rain garden to their landscapes in order to improve the water quality in the Rouge River watershed. In Washtenaw County, homeowners can volunteer for the Drain Commission's Rain Garden programme, in which volunteers are annually selected for free professional landscape design. The homeowners build the garden themselves as well as pay for landscaping material. Photos of the gardens as well as design documents and drainage calculations are available online.

The city of Atlanta, Georgia, has established a public education project, the *Clean Water Campaign* (CWC), to encourage residents to learn about stormwater management and to add rain gardens to their properties. They do this through community workshops and an official website.

The city of Portland, Oregon, has established a Clean River Rewards program, to encourage residents to disconnect downspouts from the city's combined sewer system and create rain gardens. Workshops, discounts on storm water bills, and web resources are offered.

The city of Austin, Texas, has established rain gardens as an 'Innovative Water Quality Control', per its Environmental Criteria Manual.

In Delaware, several rain gardens have been created through the work of the University of Delaware Water Resources Agency, and environmental organizations, such as the Appoquinimink River Association.

The US Fish and Wildlife Service provided a grant to the Wasilla Soil and Water Conservation District for a rain garden as a memorial for Steve Duncan, a long time advocate for soil and water conservation who recently passed away from cancer. What was to be a 20 foot by 10 foot Rain Garden, turned into over 100 feet long by 10-12 feet wide. A brass plaque is being placed in the garden to recognized Steve's work with the local community and to teach kids the importance of water conservation. A story of it aired on Wednesday May, 20 2009.

Students in the College of Architecture, Design, and Contstruction at Auburn University have just finished putting in rain gardens and bioswales around the Boykin Center in Auburn, Alabama, through a project called 'Green For Life'. The students put many native plants in the rain gardens to help make it look beautiful. The University students also taught the students in the Boykin Center about rain gardens, rain barrels, native plants, and green benefits.

Green Roof

A green roof is a roof of a building that is partially or completely covered with vegetation and a growing medium, planted over a waterproofing membrane. It may also include additional layers such as a root barrier and drainage and irrigation systems. (The use of 'green' refers to the growing trend of environment friendly and does not refer to roofs which are merely coloured green, as with green roof tiles or roof shingles.)

Container gardens on roofs, where plants are maintained in pots, are not generally considered to be true green roofs, although this is an area of debate. Rooftop ponds are another form of green roofs which are used to treat greywater.

Also known as 'living roofs', green roofs serve several purposes for a building, such as absorbing rainwater, providing insulation, creating a habitat for wildlife, and helping to lower urban air temperatures and combat the heat island effect. There are two types of green roofs: intensive roofs, which are thicker and can support a wider variety of plants but are heavier and require more maintenance, and extensive roofs, which are covered in a light layer of vegetation and are lighter than an intensive green roof.

The term *green roof* may also be used to indicate roofs that use some form of 'green' technology, such as a cool roof, a roof with solar thermal collectors or photovoltaic modules. Green roofs are also referred to as *eco-roofs*, *oikosteges*, *vegetated roofs*, *living roofs*, and *greenroofs*.

Green roofs are used to:

- Reduce heating (by adding mass and thermal resistance value)
- A 2005 study by Brad Bass of the University of Toronto showed that green roofs can also reduce heat loss and energy consumption in winter conditions.
- Reduce cooling (by evaporative cooling) loads on a building by fifty to ninety per cent especially if it is glassed in so as to act as a terrarium and passive solar heat reservoir — a concentration of green roofs in an urban area can even reduce the city's average temperatures during the summer.
- Reduce stormwater run off
- Natural Habitat Creation
- Filter pollutants and carbon dioxide out of the air which helps lower disease rates such as asthma
- Filter pollutants and heavy metals out of rainwater
- Help to insulate a building for sound; the soil helps to block lower frequencies and the plants block higher frequencies

  If installed correctly many living roofs can contribute to LEED points.
- Increase roof life span dramatically
- Increase real estate value

A green roof is often a key component of an autonomous building.

In a recent study on the impacts of green infrastructure and in particular green roofs in the Greater Manchester area, researchers found that adding green roofs will help keep temperatures down, particularly in urban areas: "adding green roofs to all buildings can have a dramatic effect on maximum surface temperatures, keeping temperatures below the 1961-1990 current form case for all time periods and emissions scenarios. Roof greening makes the biggest difference ... where the building proportion is high and the evaporative fraction is low. Thus, the largest difference was made in the town centers."

Types

Green roofs can be categorized as intensive, 'semi-intensive', or extensive, depending on the depth of planting medium and the amount of maintenance they need. Traditional roof gardens, which require a reasonable depth of soil to grow large plants or conventional lawns, are considered 'intensive' because they are labour-intensive, requiring irrigation, feeding and other maintenance. Intensive roofs are more park-like with easy access and may include anything from kitchen herbs to shrubs and small trees. 'Extensive' green roofs, by contrast, are designed to be virtually self-sustaining and should require only a minimum of maintenance, perhaps a once-yearly weeding or an application of slow-release fertiliser to boost growth. Extensive roofs are usually only accessed for maintenance. They can be established on a very thin layer of 'soil' (most use specially formulated composts): even a thin layer of rockwool laid directly onto a watertight roof can support a planting of *Sedum* species and mosses.

Another important distinction is between pitched green roofs and flat green roofs. Pitched sod roofs, a traditional feature of many Scandinavian buildings, tend to be of a simpler design than flat green roofs. This is because the pitch of the roof reduces the risk of water penetrating through the roof structure, allowing the use of fewer waterproofing and drainage layers.

A number of European countries have very active associations promoting green roofs, including Germany, Switzerland, the Netherlands, Italy, Austria, Hungary, Sweden, the UK and Greece. The City of Linz in Austria has been paying developers to install green roofs since 1983 and in Switzerland it has been a federal law since the late 1990s. In the UK their up-take has been slow but a number of cities have developed policies to encourage their use, notably in London and Sheffield.

Many green roofs are installed to comply with local regulations and government fees, often regarding stormwater runoff management. In areas with combined sewer-stormwater systems, heavy storms can overload the wastewater system and cause it to flood, dumping raw sewage into the local waterways. Green roofs decrease the total amount of runoff and slow the rate of runoff from the roof. It has been found that they can retain up to 75 per cent of rainwater, gradually releasing it back into the atmosphere via condensation and transpiration, while retaining pollutants in their soil. Elevation 314, a new development in Washington D.C., uses green roofs to filter and store some of its stormwater on site, avoiding the need for expensive underground sand filters to meet D.C. Department of Health stormwater regulations.

Combating the urban heat island effect is another reason for creating a green roof. Traditional building materials soak up the sun's radiation and re-emit it as heat, making cities at least 4 degrees Celsius (7 °F) hotter than surrounding areas. On Chicago's City Hall, by contrast, which features a green roof, roof temperatures on a hot day are typically 14-44 degrees Celsius (25-80 °F) cooler than they are on traditionally roofed buildings nearby.

Green roofs are becoming common in Chicago, as well as Atlanta, Portland, and other United States cities, where their use is encouraged by regulations to combat the urban heat island effect. In the case of Chicago, the city has passed codes offering incentives to builders who put green roofs on their buildings. The Chicago City Hall green roof is one of the earliest and most well-known examples of green roofs in the United States; it was planted as an experiment to determine the effects a green roof would have on the microclimate of the roof. Following this and other studies, it has now been estimated that if all the roofs in a major city were 'greened', urban temperatures could be reduced by as much as 7 degrees Celsius.

Green roofs have also been found to dramatically improve a roof's insulation value. A study conducted by Environment Canada found a 26 per cent reduction in summer cooling needs and a 26 per cent reduction in winter heat losses when a green roof is used. In addition, greening a roof is expected to lengthen a roof's lifespan by two or three times, according to Penn State University's Green Roof Research Center.

Roof top water purification is also being implemented in green roofs. These forms of green roofs are actually treatment ponds built unto the rooftops. They are built either from a simple substrate (as being done in Dongtan or with plant-based ponds (as being done by WaterWorks UK Grow System and Waterzuiveren.be Plants used include calamus, Menyanthes trifoliata, Mentha aquatica, etc.

Green roofs also provide habitats for plants, insects, and animals that otherwise have limited natural space in cities. Even in high-rise urban settings as tall as 19 stories, it has been found that green roofs can attract beneficial insects, birds, bees and butterflies. Rooftop greenery complements wild areas by providing 'stepping stones' for songbirds, migratory birds and other wildlife facing shortages of natural habitat.

Industrial brownfield sites can be valuable ecosystems, supporting rare species of plants, animals and invertebrates. Increasingly in demand for redevelopment, these habitats are under threat. 'Brown roofs', also known as 'biodiverse roofs', can partly mitigate this loss of habitat by covering the flat roofs of new developments with a layer of locally sourced material. Construction techniques for brown roofs are typically similar to those used to create flat green roofs, the main difference being the choice of growing medium (usually locally sourced rubble, gravel, spoil etc.) to meet a specific biodiversity objective. In Switzerland it is common to use alluvial gravels from the foundations; in London a mix of brick rubble and some concrete has been used. Although the original idea was to allow the roofs to self-colonise with plants, they are sometimes seeded to increase their biodiversity potential in the short term, although such practices are derided by purists. The roofs are colonised by spiders and insects (many of which are becoming extremely rare in the UK as such sites are developed) and provide a feeding site for insectivorous birds. Laban, a centre for contemporary dance in London, has a brown roof specifically designed to encourage the nationally rare black redstart. (In 2003 Laban won the coveted RIBA Stirling Prize.) A green roof, 160m above ground level, and claimed to be the highest in the UK and Europe 'and probably in the world' to act as nature reserve, is on the Barclays Bank HQ in Canary Wharf. Designed combining the principles of green and brown roofs, it is already home to a range of rare invertebrates.

Switzerland has one of Europe's oldest green roofs, created in 1914 at the Moos lake water-treatment plant, Wollishofen, Zürich. Its filter-tanks have 30,000 square metres (320,000 sq ft) of flat concrete roofs. To keep the interior cool and prevent bacterial growth in the filtration beds, a drainage layer of gravel and a 15 cm (6 in) layer of soil was spread over the roofs, which had been waterproofed with asphalt. A meadow developed from seeds already present in the soil; it is now a haven for many plant species, some of which are now otherwise extinct in the district, most notably 6,000 *Orchis morio* (green-winged orchid). More recent Swiss examples can be found at Klinikum 1 and Klinikum 2, the Cantonal Hospitals of Basel, and the Sihlpost platform at Zürich's main railway station.

Sweden

What is claimed to be the world's first green roof botanical garden was set up in Augustenborg, a suburb of Malmö, in May 1999. The International Green Roof Institute (IGRI) opened to the public in April 2001 as a research station and educational facility. (It has since been renamed the Scandinavian Green Roof Institute (SGRI), in view of the increasing number of similar organisations around the world.) Green roofs are well-established in Malmö: the Augustenborg housing development near the SGRI botanical garden incorporates green roofs and extensive landscaping of streams, ponds and soakaways between the buildings to deal with storm water run-off.

The new Bo01 urban residential development (in the Västra Hamnen (Western Harbour) close to the foot of the Turning Torso office and apartment block, designed by Santiago Calatrava) is built on the site of old shipyards and industrial areas, and incorporates many green roofs.

Iceland

Sod roofs are frequently found on traditional farmhouses and farm buildings in Iceland.

United Kingdom

British examples can be found at the University of Nottingham Library, and in London at the Horniman Museum and Canary Wharf. The Ethelred Estate, close to the River Thames in central London, is the British capital's largest roof-greening project to date. Toxteth in Liverpool is also a candidate for a major roof-greening project.

In the United Kingdom, green roofs are often used in built-up city areas where residents and workers often do not have access to gardens or local parks. They have also been used by companies such as Rolls-Royce Motor Cars, who have one of the biggest green roofs in Europe (covering more than 32,000m^2 to help their factory, at Goodwood, West Sussex, blend into its rural surroundings.

Canada

The city of Toronto approved a by-law in May 2009, mandating green roofs on residential and industrial buildings. There is criticism from Green Roofs for Healthy Cities that the new laws are not stringent enough, since they will only apply to residential building that are a minimum of six storeys high. By 31 January 2011, industrial buildings will be required to render 10 per cent or 2,000m^2 of their roofs green.

France

In France, a huge green roof of roughly 8,000 square metres (86,000 sq ft) has been incorporated into the new museum L'Historial de la Vendée which opened in June 2006 at Les Lucs-sur-Boulogne.

Greece

The Greek Ministry of Finance has now installed a green roof on the Treasury in Constitution Square in Athens. The so called 'oikostegi' (Greek - *oiko*, pronounced *eeko*, meaning building-ecological, and *stegi*, pronounced *staygee*, meaning roof-abode-shelter) was inaugurated in September, 2008. Studies of the thermodynamics of the roof in September 2008 concluded that the thermal performance of the building was significantly affected by the installation. In further studies, in August 2009, energy savings of 50 per cent were observed for air conditioning in the floor directly below the installation. The ten-floor building has a total floor space of 1.4 hectares. The oikostegi covers 650m^2, equalling 52 per cent of the roof space and 8 per cent of the total floor space. Despite this, energy savings totalling •5,630 per annum were recorded, which translates to a 9 per cent saving in air conditioning and a 4 per cent saving in heating bills for the whole building.

The roof to Banco Santander's headquarters in Madrid, Spain is currently home to Europe's biggest green roof at just over 100,000sqm in size. The roof was made using a mix of both extensive and intensive planting systems.

Egypt

In Egypt, soil-less agriculture is used to grow plants on the roofs of buildings. No soil is placed directly on the roof itself, thus eliminating the need for an insulating layer; instead, plants are grown on wooden tables. Vegetables and fruit are the most popular candidates, providing a fresh, healthy source of food that is free from pesticides.

A more advanced method (aquaponics), being used experimentally in Egypt, is farming fish next to plants in a closed cycle. This allows the plants to benefit from the ammonia excreted by the fish, helping the plants to grow better and at the same time eliminating the need for changing the water for the fish, because the plants help to keep it clean by absorbing the ammonia. The fish also get some nutrients from the roots of the plants.

United States of America

One of the largest expanses of extensive green roof is to be found in the USA, at Ford Motor Company's River Rouge Plant, Dearborn,

Michigan, where 42,000 square metres (450,000 sq ft) of assembly plant roofs are covered with sedum and other plants, designed by William McDonough. Built over Millennium Park Garage, Chicago's 24.5-acre (99,000 m^2) Millennium Park is considered one of the largest intensive green roofs. Other well-known American examples include Chicago's City Hall and the Gap headquarters in San Bruno, CA. Recently, the American Society of Landscape Architects retrofitted their existing headquarters building in Washington, D.C. with a green roof designed by landscape architect Michael Van Valkenburgh.

Another example of a green roof in the United States is the Ballard Library in Seattle. The landscape architect was Swift & Co. and the building architect was Bohlin Cywinski Jackson. This green roof has over 18,000 plants to help with insulation and reduce runoff. The plants used on the roof include *Achillea tomentosa* (woolly yarrow), *Armeria maritima* (sea pink, sea thrift), *Carex inops pensylvanica* (long-stoloned sedge), *Eriphyllum lanatum* (Oregon sunshine), *Festuca rubra* (red creeping fescue), *Festuca idahoensis* (Idaho fescue), *Phlox subulata* (creeping phlox), *Saxifrage cespitosa* (tufted saxifrage), *Sedum oreganum* (Oregon stonecrop), *Sedum album* (white stonecrop), *Sedum spurium* (two-row stonecrop), *Sisyrinchium idahoensis* (blue-eyed grass), *Thymus serpyllum* (wild thyme), *Triteleia hyacintha* (fool's onion).

The new California Academy of Sciences building in San Francisco's Golden Gate Park has a green roof that provides 2.5 acres (10,000 m^2) of native vegetation designed as a habitat for indigenous species, including the threatened Bay checkerspot butterfly. According to the Academy's fact sheet on the building, the building consumes 30-35 per cent less energy than required by code.An early green roofed building (completed in 1971) is the 358,000 sq ft Weyerhaeuser Corporate Headquarters building in Federal Way, Washington. Its 5 storey office roof system comprises a series of stepped back terraces covered in greenery. From the air, the building blends into the landscape.A properly designed and installed green roof system can cost 5 to 10 dollars per square foot . In Europe a well-designed and professionally installed fully integrated green roof can cost anywhere between 100 to 200 euros per square meter. The cost depends on what kind of roof it is, the structure of the building, and what plants can grow on the material that is on top of the roof. In the Spring 2007 issue of the Green Roof Infrastructure Monitor (Green Roofs for Healthy Cities web site), Jörg Breuning reflects the wind and fire loads of green roofs and how German insurance companies handle extensive green roofs. Some cost can also be attributed to maintenance. Extensive green roofs have low maintenance requirements but they are generally not maintenance free. German research has quantified the need to remove unwanted seedlings to approximately 0,1 min/(m^2*year). Maintenance of green roofs often includes fertilisation to increase flowering and succulent plant cover. If aesthetics is not an issue, fertilisation and maintenance is generally not needed. Extensive green roofs should only be fertilised with controlled release fertilisers in order to avoid pollution of the stormwater. Conventional fertilisers should never be used on extensive vegetated roofs. German studies have approximated the nutrient requirement of vegetated roofs to 5gN/m^2. It is also important to use a substrate that does not contain too much available nutrients. The FLL-guidelines specify maximum allowable nutrient content of substrates.

Disadvantages

The main disadvantage of green roofs is the higher initial cost. Some types of green roofs do have more demanding structural standards especially in seismic regions of the world. Some existing buildings cannot be retrofitted with certain kinds of green roof because of the weight load of the substrate and vegetation exceeds permitted static loading. Depending on what kind of green roof it is, the maintenance costs could be higher, but some types of green roof have little or no ongoing cost. Some kinds of green roofs also place higher demands on the waterproofing system of the structure both because water is retained on the roof and due to the possibility of roots penetrating the waterproof membrane. 'However, a sedum covering doesn't need water to be retained on the roof as these plants can tolerate long periods without rainfall, so a drainage layer will combat this particular problem' (Chris Sorrell). Moreover, properly designed and installed systems include root barriers. It is true that installing adequate waterproofing systems and root barriers can increase the initial cost of the roof, however, due to the fact that a green roof protects the waterproofing membrane from the elements, particularly UV light, the life expectancy of the membranes is doubled or even tripled, leading to recovered.

14

Water Garden

Water gardens, also known as aquatic gardens, backyard ponds and garden ponds, usually referring to a man-made feature, typically combine a pool with aquatic plants and often ornamental fish. Fixed items such as rocks, fountains, statuary, waterfalls and watercourses can be combined with the pool to add visual interest and integration with the local landscape and environment.

They have become popular in recent years. They have also been famous in Chinese and European history.

Types of Water Gardens

A water garden in a private residence.

- Containers
- Man-made ponds
- Natural ponds
- Bogs
- Wild River
- Lakes
- Halka lever

Man-made Ponds

In the sixteenth century, Europe was recovering from the Black Death and towns were growing and prospering again. Renewed interest in Greek thought and philosophy led some aristocrats to reconsider the works of Hero of Alexandria in hydraulics and pneumatics. His devices, such as temple doors operated by invisible weights or flowing liquids, and mechanical singing birds powered by steam, motivated several European princes to create similar clever devices to enhance their public image.

In Italy especially, some princes took things a stage further and constructed large water gardens incorporating mechanical devices in water settings. The best-known is the Villa d'Este at Tivoli, constructed in 1550 AD. A hill presented several fountains and dozens of grottoes, where water-driven figures moved or spouted water. Within 50 years there were imitations all over Europe; the best-known today is the Hellbrunn Palace, full of performing figures (human and animal), fountains that erupt without notice, and a water-powered puppet theatre.

In the sixteenth century, Europe was recovering from the Black Death and towns were growing and prospering again. Renewed interest in Greek thought and philosophy led some aristocrats to reconsider the works of Hero of Alexandria in hydraulics and pneumatics. His devices, such as temple doors operated by invisible weights or flowing liquids, and mechanical singing birds powered by steam, motivated several European princes to create similar clever devices to enhance their public image.

In Italy especially, some princes took things a stage further and constructed large water gardens incorporating mechanical devices in water settings. The best-known is the Villa d'Este at Tivoli, constructed in 1550 AD. A hill presented several fountains and dozens of grottoes, where water-driven figures moved or spouted water. Within 50 years there were imitations all over Europe; the best-known today is the Hellbrunn Palace, full of performing figures (human and animal), fountains that erupt without notice, and a water-powered puppet theatre.

Wild River

One chooses a spot on the banks of a fast-moving river, and places rocks in the path of the water to make a small waterfall. The rocks interfere with the waterflow, causing splashing and bubbles to form. The water splashing makes a pleasant sound and new habitat for fish, crustaceans and wildlife that feed on the fish and the crustaceans.

The river's water level may vary considerably, so proper location of the rocks requires ingenuity to achieve good aeration from the splashing. Finding a good placement of rocks is similar to arranging a

Zen garden or Japanese rock garden. A well-done, intuitive placement of rocks can stimulate a feeling of peace or Zen while also achieving a practical effect, since the splashing water adds valuable oxygen to the river and may prevent hypoxia. The more bubbles formed, the more dissolved oxygen is being placed in the river.

Typical water garden plants are divided into three main categories: submerged, marginal, and floating.

1. Submerged plants are those that live almost completely under the water, sometimes with leaves or flowers that grow to the surface such as with the water lily. These plants are placed in a pond or container usually 1-2 ft. below the water surface. Some of these plants are called oxygenators because they create oxygen for the fish that live in a pond. Examples of submerged plants are:
   - Water lily (Hardy and Tropical)
   - Hornwort (*Ceratophyllum demersum*)
2. Marginal plants are those that live with their roots under the water but the rest of the plant above the surface. These are usually placed so that the top of the pot is at or barely below the water level. Examples of these are:
   - Iris or flag
   - Water-crowfoot (*Ranunculus fluitans*)
   - Bulrush (*Scirpus lacustris*)
   - Cattail (*Typha latifolia*)
   - Taro, Elephant Ear, roots for poi (*Colocasia esculenta*)
   - Arrowhead (*Sagittaria latifolia*)
   - Lotus (*Nelumbo*)
   - Pickerelweed (*Pontederia cordata*)
3. Floating plants are those that are not anchored to the soil at all, but are free-floating on the surface. In water gardening, these are often used as a provider of shade to reduce algae

Mosquito ferns (*Azolla*) Water-spangle (*Salvinia*) Water-clover (*Marsilea vestita*) Water lettuce (Nile lettuce) (*Pistia stratiotes*) Water-hyacinth (*Eichhornia crassipes*).

Some areas of the United States do not allow certain of these plants to be sold or kept as they have become invasive species in warmer areas of the country, such as Florida.

Algae are found in all ponds. There are hundreds of species of algae that can grow in garden ponds but they are only usually noticied when they become abundant. Algae often grow in very high densities in ponds because of the high nutrient levels that are typical of garden ponds. Generally alga attaches itself to the sides of the pond and remains innocuous. Some species of algae, namely the dreaded 'blanket weed' can grow up to a foot a day under ideal conditions and can rapidly clog a garden pond. On the other hand, free floating algae are microcopic and are what cause pond water to appear green.

Often the reason for having a pond in a garden is to keep fish, often koi, though many people keep goldfish. Both are hardy, colourful fish which require no special heating, provided the pond is located in an area which does not have extremes of temperature that would affect the fish. If fish are kept, pumps and filtration devices are usually needed in order to keep enough oxygen in the water to support them. In winter, a small heater may need to be used in cold climates to keep the water from freezing solid. Examples of common pond fish include:

- Goldfish (Common, Comet, Shubunkin varieties, Wakin and the Fantail varieties. With the possible exception of some of the fantail varieties, the fancy goldfish are not suited to pond life.)
- Koi (Nishikigoi, Butterfly Koi and Ghost Koi)
- Golden Orfe
- Golden Tench
- Rosy Red Minnows
- Mosquitofish
- Eel
- Catfish
- Bass
- Acipenser
- Carp
- Crucian carp
- Bluegill

Snails

Small aquatic snails are usually in ponds which have plants. Some people purchase Apple snails to keep in their water garden. Another common variety is the Melantho snail.

Amphibian and Reptile

Ponds located in suburban and rural areas often attract amphibians such as common frogs and fire salamanders, and reptiles such as turtles, lizards, and snakes.

Predators

Garden ponds can attract attention from predators such as (in North America) raccoons, heron/birds, snakes, and domestic cats. These predators can be a danger to fish. Owners of koi are often particularly upset by this as some varieties of koi can be very expensive.

Garden Pond

A garden pond is a water feature constructed in a garden, normally either for aesthetic purposes or to provide wildlife habitat. The UK charity Pond Conservation has estimated that there are about two million garden ponds in the UK.

Garden ponds can be excellent wildlife habitats. However, knowing how to make a good wildlife pond in practice is rather a matter of trial and error at present because there is remarkably little reliable information available about how to create good wildlife ponds. Despite the popularity of garden ponds, despite dozens of books and web-sites offering advice about making garden ponds, in fact there have been virtually no studies of garden pond wildlife, the best designs for wildlife ponds or of how garden ponds should be managed to maximise their value for wildlife. As a result of this, advice about the making of ponds for wildlife is plagued by the repetition of a range of myths about ponds. These myths were first identified in the early 1990s by Pond Conservation and described in an article in the magazine *British Wildlife*. The Garden Pond Blog, started by a member of Pond Conservation, aims to dispel some of these myths and help people make better garden (or backyard) ponds.

Although people often say that garden ponds make a great contribution to the protection of freshwater wildlife there is in fact no evidence one way or the other to determine whether this is really the case. This is because there have never been any careful studies made of garden ponds compared to ponds in the rest of the landscape. Because of this garden pond owners have the potential to make many original and valuable observations about the ecology of small waterbodies because so little is known about ponds generally, and specifically about the smallest natural ponds, which garden ponds replicate.

Not everything about garden ponds is good. Although invertebrate animals such as dragonflies and water beetles, and amphibians can colonise new ponds quickly, garden ponds also cause problems. In particular, garden ponds can be pathways for the spread of invasive non-native plants. In the UK the non-native species Crassula helmsii and Myriophyllum aquaticum, which cause considerable practical problems in protecting freshwaters, are both escapees from garden ponds.

Ponds may be created by natural processes or by people; however, the origin of the hole in the ground makes little difference to the kind of wildlife that will be found in the pond. Much more important is whether the pond is polluted or clean, how close it is to other wetlands and its depth, particularly whether it dries out from time to time and how many fish (if any) there are.

Naturally, ponds vary more in their physical and chemical conditions from day to day, and even during the day, than other freshwaters, like rivers. People often install pumps in garden ponds to counter these natural tendencies, particularly to maintain higher levels of dissolved oxygen: although this is probably not necessary for wildlife generally, it may be essential to keep fish in a small pond. For ponds with polluted nutrient-rich tapwater added to them, filters can be used to reduce the abundance of algae.

Ponds outside of gardens are fed by five main water sources: rain, inflows (spring, streams, ditches), groundwater and surface runoff. The wildlife value of ponds is greatly affected by the extent to which these water sources are polluted: the less pollution the better. Garden ponds are often filled with tap water; since water supplied for drinking often has high levels of nutrients which, when too abundant, pollute the pond, this gets the pond off to a bad start. Chemical pond treatments said to maintain the 'ecological balance' in ponds have rarely been carefully tested to assess their effects: although some of these treatments may have beneficial effects (for example, adding chalk to a pond polluted by phosphorus could precipitate the nutrient from the water and prevent it from being taken up by algae) most freshwater scientists would not currently consider these an effective solution to pond management problems.

Garden ponds are generally not fed by inflows or groundwater, except in the biggest gardens. Usually the pond will be filled by a combination of rainwater and surface runoff and lost to evaporation. One can make a garden pond/ koi pond that generally ranges in size from 150 gallons to around 10,000 gallons. However, if evaporation exceeds the amount of water added from rain or surface runoff, the pond may dry out during summer. This is not harmful biologically because many freshwater plants and animals (perhaps half of all species) are well adapted to periods of drought, and worldwide so-called 'temporary ponds' (ponds which usually dry out once a year) are an important natutral habitat type. However in a garden, a pond which dries out in summer may be a bit disappointing for the owner since this is the time when most people will be spending time enjoying their pond. And of course some animals, particularly fish, cannot survive periods of drought. Indeed, drought is nature's way of telling fish they are not wanted in a particular place! Amphibians, on the other hand, often benefit from ponds which dry out because this removes the major predators of tadpoles and newtpoles (fish) and, provided the larvae emerge before the pond dries out, the drought presents no problems for the amphibians.

In soils which lack natural clay, additional water loss to drainage and permeation is prevented by a liner. Pond liners are PVC or EPDM foils that are placed between the soil of the pond bed and the water. Liners can also be made from puddled clay, and ponds on free-draining soils can even be self-sealing with fine sediments washed into the pond.

15

History of Gardening

This entry concerns the history of ornamental gardening considered as an amenity of civilized life, as a vehicle for style, for conspicuous show and even an expression of philosophy.

The history of gardening extends across at least 4,000 years of human civilization. Egyptian tomb paintings of the 1500s BC are some of the earliest physical evidence of ornamental horticulture and landscape design; they depict lotus ponds surrounded by symmetrical rows of acacias and palms. Another ancient gardening tradition is of Persia: Darius the Great was said to have had a 'paradise garden' and the Hanging Gardens of Babylon were renowned as a Wonder of the World. Persian gardens were also organized symmetrically, along a center line known as an axis.

Persian influences extended to post-Alexander's Greece: Around 350 BC there were gardens at the Academy of Athens, and Theophrastus, who wrote on botany, was supposed to have inherited a garden from Aristotle. Epicurus also had a garden where he walked and taught, and bequeathed it to Hermarchus of Mytilene. Alciphron also mentions private gardens.

The most influential ancient gardens in the western world were the Ptolemy's gardens at Alexandria and the gardening tradition brought to Rome by Lucullus. Wall paintings in Pompeii attest to elaborate development later. The wealthiest Romans built extensive villa gardens with water features, topiary and cultivated roses and shaded arcades. Archaeological evidence survives at sites such as Hadrian's Villa.

Byzantium and Moorish Spain kept garden traditions alive after the 4th century AD and the fall of Rome. By this time a separate gardening tradition had arisen in China, which was transmitted to Japan, where it developed into aristocratic miniature landscapes centered on ponds and separately into the severe Zen gardens of temples.

In Europe, gardening revived in Languedoc and the Île-de-France in the 13th century. The rediscovery of descriptions of antique Roman villas and gardens led to the creation of a new form of garden, the Italian Renaissance garden in the late 15th and early 16th century. .The formal Garden à la française, exemplified by the Gardens of Versailles, became the dominant style of garden in Europe until the middle of the 18th century when it was replaced by the English landscape garden and the French landscape garden. The 19th century saw a welter of historical revivals and Romantic cottage-inspired gardening. In England, William Robinson and Gertrude Jekyll were strong proponents of the wild garden and the perennial garden respectively. Andrew Jackson Downing and Frederick Law Olmsted adapted European styles for North America, especially influencing public parks, campuses and suburban landscapes. Olmsted's influence extended well into the 20th century.

The 20th century also saw the influence of modernism in the garden: from Thomas Church's kidney-shaped swimming pool to the bold colours and forms of Roberto Burle-Marx. A strong environmental consciousness is driving new considerations in gardening today.

All Persian gardens, from the ancient to the high classical were developed in opposition to the harsh and arid landscape of the Iranian Plateau. Unlike historical European gardens, which seemed carved or re-ordered from within their existing landscape, Persian gardens appeared as impossibilities. Their ethereal and delicate qualities emphasized their intrinsic contrast to the hostile environment.

The heart of Persia, modern day Iran, is high and dry. A series of basins and plateaus are separated by the two main mountain ranges, the Albourz and the Zagros. Since ancient times, lush gardens have grown in the region due to an ingenious engineering system of underground aqueducts called qanats. Originating in northeastern Iran around 800 BC, qanats brought the water from the snow melt to the plains for irrigation and human use. The very presence and abundance of water became the essence of the Persian garden. A rich variety of species thrived while thin channels delivered water throughout the garden, feeding fountains and pools, cooling the atmosphere and providing tender, constant music in the air. Although gardens were places for poetry, contemplation and seclusion, they were not limited to pleasure and refuge. Throughout Persia's history, gardens were central to the political life of the ruling class. The Achaemenian king Cyrus placed his throne within his garden at Pasargadae. Persian miniature paintings from the 15th to the 17th century depict kings receiving diplomats in their gardens, treaties being signed there, feasts and celebrations, and all defining moments of national identity along with portrayals of legendary loves. The illustrated history, Shahnameh, Book of Kings detail both the dreamy and the practical in court life.

The ancient gardens before Cyrus and those of his descendents show evidence of the characteristics that continued to define gardens in Persia and in places that drew on Persian ideas, from India to Spain. Gardens typically were divided into quadrants by channels of water, often punctuated by geometrically shaped basins. At a central intersection point was a platform for viewing, which later evolved into a formal open pavilion, sometimes decorated with coffered ceiling structures that represented the complexity of the heavens. Geometry as a demonstration of the ordered universe was celebrated throughout Persian gardens from the surface design features to the basic ground plane and its four-fold chahar bagh format, representing the four corners of the world in the ancient vernacular, and the four rivers of paradise more predominately associated with the Islamic period. The roots of an earthly paradise however, originate in Mesopotamia thousands of years before the Achaemenians, long before the Islamic period. Persian design aspects proved to have a natural affinity to certain Islamic concepts but because they were so deeply embedded in the culture of the area, they maintained their Persian-ness throughout the country's tumultuous history.

The relationship of architecture to the Persian garden is layered; influenced by climate and geography and infused with a sense of the ephemeral qualities of light and reflection. The border between interior and exterior spaces was permeable and often transparent through the use of carved screens, deep archways, multiple vaults and honeycomb patterned ceilings punctured with tiny windows of light. Through these devices, the stone, mud and ceramic materials appear as delicate and malleable as paper, conveying the fugitive qualities of light and shadow while playing with what is revealed and what is veiled.

Classical Persian gardens were lived spaces; one imagines that they are best seen from within. As 17th century European gardens expressed the concept of a privileged point of view as demonstrated in Renaissance painting, Persian gardens can also be viewed in relation to their classical tradition of painting during the Safavid period, contemporaneous of the

European Renaissance. Where the space of the paintings appears flat and perplexing, a balance is found in multiple entry points and equal attention to every detail whether it is the king's action, a servant's gesture or the ruby red of a bowl of pomegranates. Despite a hierarchical, feudal society, everything is painted equally and in sharp focus. As the viewer, you are at once, inside and everywhere.

The Islamic gardens of Spain constructed during the 14th century are far more elaborate and extensive than northern European gardens of that period. Featuring open garden rooms, intricate tile designs, water features and sculpture, the designs were influenced by the Moors. Unlike the mediaeval gardens depicted above, these gardens were ornate outdoor spaces where members of the court could convene and cool themselves from the intense heat of the sun. The Alhambra Palace as well as the Generalife gardens that surround the palace in Grenada, Spain survive today as well-preserved examples of the Moors mark on Spanish architecture and landscape design.

Gardens were much cherished in the Egyptian times and were kept both for secular purposes and attached to temple compounds. Gardens in private homes and villas before the New Kingdom were mostly used for growing vegetables and located close to a canal or the river. However, in the New Kingdom they were often surrounded by walls and their purpose incorporated pleasure and beauty besides utility. Garden produce made out an important part of foodstuff but flowers were also cultivated for use in garlands to wear at festive occasions and for medicinal purposes. While the poor kept a patch for growing vegetables, the rich people could afford gardens lined with sheltering trees and decorative pools with fish and waterfowl. There could be wooden structrures forming pergolas to support vines of grapes from which raisins and wine were produced. There could even be elaborate stone kiosks for ornamental reasons, with decorative statues.

Temple gardens had plots for cultivating special vegetables, plants or herbs considered sacred to a certain deity and which were required in rituals and offerings like lettuce to Min. Sacred groves and ornamental trees were planted in front of or near both cult temples and mortuary temples. As temples were representations of heaven and built as the actual home of the god, gardens were laid out according to the same principle. Avenues leading up to the entrance could be lined with trees, courtyards could hold small gardens and between temple buildings gardens with trees, vineyards, flowers and ponds were maintained.

The ancient Egyptian garden would have looked different to a modern viewer than a garden in our days. It would have seemed more like a collection of herbs or a patch of wild flowers, lacking the specially bred flowers of today. Flowers like the iris, chrysanthemum, lily and delphinium (blue), were certainly known to the ancients but do not feature much in garden scenes. Formal boquets seem to have been composed of mandrake, poppy, cornflower and or lotus and papyrus.

Due to the arid climate of Egypt, tending gardens meant constant attention and depended on irrigation. Skilled gardeners were employed by temples and households of the wealthy. Duties included planting, weeding, watering by means of a shaduf, pruning of fruit trees, digging the ground, harvesting the fruit etc.

Roman Gardens

Roman gardens were a place of peace and tranquillity, a refuge from urban life. Ornamental horticulture became highly developed during the development of Roman civilisation. The administrators of the Roman Empire (c.100 BC - AD 500) actively exchanged information on agriculture, horticulture, animal husbandry, hydraulics, and botany. Seeds and plants were widely shared. The Gardens of Lucullus (Horti Lucullani) on the Pincian Hill on the edge of Rome introduced the Persian garden to Europe, about 60 BC.

Gardens of Byzantium

The Byzantine empire span a period of more than 1000 years (330-1453 AD) and a geographic area from modern day Spain and Britain to the Middle East and north Africa. Probably due to this temporal and geographic spread and its turbulent history, there is no single dominant garden style that can be labeled 'Byzantine style'. Archaeological evidence of public, imperial, and private gardens is scanty at best and researchers over the years have relied on literary sources to derive clues about the main features of Byzantine gardens. Romance novels such as [*Hysmine and Hysminias*] *(12th century) included detailed descriptions of gardens and their popularity attests to the Byzantines' enthusiasm for pleasure gardens (locus amoenus). More formal gardening texts such as the Geoponika (10th century) were in fact encyclopaedias of accumulated agricultural practices (grafting, watering) and pagan lore (astrology, plant sympathy/antipathy relationships) going back to Hesiod's time. Their repeated publications and translations to other languages well into the 16th century is evidence to the value attributed to the horticultural knowledge of antiquity. These literary sources worked as handbooks promoting the concepts of walled gardens with plants arranged by type. Such ideals found expression in the suburban parks (Philopation, Aretai) and palatial gardens of Constantinople.*

The Byzantine garden tradition was influenced by the strong undercurrents of history that the empire itself was exposed to. The first and foremost influence was the adoption of Christianity as the empire's official religion by its founder Constantine I. The new religion signalled a departure from the ornamental pagan sculptures of the Greco-Roman garden style. The second influence was the increasing contact with the Islamic nations of the Middle East especially after the 9th century. Lavish furnishings in the emperor's palace and the adoption of automata in the palatial gardens are evidence of this influence. The third factor was a fundamental shift in the design of the Byzantine cities after the 7th century when they became smaller in size and population as well as more ruralized. The class of wealthy aristocrats who could finance and maintain elaborate gardens probably shrank as well. The final factor was a shifting view toward a more 'enclosed' garden space (hortus conclusus); a trend dominant in Europe at that time. The open views and vistas so much favored by the garden builders of the Roman villas were replaced by garden walls and scenic views painted on the inside of these walls. The concept of the heavenly paradise was an enclosed garden gained popularity during that time and especially after the iconoclastic period (7th century) with the emphasis it placed on divine punishment and repentance.

An area of horticulture that flourished throughout the long history of Byzantium was that practiced by monasteries. Although archaeological evidence has provided limited evidence of monastic horticulture, a great deal can be learned by studying the foundation documents (typikon) of the numerous Christian monasteries as well as the biographies of saints describing their gardening activities. From these sources we learn that monasteries maintained gardens outside their walls and watered them with complex irrigation systems fed by springs or rainwater. These gardens contained vineyards, broadleaf vegetables, and fruit trees for the sustenance of monks and pilgrims alike. The role of the gardener was frequently assumed by monks as an act of humility. Monastic horticultural practices established at that time are still in use in Christian monasteries throughout Greece and the Middle East.

Chinese and Japanese Gardens

Both Chinese and Japanese garden design traditionally is intended to evoke the natural landscape of mountains and rivers. However, the intended viewpoint of the gardens differs: Chinese gardens were intended to be viewed from within the garden and are intended as a setting for everyday life. Japanese gardens, with a few exceptions, were intended to be viewed from within the house, sort of like a diorama.

Additionally, Chinese gardens more often included a water feature, while Japanese gardens, set in a wetter climate, would often get by with the suggestion of water. (Such as sand or pebbles raked into a wave pattern.) Traditional Chinese gardens are also more likely to treat the plants in a naturalistic way, while traditional Japanese gardens might feature plants sheared into mountain shapes. This contrasts with the handling of stone elements: in a Japanese garden, stones are placed in groupings as part of the landscape, but in a Chinese garden, a particularly choice stone might even be placed on a pedestal in a prominent location so that it might be more easily appreciated.

Chinese Scholar Gardens

The style of Chinese garden varies among economic groups and differs by dynasties. Rocks, water, bridges and pavilions are among the most common features of scholar gardens for the wealthy classes, while courtyards, wells, and terra cotta fish tanks are common among general population. Other features such as moon gates and leaky windows (openwork screens that pierce surrounding walls) are seen in both groups.

There are two ways of looking at the signature design characteristics of the Chinese garden: first, the concept of Yin and Yang and second, the myths of longevity that arose during the Qin Dynasty.

The philosophy of Yin and Yang portrays the idea of balance and harmony. The Chinese garden expresses the relationship to nature and the idea of balance through the art of mimicking natural setting, thus the existence of mountains, rocks, water, and wind elements. Yin and Yang juxtapose complementary opposites: as hard as rock can be, the softness of water can dissolve it. Tai Hu rocks, limestone eroded by the water of Lake Tai, are the quintessential example. Water, air and light run through the rock as it sit still on display. The leaky windows of the Chinese garden wall portray both steadiness and movement. The windows create a solid painting on walls, however that steadiness changes once the wind blows or the eyes move.

Chinese garden's structure is based upon the culture's creation myth, rooted in rocks and water. To have longevity is to live among mountains and water; it is to live with nature, to live like an immortal being (Xian). The garden evokes a healthy lifestyle that makes one immortal, free from the problems of civilization. Thus, Chinese landscape is known as Shan (mountain) and Shui (water). (Add Roger's citation).

Symbolism is a key element of Chinese garden design. To the earthy tones of the Chinese garden, a touch of red or gold is often added to bring forth the Yin/Yang contrast. The colours red and gold also represent luck and wealth. Bats, dragons and other mystic creatures carved on wooden doors are also commonly found in Chinese gardens; these are signs of luck and protection.

Circles portray togetherness, especially for family members, and are depicted in moon gates and round tables placed within square backgrounds. The moon gate and other whimsical doorways also act to frame views and to force the viewer to pause for a transition into a new space.

Paths in Chinese gardens are often uneven and sometimes consciously zigzag. These paths are like the passages of a human life. There is always something new or different when seen from a different angle, while the future is unknown and unpredictable.

European Gardens: Mediaeval

Monasteries carried on a tradition of garden design and intense horticultural techniques during the mediaeval period in Europe. Rather than any one particular horticultural technique employed, it is the variety of different purposes the monasteries had for their gardens that serves as testament to their sophistication. As for gardening practices, records are limited, and there are no extant monastic gardens that are entirely true to original form. There are, however, records and plans that indicate the types of garden a monastery might have had, such as those for St. Gall in Switzerland.

Generally, monastic garden types consisted of kitchen gardens, infirmary gardens, cemetery orchards, cloister garths and vineyards. Individual monasteries might also have had a 'green court', a plot of grass and trees where horses could graze, as well as a cellarer's garden or private gardens for obedientiaries, monks who held specific posts within the monastery.

From a utilitarian standpoint, vegetable and herb gardens helped provide both alimentary and medicinal crops, which could be used to feed or treat the monks and, in some cases, the outside community. As detailed in the plans for St. Gall, these gardens were laid out in rectangular plots, with narrow paths between them to facilitate collection of yields. Often these beds were surrounded with wattle fencing to prevent animals from entry. In the kitchen gardens, fennel, cabbage, onion, garlic, leeks, radishes, and parnips might be grown, as well as peas, lentils and beans if space allowed for them. The infirmary gardens could contain savory, costmary, fenugreek, rosemary, peppermint, rue, iris, sage, bergamot, mint, lovage, fennel and cumin, amongst other herbs.

The herb and vegetable gardens served a purpose beyond that of production, and that was that their installation and maintenance allowed the monks to fulfill the manual labour component of the religious way of life prescribed by Rule of St. Benedict.

Orchards also served as sites for food production and as arenas for manual labour, and cemetery orchards, such as that detailed in the plan for St. Gall, showed yet more versatility. The cemetery orchard not only produced fruit, but manifested as a natural symbol of the garden of Paradise. This bi-fold concept of the garden as a space that met both physical and spiritual needs was carried over to the cloister garth.

The cloister garth, a claustrum consisting of the viridarium, a rectangular plot of grass surrounded by peristyle arcades, was barred to the laity, and served primarily as a place of retreat, a locus of the 'vita contempliva' . The viridarium was often bisected or quartered by paths, and often featured a roofed fountain at the center or side of the garth that served as a primary source for wash water and for irrigation, meeting yet more physical needs. Some cloister gardens contained small fish ponds as well, another source of food for the community. The arcades were used for teaching, sitting and meditating, or for exercise in inclement weather.

There is much conjecture as to ways in which the garth served as a spiritual aid. Umberto Eco describes the green swath as a sort of balm on which a monk might rest weary eyes, so as to return to reading with renewed vigour . Some scholars suggest that, though sparsely planted, plant materials found in the cloister garth might have inspired various religious visions. This tendency to imbue the garden with symbolic values was not inherent to the religious orders alone, but was a feature of mediaeval culture in general. The square closter garth was meant to represent the four points of the compass, and so the universe as a whole. As Turner puts it:

"Augustine inspired mediaeval garden makers to abjure earthliness and look upward for divine inspiration. A perfect square with a round pool and a pentagonal fountain became a microcosm, illuminating the mathematical order and divine grace of the macrocosm (the universe)."

Walking around the cloister while meditating was a way of devoting oneself to the 'path of life'; indeed, each of the monastic gardens was imbued with symbolic as well as palpable value, testifying to the ingenuity of its creators.

In the later Middle Ages, texts, art and literary works provide a picture of developments in garden design. During the late 12th through

15th centuries, European cities were walled for internal defense and to control trade. Though space within these walls was limited, surviving documents show that there were animals, fruit trees and kitchen gardens inside the city limits.

Pietro Crescenzi, a Bolognese lawyer, wrote twelve volumes on the practical aspects of farming in the 13th century and they offer a description of mediaeval gardening practices. From his text we know that gardens were surrounded with stonewalls, thick hedging or fencing and incorporated trellises and arbors. They borrowed their form from the square or rectangular shape of the cloister and included square planting beds.

Grass was also first noted in the mediaeval garden. In the *De Vegetabilibus* of Albertus Magnus written around 1260, instructions are given for planting grass plots. Raised banks covered in turf called 'Turf Seats' were constructed to provide seating in the garden. Fruit trees were prevalent and often grafted to produce new varieties of fruit. Gardens included a raised mound or mount to serve as a stage for viewing and planting beds were customarily elevated on raised platforms.

Two works from the late Middle Ages discuss plant cultivation. In the English poem 'The Feate of Gardinage' by Jon Gardener and the general household advice given in Le Ménagier de Paris of 1393, a variety of herbs, flowers, fruit trees and bushes were listed with instructions on their cultivation. The Menagier provides advice by season on sowing, planting and grafting. The most sophisticated gardening during the Middle Ages was done at the monasteries. Monks developed horticultural techniques, and cultivated herbs, fruits and vegetables. Using the medicinal herbs they grew, monks treated those suffering inside the monastery and in surrounding communities.

During the Middle Ages, gardens were thought to unite the earthly with the divine. The enclosed garden as an allegory for paradise or a 'lost Eden' was termed the *Hortus Conclusus*. Freighted with religious and spiritual significance, enclosed gardens were often depicted in the visual arts, picturing the Virgin Mary, a fountain, a unicorn and roses inside an enclosed area.

Though Mediaeval gardens lacked many of the features of the Renaissance gardens that followed them, some of the characteristics of these gardens continue to be incorporated today.

European Gardens: Italian Renaissance

The Italian Renaissance inspired a revolution in gardening. Renaissance gardens were full of scenes from ancient mythology and other learned allusions. Water during this time was especially symbolic: it was associated with fertility and the abundance of nature.

Terraced Italian Garden of the Renaissance

The Medici Villa Petraia, near Florence, laid out by Niccolò Tribolo, epitomizes the Italian garden of the early Renaissance, before the grander architectural schemes of the 16th century.

Gardens of the French Renaissance

The French Classical garden style, or Garden à la française, climaxed during the reign of Louis XIV of France (1638-1715) and his head gardener of Versailles, André Le Nôtre (1613-1700). The inspiration for these gardens initially came from the Italian Renaissance garden of the 14th and 15th centuries and ideas of French philosopher Renée Descartes (1576-1650). At this time the French opened the garden up to enormous proportions compared to their Italian predecessor. Their gardens epitomize man dominating and manipulating nature to show his authority, wealth, and power.

Renée Descartes, the founder of analytical geometry, believed that the natural world was objectively measurable and that space is infinitely divisible. His belief that "all movement is a straight line therefore space is a universal grid of mathematical coordinates and everything can be located on its infinitely extendable planes" gave us Cartesian mathematics. Through the classical French gardens this coordinate system and philosophy is now given a physical and visual representation.

This formal and symmetrical garden style placed the house centrally on an enormous and mainly flat property. A large central axis that gets narrower further from the main house, forces the viewer's perspective to the horizon line, making the property look even larger. The viewer is to see the property as a cohesive whole but at the same time is unable to see all the components of the garden. One is to be led through a logical progression or story and be surprised by elements that aren't visible until approached. There is an allegorical story referring to the owner through statues and water features which have mythological references. There are small, almost imperceptible grade changes that help conceal the gardens surprises as well as elongate the gardens views.

These grand gardens have organized spaces meant to be elaborate stages for entertaining guests or the court with plays, concerts and fireworks displays. The following list of garden features were used:

- Allée
- Axis
- Bosquet
- Canal
- Cul de sac
- Fountains
- Grottos with rocaille
- Orangerie
- Parterre de broderie
- Patte d'oie (Goose foot)
- Tapis Vert
- Topiary

European Gardens: Anglo-Dutch Gardens

Anglo-Dutch formal gardens

Landscape Gardens

English landscape garden and its imitators, called ' English gardens.'

French landscape garden

Picturesque Gardens

The picturesque garden style emerged in England in the 18th century, one of the growing currents of the larger Romantic movement. Garden designers like William Kent and Capability Brown emulated the allegorical landscape paintings of European artists, especially Claude Lorraine, Poussin and Salvator Rosa. The manicured hills, lakes and trees dotted with allegorical temples were sculpted into the land.

By the 1790s there was a reaction against these stereotypical compositions; a number of thinkers began to promote the idea of picturesque gardens. The leader of the movement was landscape theorist William Gilpin, an accomplished artist known for his realistic depictions of Nature. He preferred the natural landscape over the manicured and urged designers to respond to the topography of a given site. He also noted that while classical beauty was associated with the smooth and neat, picturesque beauty had a wilder, untamed quality. The picturesque style also incorporated architectural follies—castles, Gothic ruins, rustic cottages—built to add interest and depth to the landscape.

Controversy between the picturesque school and proponents of the more manicured garden raged well into the 19th century. Landscape designer Humphrey Repton supported Gilpin's ideas, particularly that of the garden harmonizing with surrounding landforms. He was attacked in the press by two rival theorists, Richard Payne Knight and Uvedale Price. Repton countered by highlighting the differences between painting and landscape gardening. Unlike a painting, the viewer moves through a garden, constantly shifting viewpoints.

The French landscape garden, also called the *jardin anglais*, was influenced by, yet separate from contemporary English gardens. Rococo features like Turkish tents and Chinese bridges are prevalent in French gardens in the 18th century. The French Picturesque garden style falls into two categories: those that were staged, almost like theatrical scenery, usually rustic and exotic, called *jardin anglo-chinois*, and those filled with pastoral romance and bucolic sentiment, influenced by Jean-Jacques Rousseau. The former style is represented by the Parc Monceau, the latter by the Moulin Jolie.

The rusticity found in French Picturesque gardens is also derived from an admiration of Dutch 17th century landscape painting and works of French 18th century artists Claude-Henri Watelet, François Boucher and Hubert Robert.

'Gardenesque' Gardens

The 'Gardenesque' style of English garden design evolved during the 1820s from Humphry Repton's Picturesque or 'Mixed' style, largely under the impetus of J. C. Loudon, who invented the term.

In a Gardenesque plan, all the trees, shrubs and other plants are positioned and managed in such a way that the character of each plant can be displayed to its full potential. With the spread of botany as a suitable avocation for the enlightened, the Gardenesque tended to emphasize botanical curiosities and a collector's approach. New plant material that would have seemed bizarre and alien in earlier gardening found settings: Pampas grass from Argentina and Monkey-puzzle trees. Winding paths linked scattered plantings. The Gardenesque approach involved the creation of small-scale landscapes, dotted with features and vignettes, to promote beauty of detail, variety and mystery, sometimes to the detriment of coherence. Artificial mounds helped to stage groupings of shrubs, and island beds became prominent features.

PATTERN GARDENS: REVIVED PARTERRES

'Wild' Gardens and Herbaceous Borders

The books of William Robinson describing his own 'wild' gardening at Gravetye Manor, Sussex, and the sentimental picture of a rosy, idealized 'cottage garden' of the kind pictured by Kate Greenaway, which had scarcely existed historically, both influenced the development of the mixed herbaceous borders that were advocated by Gertrude Jekyll from the 1890s. Her plantings, which mixed shrubs with perennial and annual plants and bulbs in deep beds within more formal structures of terraces and stairs designed by Edwin Lutyens, set the model for high-style, high-maintenance gardening until the Second World War. Vita Sackville-West's garden at Sissinghurst Castle, Kent is the most famous and influential garden of this last blossoming of romantic style, publicized by the gardener's own gardening column in *The Observer*. In the last quarter of the 20th century, less structured Wildlife gardening emphasized the ecological framework of similar gardens using native plants.

Modern Gardens

In the twentieth century, modern garden design became important as architects began to design buildings and residences with an eye toward innovation, problem solving and streamlining the formalized Beaux Arts style, removing unnecessary embellishment. Garden design inspired by modern architecture naturally followed in the same philosophy of form following function. Thus concerning the many philosophies of plant maturity.

Garrett Eckbo, James Rose, and Dan Kiley the 'bad boys of Harvard' who met while studying traditional landscape architecture became notable pioneers in the design of modern gardens. As Harvard embraced modern design in their school of architecture, the 'boys' too wanted to incorporate those same ideas in landscape design. They became interested in developing functional space for outdoor living with designs echoing natural surroundings. Modern gardens feature a fresh mix of curved and linier designs and many include abstract art in geometrics and sculpture. Spaces are defined with the thoughtful placement of trees and plantings. A kidney-shape pool, introduced by Thomas Church in 1948 became a hallmark of modern outdoor living.

Frank Lloyd Wright also demonstrated his interpretation for the modern garden by designing homes in complete harmony with natural surroundings. Taliesin and Fallingwater are both examples of careful placement of architecture in nature so the relationship between the residence and surroundings become seamless.

NOTABLE HISTORIC GARDENS

China

- Gardens of Suzhou
- Summer Palace
- Beihai Park
- Yuyuan Garden
- Prince Gong Mansion

England

- Blenheim Palace
- Chatsworth
- Fountains Abbey
- Hidcote Manor Garden
- Lost gardens of Heligan
- Sissinghurst castle
- Stourhead
- Stowe house

France

- Chateau Fontainebleau
- Marly-le-Roi
- Chateau Villandry
- Ermenonville
- Giverny
- Versailles
- Vaux-le-Vicomte

India

- Shalimar Gardens (Jammu and Kashmir)
- Vrindavan Garden (Mysore)
- Mughal Garden (Rashtrapati Bhavan, Delhi)

Iraq

- Hanging Gardens of Babylon

Ireland

- Historic Cork Gardens

- Powerscourt Gardens
- Mount Usher Gardens

Italy

- Bomarzo
- Hadrian's villa
- Villa d'Este
- Hadrian's villa
- Reggia di Caserta
- Boboli Gardens

Japan

- Daisen-in

Netherlands

- Het Loo

Pakistan

- Shalimar Gardens (Lahore)

Poland

- Arkadia
- Baranów Sandomierski
- Krasiczyn
- Lazienki Park, Warsaw
- Muskauer Park
- Nieborów
- Saxon garden, Warsaw
- Wilanów

Russia

- Kuskovo
- Arkhangelskoye Estate
- Tsaritsyno
- Ostafyevo
- Vlakhernskoye-Kuzminki
- Pavlovsk
- Peterhof

- Summer Garden
- Monrepo
- Vybiti
- Lyublino

Spain

- Alhambra
- Reales Alcázares de Sevilla
- Monforte
- Laberinto de Horta
- Real Jardín Botánico de Madrid
- El Capricho de la Alameda de Osuna
- La Concepción
- El Retiro
- Fábrica de Paños de Brihuega
- Pazo de Oca

Ukraine

- Sofiówka, Ukraine

United States

- Central Park, New York City
- Dumbarton Oaks

16

Cottage Garden

The 'cottage garden' is a distinct style of garden that uses an informal design, traditional materials, dense plantings, and a mixture of ornamental and edible plants. English in origin, the cottage garden depends on grace and charm rather than grandeur and formal structure. Homely and functional gardens connected to working-class cottages go back several centuries, but their reinvention in stylized versions grew in 1870s England, in reaction to the more structured and rigorously maintained English estate gardens that used formal designs and mass plantings of brilliant greenhouse annuals.

The earliest cottage gardens were more practical than their modern descendants — with an emphasis on vegetables and herbs, along with some fruit trees, perhaps a beehive, and even livestock. Flowers were used to fill any spaces in between. Over time, flowers became more dominant. The traditional cottage garden was usually enclosed, perhaps with a rose-bowered gateway. Flowers common to early cottage gardens included hollyhocks, pansies and delphinium, all three essentially nineteenth-century flowers. Others were the old-fashioned roses that bloomed once a year with rich scents, simple flowers like daisies, and flowering herbs. A well-tended topiary of traditional form, perhaps a cone-shape in tiers, or a conventionalised peacock, would be part of the repertory, to which the leisured creators of 'cottage gardens' would add a sun-dial, crazy paving on paths with thyme in the interstices, and a rustic seat, generally missing in the earlier cottage gardens. Over time, even large estate gardens had sections they called 'cottage gardens'.

Modern-day cottage gardens include countless regional and personal variations of the more traditional English cottage garden, and embrace plant materials, such as ornamental grasses or native plants, that were never seen in the rural gardens of cottagers. Traditional roses, with their full fragrance and lush foliage, continue to be a cottage garden mainstay — along with modern disease-resistant varieties that keep the traditional attributes. Informal climbing plants, whether traditional or modern hybrids, are also a common cottage garden plant. Self-sowing annuals and freely spreading perennials continue to find a place in the modern cottage garden, just as they did in the traditional cottager's garden.

Cottage gardens, which emerged in Elizabethan times, appear to have originated as a local source for herbs and fruits. One theory is that they arose out of the Black Death of the 1340s, when the death of so many labourers made land available for small cottages with personal gardens. According to the late nineteenth-century legend of origin, these gardens were originally created by the workers that lived in the cottages of the villages, to provide them with food and herbs, with flowers planted in for decoration. Helen Leach analysed the historical origins of the romanticized cottage garden, subjecting the garden style to rigorous historical analysis, along with the ornamental potager and the herb garden. She concluded that their origins were less in workingmen's gardens in the nineteenth century and more in the leisured classes' discovery of simple hardy plants, in part through the writings of John Claudius Loudon. Loudon helped to design the estate at Great Tew, Oxfordshire, where farm workers were provided with cottages that had architectural quality set in a small garden—about an acre—where they could grow food and keep pigs and chickens.

Authentic gardens of the yeoman cottager would have included a beehive and livestock, and frequently a pig and sty, along with a well. The peasant cottager of medieval times was more interested in meat than flowers, with herbs grown for medicinal use rather than for their beauty. By Elizabethan times there was more prosperity, and thus more room to grow flowers. Even the early cottage garden flowers typically had their practical use—violets were spread on the floor (for their pleasant scent and keeping out vermin); calendulas and primroses were both attractive and used in cooking. Others, such as sweet william and hollyhocks were grown entirely for their beauty.

Evolution

The 'naturalness' of informal design began to be noticed and developed by the British leisured class. Alexander Pope was an early proponent of less formal gardens, calling in a 1713 article for gardens with the "amiable simplicity of unadorned nature". Other writers in the 18th century who encouraged less formal, and more natural, gardens included Joseph Addison and Lord Shaftesbury. The evolution of cottage gardens can be followed in the issues of *The Cottage Gardener* (1848-61), edited by George William Johnson, where the emphasis is squarely on the "florist's flowers", carnations and auriculas in fancy varieties that were originally cultivated as a highly-competitive blue-collar hobby.

William Robinson and Gertrude Jekyll helped to popularize less formal gardens in their many books and magazine articles. Robinson's *The Wild Garden*, published in 1870, contained in the first edition an essay on 'The Garden of British Wild Flowers', which was eliminated from later editions. In his *The English Flower Garden*, illustrated with cottage gardens from Somerset, Kent and Surrey, he remarked, "One lesson of these little gardens, that are so pretty, is that one can get good effects from simple materials." From the 1890s his lifelong friend Jekyll applied cottage garden principles to more structured designs in even quite large country houses. Her *Colour in the Flower Garden* (1908) is still in print today.

Robinson and Jekyll were part of the Arts and Crafts Movement, a broader movement in art, architecture, and crafts during the late 1800s which advocated a return to the informal planting style derived as much from the Romantic tradition as from the actual English cottage garden. The Arts and Crafts Exhibition of 1888 began a movement toward an idealized natural country garden style. The garden designs of Robinson and Jekyll were often associated with Arts and Crafts style houses. Both were influenced by William Morris, one of the leaders of the Arts and Crafts Movement—Robinson quoted Morris's views condemning carpet bedding; Jekyll shared Morris's mystical view of nature and drew on the floral designs in his textiles for her gardening style. When Morris built his Red House in Kent, it influenced new ideas in architecture and gardening—the 'old-fashioned' garden suddenly became a fashion accessory among the British artistic middle class, and the cottage garden esthetic began to emigrate to America.

In the early twentieth century the term 'cottage garden' might be applied even to as large and sophisticated a garden as Hidcote Manor, which Vita Sackville-West described as 'a cottage garden on the most glorified scale' but where the colour harmonies were carefully contrived and controlled, as in the famous 'Red Borders'. Sackville-West had taken similar models for her own 'cottage garden', one of many 'garden rooms' at Sissinghurst Castle—her idea of a cottage garden was a place where "the plants grow in a jumble, flowering shrubs mingled with Roses, herbaceous plants with bulbous subjects, climbers scrambling over hedges, seedlings coming up wherever they have chosen to sow themselves". The cottage garden ideal was also spread by artists such as water-colourist Helen Allingham (1848-1926).

The cottage garden in France is a development of the early twentieth century. Monet's garden at Giverny is a prominent example, a sprawling garden full of varied plantings, rich colors, and water gardens. In modern times, the term 'cottage garden' is used to describe any number of informal garden styles, using design and plants very different from their traditional English cottage garden origins. Examples include regional variations using a grass prairie scheme (in the American midwest) and California chapparal cottage gardens.

While the classic cottage garden is built around a cottage, many cottage-style gardens are created around houses and even estates such as Hidcote Manor, with its more intimate 'garden rooms'. The cottage garden design is based more on principles than formulae: it has an informal look, with a seemingly casual mixture of flowers, herbs, and vegetables often packed into a small area. In spite of their appearances, cottage gardens have a design and formality that help give them their grace and charm. Due to space limitations, they are often in small rectangular plots, with practical functioning paths and hedges or fences. The plants, layout, and materials are chosen to give the impression of casualness and a country feel. Modern cottage gardens frequently use local flowers and materials, rather than those of the traditional cottage garden. What they share with the tradition is the unstudied look, the use of every square inch, and a rich variety of flowers, herbs, and vegetables.

The cottage garden is designed to appear artless, rather than contrived or pretentious. Instead of artistic curves, or grand geometry, there is an artfully designed irregularity. Borders can go right up to the house, lawns are replaced with tufts of grass or flowers, and beds can be as wide as needed. Instead of the discipline of large scale colour schemes, there is the simplicity of harmonious color combinations between neighbouring plants. The overall appearance can be of 'a vegetable garden that has been taken over by flowers'. The method of planting closely packed plants was supposed to reduce the amount of weeding and watering required, but planted stone pathways or turf paths, and clipped hedges overgrown with wayward vines, are cottage garden features requiring well-timed maintenance.

Materials

Paths, arbors, and fences use traditional or antique looking materials. Wooden fences and gates, paths covered with locally made bricks or stone, and arbors using natural materials all give a more casual–and less formal–look and feel to a cottage garden. Pots, ornaments, and furniture also use natural looking materials with traditional finishes–everything is chosen to give the impression of an old-fashioned country garden.

Cottage garden plants are chosen for their old-fashioned and informal appeal. Many modern day gardeners use heirloom or 'old-fashioned' plants and varieties—even though these may not have been authentic or traditional cottage garden plants. In addition, there are modern varieties of flowers that fit into the cottage garden look. For example, modern roses developed by David Austin have been chosen for cottage gardens because of their old-fashioned look (multi-petaled form and rosette-shaped flowers) and fragrance—combined with modern virtues of hardiness, repeat blooming, and disease-resistance. Modern cottage gardens often use native plants and those adapted to the local climate, rather than trying to force traditional English plants to grow in an incompatible environment—though many of the old favourites thrive in cottage gardens throughout the world.

Cottage gardens are always associated with roses: shrub roses, climbing roses, and old garden roses with lush foliage, in contrast to the gangly modern hybrid tea roses. Old cottage garden roses include the Gallica rose, which form dense mounded shrubs 3-4 ft high and wide, with pale pink to purple flowers—with single form to full double form blooms. They are also very fragrant, and include the ancient Apothecary's rose, whose magenta flowers were preserved solely for their fragrance. Another old fragrant cottage garden rose is the Damask rose, which is still grown in Europe for use in perfumes. The damasks grow 6 ft or higher, with gently arching canes that help give an informal look to a garden. Even taller are the Alba roses, which are not always white, and which bloom well even in partial shade.

The Provence rose or *Rosa centifolia* is the full and fat rose made famous by Dutch masters in their seventeenth century paintings. These very fragrant shrub roses grow 5 ft tall and wide, with a floppy habit that is aided by training on an arch or pillar. The centifolia roses have produced many descendants that are also cottage garden favourites, including the moss rose. Unlike most modern hybrids, the older roses bloom on the previous year's wood, so they aren't pruned back severely each year like the modern varieties. Because they don't bloom continuously, like their modern counterparts, they can share their branches with Clematis vines, which use the branches for support. A rose in the cottage garden is not segregated with other roses, with bare earth or mulch underneath—but is casually blended with other flowers, vines, and groundcover.

With the introduction of China roses (*rosa chinensis*) late in the eighteenth century, many hybrids were introduced that had the repeat blooming of the China roses, but maintained the informal old rose shape and flower. These included the Bourbon rose and the Noisette rose, which were added to the rose repertoire of the cottage garden. More recently, hybrid 'English' roses introduced by David Austin have become popular cottage garden-style roses. His shrub roses combine the best traits of modern hybrid tea and floribunda roses, with the old garden roses.

Many of the old roses had cultivars that grew very long canes, which could be tied to trellises or against walls. These older varieties are called 'ramblers', rather than 'climbers'. Climbing plants in the traditional cottage garden included European honeysuckle (*Lonicera periclymenum*) and Traveller's Joy (*Clematis vitalba*). The modern cottage garden includes many Clematis hybrids that have the old appeal, with sparse foliage that allows them to grow through roses and trees, and along fences and arbors. There are also many Clematis species used in the modern cottage garden, including *Clematis armandii*, *Clematis chrysocoma*, and *Clematis flammula*. Popular honeysuckles for cottage gardens include Japanese honeysuckle and *Lonicera tragophylla*.

Hedging Plants

In the traditional cottage garden, hedges served as fences on the perimeter to keep out marauding livestock and for privacy, along with other practical uses. Hawthorn leaves made a tasty snack or tea, while the flowers were used for making wine. The fast-growing Elderberry, in addition to creating a hedge, provided berries for food and wine, with the flowers being fried in batter or made into lotions and ointments. The wood had many uses, including toys, pegs, skewers, and fishing poles. Holly was another hedge plant, useful because it quickly spread and self-seeded. Privet was also a convenient and fast growing hedge. Over time, more ornamental and less utilitarian plants became popular cottage garden hedges, including laurel, lilac, snowberry, japonica, and others.

Flowers and Herbs

Popular flowers in the traditional cottage garden included florist's flowers which were grown by enthusiasts—such as violets, pinks, and primroses—and those grown with a more practical purpose. For example, the calendula, grown today almost entirely for its bright orange flowers, was primarily valued for eating, for adding color to butter and cheese, for adding smoothness to soups and stews, and for all kinds of healing salves and preparations. Like many old cottage garden annuals and herbs, it freely self-sowed, making it easier to grow and share. Other popular cottage garden annuals included violets, pansies, stocks, and mignonette.

Perennials were the largest group of traditional cottage garden flowers—those with a long cottage garden history include hollyhocks, carnations, sweet williams, marguerites, marigolds, lilies, peonies, tulips, crocus, daisies, foxglove , monkshood, lavender, campanulas, Solomon's seal, evening primrose, lily-of-the-valley, primrose, cowslips, and many varieties of roses.

Today herbs are typically thought of as culinary plants, but in the traditional cottage garden they were considered to be any plant with household uses. Herbs were used for medicine, toiletries, and cleaning products. Scented herbs would be spread on the floor along with rushes to cover odours. Some herbs were used for dying fabrics. Traditional cottage garden herbs included sage, thyme, southernwood, wormwood, catmint, feverfew, lungwort, soapwort, hyssop, sweet woodruff, and lavender.

Fruits

Fruit in the traditional cottage garden would have included an apple and a pear, for cider and perry, gooseberries and raspberries. The modern cottage garden includes many varieties of ornamental fruit and nut trees, such as crabapple and hazel, along with non-traditional trees like dogwood.

17

Mughal Gardens

'Mughal gardens' are a group of gardens built by the Mughals in the Islamic style of architecture. This style was influenced by Persian gardens and Timurid gardens. Significant use of rectilinear layouts are made within the walled enclosures. Some of the typical features include pools, fountains and canals inside the gardens.

The founder of the Mughal empire, Babur, described his favourite type of garden as a charbagh. This word developed a new meaning in India, because as Babur explains, India lacked the fast-flowing streams required for the Central Asian charbagh. The Agra garden, now known as the Ram Bagh, is thought to have been the first charbagh. India, Bangladesh and Pakistan have a number of Mughal gardens which differ from their Central Asian predecessors with respect to 'the highly disciplined geometry'. An early textual references about Mughal gardens are found in the memoirs and biographies of the Mughal emperors, including those of Babur, Humayun and Akbar. Later references are found from 'the accounts of India' written by various European travellers (Bernier for example). The first serious historical study of Mughal gardens was written by Constance Villiers-Stuart, with the title *Gardens of the Great Mughals* (1913). Her husband was a Colonel in Britain's Indian army. This gave her a good network of contacts and an opportunity to travel. During their residence at Pinjore Gardens, Mrs. Villiers-Stuart also had an opportunity to direct the maintenance of an important Mughal garden. Her book makes reference to the forthcoming design of a garden in the Government House at New Delhi (now known as Rashtrapati Bhavan). She was consulted by Edwin Lutyens, and this may have influenced his choice of Mughal style for this project. Recent scholarly work on 'the history of Mughal gardens' has been carried out under the auspicious guidance of Dumbarton Oaks (including *Mughal Gardens: Sources, Places, Representations, and Prospects* edited by James L. Wescoat, Jr. and Joachim Wolschke-Bulmahn) and the Smithsonian Institution. Some examples of Mughal gardens are Shalimar Gardens (Lahore), Lalbagh Fort at Dhaka, and Shalimar Gardens (Jammu and Kashmir).

From the beginnings of the Mughal Empire, the construction of gardens was a beloved imperial pastime. Babur, the first Mughal conqueror-king, had gardens built in Lahore and Dholpur. Humayun, his son, does not seem to have had much time for building—he was busy reclaiming and increasing the realm—but he is known to have spent a great deal of time at his father's gardens. Akbar built several gardens first in Delhi, then in Agra, Akbar's new capital. These tended to be riverfront gardens rather than the fortress gardens that his predecessors built. Building riverfront rather than fortress gardens influenced later Mughal garden architecture considerably. Akbar's heir, Jahangir, did not build as much, but he helped to lay out the famous Shalimar garden and was known for his great love for flowers. Indeed, his trips to Kashmir are believed to have begun a fashion for naturalistic and abundant floral design.

Jahangir's son, Shah Jahan, marks the apex of Mughal garden architecture and floral design. He is famous for the construction of the Taj Mahal, a sprawling funereal paradise in memory of his favourite wife, Mumtaz Mahal. He is also responsible for the Red Fort at Delhi which contains the Mahtab Bagh, a night garden that was filled with night-blooming jasmine and other pale flowers. The pavilions within are faced with white marble to glow in the moonlight. This and the marble of the Taj Mahal are inlaid with semi-precious stone depicting scrolling naturalistic floral motifs, the most important being the tulip, which Shah Jahan adopted as a personal symbol.

The Mughals were obsessed with symbol and incorporated it into their gardens in many ways. The standard Quranic references to paradise were in the architecture, layout, and in the choice of plant life; but more secular references, including numerological and zodiacal significances connected to family history or other cultural significance, were often juxtaposed. The numbers eight and nine were considered auspicious by the Mughals and can be found in the number of terraces or in garden architecture such as octagonal pools.

Mughal garden design derives primarily from the medieval Islamic garden, although there are nomadic influences that come from the Mughals' Turkish-Mongolian ancestry. Julie Scott Meisami describes the medieval Islamic garden as "a hortus conclusus, walled off and protected from the outside world; within, its design was rigidly formal, and its inner space was filled with those elements that man finds most pleasing in nature. Its essential features included running water (perhaps the most important element) and a pool to reflect the beauties of sky and garden; trees of various sorts, some to provide shade merely, and others to produce fruits; flowers, colourful and sweet-smelling; grass, usually growing wild under the trees; birds to fill the garden with song; the whole cooled by a pleasant breeze. The garden might include a raised hillock at the center, reminiscent of the mountain at the center of the universe in cosmological descriptions, and often surmounted by a pavilion or palace." The Turkish-Mongolian elements of the Mughal garden are primarily related to the inclusion of tents, carpets and canopies reflecting nomadic roots. Tents indicated status in these societies, so wealth and power were displayed through the richness of the fabrics as well as by size and number.

SITES OF MUGHAL GARDENS

Afghanistan

- Bagh-e Babur (Kabul)

India

- Humayun's Tomb, Delhi (Nizamuddin)
- Taj Mahal, Agra
- Ram Bagh, Agra
- Mehtab Bagh, Agra
- Safdarjung's Tomb
- Shalimar Bagh (Srinagar), Jammu and Kashmir
- Nishat Gardens, Jammu and Kashmir
- Yadvindra Gardens, Pinjore
- Khusro Bagh, Allahabad
- Roshanara Bagh

Pakistan

- Chauburji (The Gate to the Mughal Gardens)
- Lahore Fort

- Shahdara Bagh
- Shalimar Gardens (Lahore)
- Hazuri Bagh
- Hiran Minar (Sheikhupura)
- Mughal Garden Wah
- Vernag

18

Italian Renaissance Garden

The Italian Renaissance garden was a new style of garden which emerged in the late fifteenth century at villas in Rome and Florence, inspired by classical ideals of order and beauty, and intended for the pleasure of the view of the garden and the landscape beyond, for contemplation, and for the enjoyment of the sights, sounds and smells of the garden itself.

In the late Renaissance, the gardens became larger, grander and more symmetrical, and were filled with fountains, statues, grottoes, water organs and other features designed to delight their owners and amuse and impress visitors. The style was imitated throughout Europe, influencing the gardens of the French Renaissance and the English garden.

Prior to the Italian Renaissance, Italian Medieval gardens were enclosed by walls, and were devoted to growing vegetables, fruits and medicinal herbs, or, in the case of monastery gardens, for silent meditation and prayer. The Italian Renaissance garden broke down the wall between the garden, the house, and the landscape outside.

The Italian Renaissance garden, like Renaissance art and architecture, emerged from the rediscovery by Renaissance scholars of classical Roman models. They were inspired by the descriptions of ancient Roman gardens given by Ovid in his *Metamorphoses*; by the letters of Pliny the Younger, by Pliny the Elder's *Naturalis Historia*; and in *Rerum Rusticanum* by Varro, all of which gave detailed and lyrical description of the gardens of Roman villas.

Pliny the Younger described his life at his villa at Laurentum: ... a good life and a genuine one, which is happy and honourable, more rewarding than any 'business' can be. You should take the first opportunity to leave the din, the futile bustle and useless occupations of the city and devote yourself to literature or to leisure.". The purpose of a garden, according to Pliny, was 'otium', which could be translated as seclusion, serenity, or relaxion. A garden was a place to think, read, write and relax.

Pliny described shaded paths bordered with hedges, ornamental parterres, fountains, and trees and bushes trimmed to geometric or fantastic shapes; all features which would become part of the future Renaissance garden.

Alberti and the Principles of the Renaissance Garden

The first Renaissance text to include garden design was *De Re Aedificatoria* ('The Ten Books of Architecture'), by Leon Battista Alberti (1404-1472). He drew upon the architectural principles of Vitruvius, and used quotations from Pliny the Older and Younger to describe what a garden should look like and how it should be used. He argued that a villa should both be looked at and a place to look from; that the house should be placed above the garden, where it could be seen and the owner could look down into the garden.

Alberti wrote:

> "The construction will give pleasure to the visitor if, when they leave the city, they see the villa in all its charm, as if to seduce and welcome the new arrivals. Toward this end, I would place it on a slightly elevated place. I would also have the road climb so gently that it fools those who take it to the point that they do not realize how high they have climbed until they discover the countryside below."

Within the garden, Alberti wrote: '... You should place porticos for giving shade, planters where vines can climb, placed on marble columns; vases and amusing statues, provided they are not obscene. You should also have rare plants ... Trees should be aligned and arranged evenly, each tree aligned with its neighbours'.

The Literary Influence on the Italian Renaissance Garden

A popular romance, *The Hypnerotomachia Poliphili,* (Poliphilo's strife of love in a dream), published in 1499 in Venice by the monk Francesco Colonna, also had an important influence on the gardens of the Renaissance. It described the voyage and adventures of a traveller,

Poliphile, through fantastic landscapes, looking for his love, Polia. The scenes described in the book and the accompanying woodcut illustrations influenced many Renaissance gardens; they included a lake-island (as at the Boboli Gardens), giants emerging from the earth (as at Villa Pratolino), the labyrinth, and the fountain of Venus (as at Villa Castello) where Poliphile and Polia were reconciled.

While the early Italian Renaissance gardens were designed for contemplation and pleasure with tunnels of greenery, trees for shade, an enclosed *giardino segreto* (secret garden) and fields for games and amusements, the Medici, the ruling dynasty of Florence, used gardens to demonstrate their own power and magnificence. "During the first half of the sixteenth century, magnificence came to be perceived as a princely virtue, and all over the Italian peninsula architects, sculptors, painters, poets, historians and humanist scholars were commissioned to concoct a magnificent image for their powerful patrons." The central fountain at Villa Castello featured a statue of Hercules, symbolizing Cosimo de Medici, the ruler of Florence, and the fish-tailed goat that was an emblem of the Medicis; the garden represented the power, wisdom, order, beauty and glory that the Medici had brought to Florence.

Glossary of the Italian Renaissance Garden

- *Fontaniere:* The fountain-maker, a hydraulic engineer who designed the water system and fountains.
- *Giochi d'acqua:* Water tricks. Concealed fountains which drenched unsuspecting visitors.
- *Bosco Sacro:* Sacred wood. A grove of trees inspired by the groves where pagans would worship. In Renaissance and especially mannerist gardens, this section was filled with allegorical statues of animals, giants and fantastic creatures.
- *Giardino Segreto:* The Secret Garden. An enclosed private garden within the garden, inspired by the cloisters of Mediaeval monasteries. A place for reading, writing or quiet conversations.
- *Semplici:* 'Simples', or medicinal plants and herbs.

The Medici Villa at Fiesole (1455-1461)

The oldest existing Italian Renaissance garden is at the Villa Medici in Fiesole, north of Florence. It was created sometime between 1455 and 1461 by Giovanni de' Medici (1421-1463) the son of Cosimo de' Medici, the founder of the Medici dynasty. Unlike other Medici family villas that were located on flat farmland, this villa was located on a rocky hillside with a view over Florence.

The Villa Medici followed Alberti's precepts that a villa should have a view 'that overlooks the city, the owner's land, the sea or a great plain, and familiar hills and mountains,' and that the foreground have 'the delicacy of gardens.'. The garden has two large terraces, one at the ground floor level and the other at the level of the first floor. From the reception rooms on the first floor, guests could go out to the loggia and from there to the garden so the loggia was a transition space connecting the interior with the exterior. Unlike later gardens, the Villa Medici did not have a grand staircase or other feature to link the two levels.

The garden was inherited by his nephew, Lorenzo de' Medici, who made it a meeting place for poets, artists, writers and philosophers. In 1479, the poet Angelo Poliziano, tutor to the Medici children, described the garden in a letter: '... Seated between the sloping sides of the mountains we have here water in abundance and being constantly refreshed with moderate winds find little inconvenience from the glare of the sun. As you approach the house it seems embosomed in the wood, but when you reach it you find it commands a full prospect of the city."

The Palazzo Piccolomini at Pienza, was built by Enea Silvio Piccolomini, who was Pope from 1458 to 1464, under the name of Pius II. He was a scholar of Latin and wrote extensively on education, astronomy and social culture. In 1459, he constructed a palace for himself and his Cardinals and court in his small native town of Pienza. Like the Villa Medici, a major feature of the house was the commanding view to be had from the loggia over the valley, the Val d'Orcia, to the slopes of Monte Amiata. Closer to the house, there were terraces with geometric flowerbeds surrounding fountains and ornamented with bushes trimmed into cones and spheres similar to the garden of Pliny described in Alberti's *De Re Aedificatoria*. The garden was designed to open to the town, the palace and the view.

The Cortile del Belvedere in the Vatican Palace, Rome, (1504-1513)

In 1504 Pope Julius II commissioned the architect Donato Bramante to recreate a classical Roman pleasure garden in the space between the old papal Vatican palace in Rome and the nearby Villa Belvedere. His model was the ancient sanctuary of Fortuna Primigenia at Palestrina or ancient Praeneste, and he used the classical ideals of proportion, symmetry and perspective in his design. He created a central axis to link the two buildings, and a series of terraces connected by double ramps, modelled after those at Palestrina. The terraces were divided into squares and rectangles by paths and flowerbeds, and served as an outdoor setting for Pope Julius's extraordinary collection of classical sculpture, which included the famous Laocoön and the Apollo Belvedere.

The heart of the garden was a courtyard surrounded by a three-tiered loggia, which served as a theater for entertainments. A central exedra formed the dramatic conclusion of the long perspective up the courtyard, ramps and terraces.

The Venetian Ambassador described the Cortile del Belvedere in 1523: "One enters a very beautiful garden, of which half is filled with growing grass and bays and mulberries and cypresses, while the other half is paved with squares of bricks laid upright, and in every square a beautiful orange tree grows out of the pavement, of which there are a great many, arranged in perfect order. ... On one side of the garden is a most beautiful loggia, at one end of which is a lovely fountain that irrigates the orange trees and the rest of the garden by a little canal in the center of the loggia."

Unfortunately the construction of the Vatican Library in the late sixteenth century across the centre of the *cortile* means that Bramante's design is now obscured but his ideas of proportion, symmetry and dramatic perspectives were used in many of the great gardens of the Italian Renaissance.

The Villa Madama, Rome (1516)

The Villa Madama, situated on the slopes of Monte Marioand overlooking Rome, was begun by Pope Leo X and continued by Cardinal Giulio de' Medici (1478-1534). In 1516 Leo X gave the commission to Raphael who was at that time the most famous artist in Rome. Using the ancient text of *De Architectura* by Vitruvius and the writings of Pliny the Younger, Raphael imagined his own version of an ideal classical villa and garden. His villa had a great circular courtyard, and was divided into a winter apartment and a summer apartment. Passages led from the courtyard to the great loggia from which views could be gained of the garden and Rome. A round tower on the east side was intended as garden room in winter, warmed by the sun coming through glazed windows. The villa overlooked three terraces, one a square, one a circle, and one an oval. The top terrace was to be planted in chestnut trees and firs while the lower terrace was intended for plant beds.

Work on the Villa Madama stopped in 1520 after the death of Raphael but was then continued by other artists until 1534. They finished one-half of the villa including half of the circular courtyard, and the northwest loggia that was decorated with grotesque frescoes by Giulio Romano and stucco by Giovanni de Udine. Fine surviving features include a fountain of the head of an elephant by Giovanni da Udine and two gigantic stucco figures by Baccio Bandinelli at the entrance of the *giardino segreto*, the secret garden. The villa is now a state guest house for the Government of Italy.

Gardens of the High Renaissance

The middle of the 16th century saw the construction by the Medicis and other wealthy families and individuals, of a series of magnificent gardens that followed the principles of Alberti and Bramante; they were usually sited on a hilltop or slopes of a mountain; had a series of symmetrical terraces, one above the other, along a central axis; the house looked over the garden and landscape beyond and it could itself be seen from the bottom of the garden. Developments in hydrology meant that the gardens were equipped with increasingly elaborate and majestic cascades and fountains, and statues which recalled the grandeur of Ancient Rome.

Villa Castello, Tuscany, (1538)

Villa Castello was the project of Cosimo de' Medici, first Duke of Tuscany, begun when he was only seventeen. It was designed by Niccolò Tribolo who designed two other gardens: the Giardino dei Semplici (1545) and the Boboli Gardens (1550) for Cosimo.

The garden was laid out on a gentle slope between the villa and the hill of Monte Morello. Tribolo first built a wall across the slope, dividing it into an upper garden filled with orange trees, and a lower garden that was subdivided into garden rooms with walls of hedges, rows of trees and tunnels of citrus trees and cedars. A central axis, articulated by a series of fountains, extended from the villa up to the base of Monte Morello. In this arrangement, the garden had both grand perspectives and enclosed, private spaces.

The lower garden had a large marble fountain that was meant to be seen against a backdrop of dark cypresses, with figures of Hercules and Antaeus. Just above this fountain, in the center of the garden, was a labyrinth formed by cypress, laurel, myrtle, roses and box hedges. Concealed in the middle of the labyrinth was another fountain, with a statue of Venus. Around this fountain, Cosimo had bronze pipes installed under the tiles for *giochi d'acqua* ('water tricks'), which were concealed conduits which could be turned on with a key to drench unsuspectng guests. Another unusual feature was a treehouse concealed in an ivy-covered oak tree, with a square dining room inside the tree.

At the far end of the garden and set against a wall, Tribolo created an elaborate grotto, decorated with mosaics, pebbles, sea shells, imitation stalactites, and niches with groups of statues of domestic and exotic animals and birds, many with real horns, antlers and tusks. The animals symbolized the virtues and accomplishments of past members of Medici family. Water flowed from the beaks, wings and claws of the animals into marble basins below each niche. A gate could close suddenly behind visitors, and they would be soaked by hidden fountains.

Above the grotto, on the hillside, was small wood, or *bosco*, with a pond in the center. In the pond is a bronze statue of a shivering giant, with cold water running down over his head, which represents either the month of January or the Apennine Mountains.

When the last of the Medicis died in 1737, the garden began to be altered by its new owners, the House of Lorraine; the labyrinth was demolished and the statue of Venus was moved to the Villa Petraia. But long before then, the garden had been described by many ambassadors and foreign visitors and had become famous throughout Europe. Its principles of perspective, proportion and symmetry, its geometric planting beds and rooms with walls of trees and hedges, were adapted in both the gardens of the French Renaissance and the [garden *à la française*] which followed.

Villa d'Este at Tivoli (1550-1572)

The Villa d'Este at Tivoli is one of the grandest and best-preserved of the Italian Renaissance gardens. It was created by Cardinal Ippolito II d'Este, son of Alfonso I d'Este, the Duke of Ferrara, and Lucretia Borgia. He was made a Cardinal at the age of twenty-nine and became governor of Tivoli in 1550. To develop his residence, he took over a former Franciscan convent, and for the garden he bought the adjoining steep hillside and the valley below. His chosen architect was Pirro Ligorio, who had been carrying out excavations for Ippolito at the nearby ruins of the ancient *Villa Adriana*, or Hadrian's Villa, the extensive country residence of the Emperor Hadrian that had numerous elaborate water features.

Ligorio created the garden as a series of terraces descending the steep hillside at the edge of the mountains overlooking the plain of Latium. The terraces were connected by gates and grand stairways starting from a terrace below the villa and traversing down to the Fountain of Dragons at the foot of the garden. The stairway was crossed by five traversal alleys on the different levels, which were divided into rooms by hedges and trellises covered with vines. At the crossing points of the stairway and the alleys there were pavilions, fruit trees, and aromatic plants. At the top, the promenade used by the Cardinal passed below the villa and led in one direction to the grotto of Diana, and in the other to the grotto of Aesclepius.

The glory of the Villa d'Este was the system of fountains, fed by two aqueducts that Ligorio constructed from the River Aniene. In the center of the garden, the alley of one hundred fountains (which actually had two hundred fountains), crossed the hillside, connecting the Oval Fountain with the Fountain of Rome, which was decorated with models of the famous landmarks of Rome. On a lower level, another alley passed by the Fountain of Dragons and joined the fountain of Proserpine with the Fountain of the Owl. Still lower, an alley of fishponds connected the Fountain of the Organ to the site of a proposed Fountain of Neptune.

Each fountain and path told a story, linking the d'Este family to the legends of Hercules and Hippolytus or *Ippolito*, the mythical son of Theseus and the Queen of the Amazons. The central axis led to the Fountain of Dragons, which illustrated one of the labours of Hercules, and three other statues of Hercules were found in the garden. The myth of Ippolito, the mythical namesake of the owner, was illustrated by two grottos, that of Aesclepius and Diana.

The Fountain of the Owl used a series of bronze pipes like flutes to make the sound of birds but the most famous feature of the garden was the great Organ Fountain. It was described by the French philosopher Montaigne, who visited the garden in 1580: "The music of the Organ Fountain is true music, naturally created ... made by water which falls with great violence into a cave, rounded and vaulted, and agitates the air, which is forced to exit through the pipes of an organ. Other water, passing through a wheel, strikes in a certain order the keyboard of the organ. The organ also imitates the sound of trumpets, the sound of cannon, and the sound of muskets, made by the sudden fall of water.

The garden was substantially changed after the death of the Cardinal and in the 17th century, and many statues were sold, but the basic features remain, and the Organ fountain has recently been restored and plays music once again.

Mannerism and the Gardens of the Late Renaissance

Mannerism was a style which developed in painting in the 1520s, which defied the traditional rules of Renaissance painting. "Mannerist paintings were intensely stylish, polished and complex, their composition bizarre, the subject matter fantastic." This also describes other mannerist gardens which appeared beginning about 1560.

Villa della Torre (1559)

The Villa della Tore, built for Giulio della Torre (1480-1563), a law professor and humanist scholar in Verona, was a parody of the classical rules of Vitruvius; the peristyle of the building was in the perfectly harmonious Vitruvius style, but some of the stones were rough-cut and of different sizes and decorated with masks which sprayed water, which jarred the classical harmony. "The building was deformed: it seemed to be caught in a strange, amorphous condition, somewhere crude rustic simplicity and classical perfection." The fireplaces inside were in the forms of the mouths of gigantic masks. Outside, the garden was filled with disturbing architectural elements, including a grotto whose entrance represented the mouth of hell, with eyes that showed fires burning inside.

Sacro Bosco at Bomarzo, Lazio (1552-1584)

The Sacro Bosco, or 'Sacred Wood', was the most famous and extravagant of the Mannerist gardens. It was created for Pier Francesco Orsini (1523-84) near the village of Bomarzo. It was witty and irreverent, and violated all the rules of Renaissance gardens; it had no symmetry, no order, and no focal point. An inscription in the garden said: "You who have travelled the world in search of great and stupendous marvels, come here, where there are horrendous faces, elephants, lions, ogres and dragons."

The garden was filled with enormous statues, reached by wandering paths. It included a mouth of hell, a house that seemed to be falling over, fantastic animals and figures, many of them carved of rough volcanic rock in place in the garden. Some of the scenes were taken from the romantic epic poem Orlando Furioso by Ludovico Ariosto, others from works by Dante Alighieri and Francesco Petrarch. As one inscription in the garden notes, the *Sacro Bosco* 'resembles only itself, and nothing else'.

The Italian Renaissance also saw a revolution in the study of botany through the systematic classification of plants and the creation of the first botanical gardens. During the Middle Ages, plants were studied for the medicinal uses. Until the sixteenth century, the standard work on botany was *De Materia Medica* written in the 1st century AD by a Greek physician, Dioscorides, that described six hundred plants but lacked many of the native plants of Italy and had vague descriptions with stylized and inexact illustrations.

In 1533, the University of Padua created the first chair of botany and appointed Francesco Bonafede as the first *Professore Similicium*-professor of 'simples,' or medicinal plants. In 1545, a scholar from the medical school of the University of Padua, Pietro Andrea Mattioli, wrote a new book on medicinal herbs *Commentarii in Sex Libros Pedacii*

Dioscordis, which, in successive editions, systematically described and gave the medicinal uses of twelve hundred different plants. Such scientific work was aided by sailors and explorers returning from the New World, Asia and Africa, who brought back samples of plants unknown in Europe.

In June 1543, the University of Padua created the world's first botanical garden, and the University of Pisa followed with its own garden, the Orto Botanico', in 1545. By 1591, the garden at Padua had over 1,168 different plants and trees, including a fan palm tree brought from Egypt. In 1545, in Florence, Cosimo de' Medici founded the *Giardino dei Semplici*, the garden of medicinal herbs. Soon the medical schools of the universities of Bologna, Ferrara and Sassari all had their own botanical gardens filled with exotic plants from around the world.

19

Chinese Garden

The Chinese Classical Garden (zhong guó gu dian yuán lín), also called Chinese Scholar's Garden, is a place for solitary or social contemplation of nature. Chinese gardens were created in the same way as a combination of landscape and paintings together with poems — this was the so-called 'poetic garden'. The design of Chinese gardens was to provide a spiritual utopia for one to connect with nature, to come back to one's inner heart, to come back to ancient idealism. Chinese gardens are a spiritual shelter for people, a place they could be far away from their real social lives, and close to the ancient way of life, their true selves, and nature. This was an escape from the frustration and disappointment of the political problems in China. They used plants as symbols. Bamboo was used in every traditional Chinese garden. This is because bamboo represents a strong but resilient character. Often pine is used to represent longevity, persistence, tenacity and dignity. The lotus is used to symbolize purity. The flowering plum is one of the most important aspects of a Chinese garden, as it represents renewal and strength of will. Flowering peaches are grown for spring colour, and sweet olive as well. The chrysanthemum is use to symbolize splendour, luster and 'the courage to make sacrifices for a natural life'. Peonies symbolize wealth and banana trees are used simply for the sound they make in the breeze.

The Chinese Classical Garden, sometimes called a Scholar's garden or simply Chinese garden, appeared as a stylistically distinct creation within the historic stream of Chinese landscape architecture during the Jin Dynasty.

Beginning with the first historic records of the Shang Dynasty, two types of Landscape architecture are recorded. The royal park of the Shang kings in Yin and agriculture of the common people. The royal park was designed as a raised platform surrounded by lush vegetation in the palace where feasts were held. Successive dynasties expanded this idea into imperial hunting parks with scenic compositions of rocks and plants. During the Warring States a nature park called Tiger Hill (Chinese: Pinyin) was built in the state of Wu. It was a notable exception to the aesthetic of the large scale royal park as an expression of worldly power. It is the earliest example of Landscape Architecture to commune with nature in China. The ultimate realization of the power aesthetic was realized by Qin Shihuangdi who turned the entire Wei Valley into a regional park dotted with 300 palaces connected by raised walkways in a microcosmic model of the universe.

During the Western Han Dynasty, Han Wudi built a large walled royal park called Upper-Forest Garden (Shànglín Yuán). This park combined the features of botanical and zoological gardens, as well as the traditional hunting grounds. Another innovation was Kunming Lake with a recreation of the three fairy islands in the center, a motif that would become a common feature of later designs. The memory of this park would continue to inspire garden design for centuries. The Eastern Han Dynasty was controlled by Confucian scholars who disapproved of the excesses of their ancestors and promoted an aesthetic of elegant simplicity to match an ethic of moderation. Thus the idea of *small is beautiful* became the new measure of a garden's success. It was at this time temple grounds, and *siheyuan* courtyards began a conversion to designed gardens.

By the end of the Han Dynasty, Chinese gardens could be classified by scale and programme as either royal parks, enclosed temple gardens, or enclosed private (scholar) gardens. The private or scholar's garden belonging to the scholar class was the beginning of the Classical Garden in China. The Chinese classical garden is considered a work of art elevated beyond the other two, to the degree that the term *Chinese garden* refers to the private Chinese classical gardens exclusively.

'Divine Trace' in the Eastern Suburb of Nanjing

Chinese Classical gardens were built by and for the scholar class (shenshì), many of whom were also civil servants. They, along with their gardens, first appeared during the Eastern Han Dynasty in parallel with the rise of Confucian ideology. When the Han Dynasty ended a strict class division virtually ended advancement in the civil service and caused the scholar class to retreat into a more contemplative life in their gardens. It was during the long period between the Eastern Han Dynasty and the Tang Dynasty that the Chinese Classical Garden as a built form fully developed. The economic expansion of the Tang Dynasty multiplied the number of these gardens across China. By the Song Dynasty, Classical garden design had been elevated beyond a mere craft into high art and the static forms of the Tang Dynasty were subject to new experimentation. It was at this time Suzhou became the center of all intellectual life and garden design in China. Finally, during the Ming Dynasty gardens had reached peak of design and the first Treatsies on garden design appeared. The following Qing Dynasty was marked by degeneration of design with an emphasis on ostentation and ornament. The scholar class and their gardens ended with the Republican Period. The Classical Chinese Garden as a built form is largely extinct in modern China.

Culturally, the scholar class was under immense pressure in their Confucian public lives and so sought a more carefree Daoist existence in their private lives. The design of a garden drew on such diverse fields as *fengshui*, botany, hydraulics, history, literature, and architecture. The task was considered so complex that only a scholar was capable of completing it, thus his garden was a measure of his knowledge. For the same reason poetry was a primary part of the garden design, as knowledge and composition of poetry served as an intelligence test for the scholar class.

The garden served multiple functions as semi-public extension of the house and a place; of retreat, for festivity, for study of poetry, for romance. The social and cultural importance of the garden is attested in Chinese literature, particularly the classic Novel *Dream of the Red Chamber* which unfolds almost exclusively in a garden.

The Chinese classical garden evolved into several major regional styles; North China gardens, Central China gardens, Yangtze Delta gardens, and South China (Lingnan) gardens. Of these regional styles, the most influential was the Yangtze Delta style, centered on Suzhou.

The original character for garden (yuán) is: This decomposition of this pictograph shows a wall surrounding a hall, a pool, and a mountain with a tree. This is a summary of the essential elements in the garden. Later the number was expanded to seventeen essential elements:

1. proximity to the home;
2. small;
3. walled;

4. small individual sections;
5. asymmetrical;
6. various types of spatial connections;
7. architecture;
8. rocks;
9. water;
10. trees;
11. plants;
12. sculpture;
13. jie jing (borrowed scenery);
14. chimes;
15. incense burners;
16. inscriptions;
17. use of feng shui for choosing site.

The variety of sensory features enhance a garden's appeal. Windows frame garden views. Trees and flowers provide aroma. Even the intricate designs of pavement and gravel offer tactile enjoyment. Suzhou, in eastern China is widely known for its numerous classical private scholar gardens.

The aesthetics of the garden are judged by its conception, approach, layout, scenes, and borrowing. The conception is the measure of how well the garden reflects a painting or poem. The approach describes how the garden may express the idea of nature beyond the theme. The layout is the use of multiple layers of scenery to create a sense of the infinite in the finite. the scene is how well paired two opposite scene are and how they create harmony. finally the borrowing or borrowed view is how artfully distant views are incorporated into the whole.

Chinese gardens are built not planted. The basic form of the garden is created by ponds and mounds. China is mostly covered in mountains, thus they have occupied a special place in the collective imagination since the Neolithic. The mountain in the Chinese imagination is magical place. An axis mundi where ancient wise men live on a diet of minerals and rare high altitude herbs. These men called immortals have access to knowledge and skills unknown to ordinary men. A mountain of the right type is a *dragon* of Qi and all its associated benefits. In myth certain mountains are themselves sacred. The elaborate grottoes of rock serve the same function, a small piece of the mountain through which to stroll, full of caves where immortals live. The pits dug to heap these mounds are used as ponds and streams. With the right properties such a pond may be the home of a *dragon* of Qi. The pavilions are placed in this landscape of mounds and ponds at auspicious points. Together the mound, pond, and pavilion create the primary form of the garden. A secondary layer is created by plants. In literature this secondary role is well attested. Finally, individual taihu rock is added for accent, like sculpture in a European garden.

Architecture is the primary element of design. The garden scenes are all constructed to be best viewed from a pavilion. A more dynamic although inferior scene may be scene from a path. It is the location of the building; however, that determines the circulation of paths. The path itself can become architectonic by the addition of roof and screen walls. These screen walls often have have moon-shaped doorways and small windows in the shapes of vases and apples.

Rock

Decorative Chinese scholar's rocks, are used both for structural and sculptural purposes. The sculptural Taihu rock is especially prized because it represents wisdom and immortality, and is only procurable from Tai Lake, just west of Suzhou. During the Song dynasty, they were the most expensive objects in the empire [citation needed]. Such rocks, combined with streams and pools, form the basis of a garden's plan. The Chinese word for landscape, shan shui, literally means 'mountains and waters' while a common phrase for making a garden means 'digging ponds and piling mountains'.

Chinese gardens usually feature a central pond and several offshooting streams. The softness of water offsets the solidity of the rocks, while also acting to reflect the constantly changing sky above. Goldfish, carp, and mandarin ducks are three of the most commonly raised fauna. The goal of the design is to make the scenery beautiful, the surrounding is quiet and cool, and the landscape wonderful. Temples, resthouses and short bridges are common features. Also, small fountains were a favourite.

Plants

Many garden plants have essential symbolism. Pine trees represent wisdom and bamboo represents strength and upright morality. Plum trees are also extremely valuable to the Chinese for their beautiful pink and white blooms during winter. Chrysanthemums were also extremely well-loved because of their autumn bloom (when most plants wither and die) and symbolize the perfect Confusician scholar. Peonies symbolize wealth and power, and the lotus symbolizes purity (and is also a revered Buddhist plant). Climbing roses, camellias, ginkgos, magnolias, jasmine, willows, sweet osmanthus, and maples were also planted. The plum blossom is one of the 'Four Junzi Flowers' in China (the others being orchid, chrysanthemum, and bamboo) and symbolized nobleness. The Chinese see the blossoms as more of a symbol for winter rather than a harbinger of spring. It is precisely for this reason that the blossoms are so beloved, because they bloom most vibrantly amidst the winter snow while all other flowers have long since succumbed to the cold and died. Thus, they are seen as an example of resilience and perseverance in the face of adversity, and thus has also been used as a metaphor to symbolize revolutionary struggle. Because they blossom in winter, the plum, the pine, and the bamboo together have been called the 'Three Friends of the Cold'.

The pavement of a Chinese Scholar's Garden might include intricate natural patterns or simply dirt depending on the wealth and mission of the owner. Decoration consists of calligraphy carved into rocks or walls, and lattice windows. Some windows have the shape of different objects such as apples, pears, circles, pentagons etc.

The Classical Gardens of Suzhou

Suzhou is located in the south-eastern part of Jiangsu Province. When the Grand Canal linking many older canals in China was constructed during the Sui dynasty, Suzhou prospered, becoming a center of the silk trade. During the Song dynasty, nearby Hangzhou became the imperial capital and Suzhou grew as well, a convenient retreat for scholars, officials and merchants.

Gardening in Suzhou reached its height during the Ming and Qing dynasties. Suzhou became the center for a garden supply industry. It is for the reason the gardens of Suzhou are considered classical standards of design. There were over 280 private gardens then in Suzhou and landscaping became an art with established masters. The mild climate, along with 230 frost-free days and around 43 inches (1,100 mm) of rain annually the area is perfect for gardening endeavours. Sixty-nine gardens in and around Suzhou are preserved as important national cultural heritage sites. In 1997, UNESCO added four of the largest private gardens of Suzhou to the World Heritage List, and in 2000 UNESCO added the historic section of the city and five more gardens in Suzhou as extensions to the World Heritage Site.

20

Bonsai

Bonsai (help·info) (Japanese) (lit. *tray cultivation*) is the art of growing trees, or woody plants shaped as trees, in containers. Bonsai is sometimes confused with dwarfing, but dwarfing more accurately refers to researching and creating cultivars of plant material that are permanent, genetic miniatures of existing species. Bonsai does not require genetically dwarfed trees, but rather depends on growing small trees from regular stock and seeds. Bonsai uses cultivation techniques like pruning, root reduction, potting, defoliation, and grafting to produce small trees that mimic the shape and style of mature, full-sized trees.

The purposes of bonsai are primarily contemplation (for the viewer) and the pleasant exercise of effort and ingenuity (for the grower). By contrast with other plant-related practices, bonsai is not intended for production of food, for medicine, or for creating yard-sized or park-sized landscapes. As a result, the scope of bonsai practice is narrow and focussed on long-term cultivation and shaping of one or more small trees in a single container.

'Bonsai' is a Japanese pronunciation of the earlier Chinese term *penzai*. A 'bon' is a tray-like pot typically used in bonsai culture. The word *bonsai* is sometimes used as an umbrella term for all miniature trees in containers or pots, but this article focuses primarily on bonsai as defined in the Japanese tradition. Similar practices in other cultures include the Chinese tradition of *penjing* and the miniature living landscapes of Vietnamese.

Container-grown plants, including trees and many other plant types, have a history stretching back at least to the early times of Egyptian culture. Pictorial records from around 4000 BC show trees growing in containers cut into rock. Pharaoh Ramesses III donated gardens consisting of potted olives, date palms, and other plants to hundreds of temples. Pre-Common-Era India used container-grown trees for medicine and food.

The word *penzai* first appeared in writing in China during the Jin Dynasty, in the period 265AD — 420AD. Over time, the practice developed into new forms in various parts of China, Japan, Korea, Vietnam and Thailand. Notably, container-grown trees were popularized in Japan during Heian period, a period of cultural growth when the Japanese experienced and adopted their own versions of many Chinese practices. At this time, the term for dwarf potted trees was 'the bowl's tree' (*hachi-no-ki*), denoting the use of a deep pot. The c.1300 rhymed prose essay, *Rhymeprose on a Miniature Landscape Garden*, by the Japanese Zen monk Kokan Shiren, outlines aesthetic principles for bonsai, bonseki, and garden architecture itself.

At first, the Japanese used miniaturized trees grown in containers to decorate their homes and gardens. During the Tokugawa period, landscape gardening attained new importance. Cultivation of plants such as azalea and maples became a pastime of the wealthy. Growing dwarf plants in containers was also popular. Around 1800, the Japanese changed the term they used for this art to their pronunciation of the Chinese *penzai* with its connotation of a shallower container in which the Japanese could now style small trees.

One of the oldest-known living bonsai trees, considered one of the National Treasures of Japan, is in the Tokyo Imperial Palace collection. A five-needle pine (*Pinus pentaphylla* var. *negishi*) known as Sandai-Shogun-No Matsu is documented as having been cared for by Tokugawa Iemitsu. The tree is considered to be at least 500 years old and was first trained as a bonsai by 1610. Older plants have been made more recently into bonsai as well.

Bonsai can be created from nearly any perennial woody-stemmed tree or shrub species which produces true branches and remains small through pot confinement with crown and root pruning. Some species are popular as bonsai material because they have characteristics, such as small leaves or needles, that make them appropriate for the compact visual scope of bonsai.

Sources of Bonsai Material

All bonsai start with a specimen of source material, a plant that the grower wishes to train into bonsai form. Bonsai practice is an unusual form of plant cultivation in that growth from seeds is rarely used to obtain source material. To display the characteristic aged appearance of a bonsai within a reasonable time, the source plant is often partially-grown or mature stock. A specimen may be selected specifically for bonsai aesthetic characteristics it already possesses, such as great natural age for a specimen collected in the wild, or a tapered, scar-free trunk from a nursery specimen. Alternatively, it may be selected for non-aesthetic reasons, such as known hardiness for the grower's local climate or low cost (in the case of collected materials).

Propagation

While any form of plant propagation could generate bonsai material, a few techniques are favored because they can quickly produce a relatively mature trunk with well-placed branches.

Cuttings

In taking a cutting, part of a growing plant is cut off and placed in a growing medium to develop roots. If the part that is cut off is fairly thick, like a mature branch, it can be grown into an aged-looking bonsai more quickly than can a seed. Unfortunately, thinner and younger cuttings tend to strike roots more easily than thicker or more mature ones. In bonsai propagation, cuttings usually provide source material to be grown for some time before training.

Layering

Layering is a technique in which rooting is encouraged from part of a plant, usually a branch, while it is still attached to the parent plant. After rooting, the branch is removed from the parent and grown as an independent entity. For bonsai, both ground layering and air layering can create a potential bonsai, by transforming a mature branch into the trunk of a new tree. The point at which rooting is encouraged can be close to the location of side branches, so the resulting rooted tree can immediately have a thick trunk and low branches, characteristics that complement bonsai aesthetics.

Commercial Bonsai Growers

Commercial bonsai growers may use any of the other means of obtaining starter bonsai material, from seed propagation to collecting expeditions, but they generally sell mature specimens that display bonsai aesthetic qualities already. The grower trains the source specimens to a greater or lesser extent before sale, and the trees may be ready for display as soon as they are bought. Those who purchase commercially-grown bonsai face some challenges, however, particularly of buying from another country. If the purchaser's local climate does not closely match the climate in which the bonsai was created, the plant will have difficulties surviving and thriving. As well, importing living plant material from a foreign source is often closely controlled by customs regulations and may require a licence or other special customs arrangement on the buyer's part. If a local commercial bonsai grower does not exist, buying from a distant one may be unsatisfactory.

Nursery Stock

A plant nursery is an agricultural operation where (non-bonsai) plants are propagated and grown to usable size. Nursery stock may be available directly from the nursery, or may be sold in a garden centre or similar resale establishment. Nursery stock is usually young but fully viable, and is often potted with sufficient soil to allow plants to survive a season or two before being transplanted into a more permanent location. Because the nursery tree is already pot-conditioned, it can be worked on as a bonsai immediately. The large number of plants that can be viewed in a single visit to a nursery or garden centre allows the buyer to identify plants with better-than-average bonsai characteristics. According to Peter Adams, a nursery visit 'offers the opportunity to choose an instant trunk'. One issue with nursery stock is that many specimens are shaped into popular forms, such as the standard or half-standard forms, with several feet of clear trunk rising from the roots. Without branches low on the trunk, it is difficult for a source specimen to be trained as bonsai.

Collecting

Collecting bonsai is the process of finding suitable bonsai material in its original wild situation, successfully moving it, and replanting it in a container for development as bonsai. Collecting may involve wild materials collected from naturally treed areas, or cultivated specimens found growing in yards and gardens. Mature landscape plants which are being discarded from a building site can provide excellent material for bonsai. In Great Britain, hedgerow trees that have grown for many years but have been continually trimmed down to hedge height provide heavy, gnarled trunks for bonsai growers.

Some regions have plant material that is known for its suitability in form. In North America, for example, the California Juniper and Sierra Juniper found in the Sierra Mountains, the Ponderosa pine and Rocky

Mountain Juniper found in the Rocky Mountains, and the Bald Cypress found in the swamps of the Everglades. In Western Canada near the Rocky Mountains, wild larch are widely collectible and well-suited to bonsai cultivation.

The benefit of collecting bonsai specimens is that the collected materials can be mature, and will display the natural marks and forms of age, which makes them more suitable for bonsai development than the young plants obtained through nurseries. Some of the difficulties of collecting include getting permission to remove the specimens, and the challenges of keeping a mature tree alive while transplanting it to a bonsai pot.

The practice of bonsai development incorporates a number of techniques either unique to bonsai or, if used in other forms of cultivation, applied in unusual ways that are particularly suitable to the bonsai domain.

Leaf Trimming

This technique involves the selective removal of leaves (for most varieties of deciduous tree) or needles (for coniferous trees and some others) from a bonsai's trunk and branches. A common aesthetic technique in bonsai design is to expose the tree's branches below groups of leaves or needles (sometimes called 'pads'). In many species, particularly coniferous ones, this means that leaves or needles projecting below their branches must be trimmed off. For some coniferous varieties, such as spruce, branches carry needles from the trunk to the tip and many of these needles may be trimmed to expose the branch shape and bark. Needle and bud trimming can also be used in coniferous trees to force back-budding or budding on old wood, which may not occur naturally in many conifers. Along with pruning, leaf trimming is the most common activity used for bonsai development and maintenance, and the one that occurs most frequently during the year.

Pruning

The small size of the tree and some dwarfing of foliage result from pruning the trunk, branches, and roots. Pruning is often the first step in transforming a collected plant specimen into a candidate for bonsai. The top part of the trunk may be removed to make the tree more compact. Major and minor branches that conflict with the designer's plan will be removed completely, and others may be shortened to fit within the planned design. Pruning later in the bonsai's life is generally less severe, and may be done for purposes like increasing branch ramification or encouraging growth in non-pruned branches. Although pruning is an important and common bonsai practice, it must be done with care, as improper pruning can weaken or kill trees. Careful pruning throughout the tree's life is necessary, however, to maintain a bonsai's basic design, which can otherwise disappear behind the uncontrolled natural growth of branches and leaves.

Wiring

Wrapping copper or aluminium wire around branches and trunks allows the bonsai designer to create the desired general form and make detailed branch and leaf placements. When wire is used on new branches or shoots, it holds the branches in place until they lignify (convert into wood), usually 6-9 months or one growing season for deciduous, but several years for pines (which maintain their branch flexibility through multiple growing seasons). Wires are also used to connect a branch to another object (e.g., another branch, the pot itself) so that tightening the wire applies force to the branch. Some species do not lignify strongly, and some specimens' branches are too stiff or brittle to be bent easily. These cases are not conducive to wiring, and shaping them is accomplished primarily through pruning.

Clamping

For larger specimens, or species with stiffer wood, bonsai artists also use mechanical devices for shaping trunks and branches. The most common are screw-based clamps, which can straighten or bend a part of the bonsai using much greater force than wiring can supply. To prevent damage to the tree, the clamps are tightened a little at a time and make their changes over a period of months or years.

Grafting

In this technique, new growing material (typically a bud, branch, or root) is introduced to a prepared area on the trunk or under the bark of the tree. There are two major purposes for grafting in bonsai. First, a number of favourite species do not thrive as bonsai on their natural root stock and their trunks are often grafted onto hardier root stock. Examples include Japanese red maple and Japanese black pine. Second, grafting allows the bonsai artist to add branches (and sometimes roots) where they are needed to improve or complete a bonsai design. There are many applicable grafting techniques, none unique to bonsai, including branch grafting, bud grafting, thread grafting, and others.

Defoliation

Short-term dwarfing of foliage can be accomplished in certain deciduous bonsai by partial or total defoliation of the plant partway through the growing season. Not all species can survive this technique. In defoliating a healthy tree of a suitable species, most or all of the leaves are removed by clipping partway along each leaf's petiole (the thin stem that connects a leaf to its branch). Petioles later dry up and drop off or are manually removed once dry. The tree responds by producing a fresh crop of leaves. The new leaves are generally much smaller than those from the first crop, sometimes as small as half the length and width. If the bonsai is shown at this time, the smaller leaves contribute greatly to the bonsai esthetic of dwarfing. This change in leaf size is usually not permanent, and the leaves of the following spring will often be the normal size. Defoliation weakens the tree and should not be performed in two consecutive years.

Deadwood

Bonsai growers use deadwood bonsai techniques called *jin* and *shari* to simulate age and maturity in a bonsai. Jin is the term used when the bark from an entire branch is removed to create the impression of a snag of deadwood. Shari denotes stripping bark from areas of the trunk to simulate natural scarring from a broken limb or lightning strike. In addition to stripping bark, this technique may also involve the use of tools to scar the deadwood or to raise its grain, and the application of chemicals (usually lime sulfur) to bleach and preserve the exposed deadwood.

Care: Watering

With limited space in a bonsai pot, regular attention is needed to ensure the tree is correctly watered. Sun, heat and wind exposure can dry bonsai trees to the point of drought in a short period of time. While some species can handle periods of relative dryness, others require near-constant moisture. Watering too frequently, or allowing the soil to remain soggy, promotes fungal infections and root rot. Free draining soil is used to prevent waterlogging. Deciduous trees are more at risk of dehydration and will wilt as the soil dries out. Evergreen trees, which tend to cope with dry conditions better, do not display signs of the problem until after damage has occurred.

Repotting

Bonsai are repotted and root-pruned at intervals dictated by the vigour and age of each tree. In the case of deciduous trees, this is done as the tree is leaving its dormant period, generally around springtime. Bonsai are often repotted while in development, and less often as they become more mature. This prevents them from becoming pot-bound and encourages the growth of new feeder roots, allowing the tree to absorb moisture more efficiently.Specimens meant to be developed into bonsai are often placed in "growing boxes", which have a much larger volume of soil per plant than a bonsai pot does. These large boxes allow the roots to grow freely, increasing the vigor of the tree and helping the trunk and branches grow thicker. After using a grow box, the tree may be replanted in a more compact 'training box' that helps to create a smaller, denser root mass which can be more easily moved into a final presentation pot.

Special tools are available for the maintenance of bonsai. The most common tool is the concave cutter (5th from left in picture), a tool designed to prune flush, without leaving a stub. Other tools include branch bending jacks, wire pliers and shears of different proportions for performing detail and rough shaping.

Soil and Fertilization

Bonsai soil is usually a loose, fast-draining mix of components, often a base mixture of coarse sand or gravel, fired clay pellets, or expanded shale combined with an organic component such as peat or bark. The inorganic components provide mechanical support for bonsai roots, and—in the case of fired clay materials—also serve to retain moisture. The organic components retain moisture and may release small amounts of nutrients as they decay.

In Japan, bonsai soil mixes based on volcanic clays are common. The volcanic clay has been fired at some point in time to create porous, water-retaining pellets. Varieties such as akadama, or 'red ball' soil, and kanuma, a type of yellow pumice used for azaleas and other calcifuges, are used by many bonsai growers. Similar fired clay soil components are extracted or manufactured in other countries around the world, and other soil components like diatomaceous earth can fill a similar purpose in bonsai cultivation.

Opinions about fertilizers and fertilization techniques vary widely among practitioners. Some promote the use of organic fertilizers to augment an essentially inorganic soil mix, while others will use chemical fertilizers freely. Many follow the general rule of little and often, where a dilute fertilizer solution or a small amount of dry fertilizer are applied relatively frequently during the tree's growing season. The flushing effect of regular watering moves unmetabolized fertilizer out of the soil, preventing the potentially toxic build-up of fertilizer ingredients.

Bonsai are sometimes marketed or promoted as house plants, but few of the traditional bonsai species can thrive or even survive inside a typical house. The best guideline to identifying a suitable location for a bonsai is its native hardiness. If the bonsai grower can closely replicate the full year's temperatures, relative humidity, and sunlight, the bonsai should do well. In practice, this means that trees from a hardiness zone closely matching the grower's location will generally be the easiest to grow outdoors, and others will require more work or will not be viable at all.

Outdoors

Most bonsai species are outdoor trees and shrubs by nature, and they require temperature, humidity, and sunlight conditions approximating their native climate year round. The skill of the gardener can help plants from outside the local hardiness zone to survive and even thrive, but doing so takes careful watering, shielding of selected bonsai from excessive sunlight or wind, and possibly protection from winter conditions (e.g., through the use of cold boxes or winter greenhouses).

Common bonsai species (particularly those from the Japanese tradition) are temperate climate trees from hardiness zones 7 to 9, and require moderate temperatures, moderate humidity, and full sun in summer with a dormancy period in winter that may need be near freezing. They do not thrive indoors, where the light is generally too dim, and humidity often too low, for them to grow properly. Only in the dormant period can they safely be brought indoors, and even then the plants require cold temperatures, reduced watering, and lighting that approximates the number of hours the sun is visible. Raising the temperature or providing more hours of light than available from natural daylight can cause the bonsai to break dormancy, which often weakens or kills it.

Tropical and Mediterranean species typically require consistent temperatures close to room temperature, and with correct lighting and humidity many species can be kept indoors all year. Those from cooler climates may benefit from a winter dormancy period, but temperatures need not be dropped as far as for the temperate climate plants and a north-facing windowsill or open window may provide the right conditions for a few winter months.

Display

A bonsai display presents one or more bonsai specimens in a way that allows a viewer to see all the important features of the bonsai from the most advantageous position. That position emphasizes the bonsai's defined 'front', which is designed into all bonsai. It places the bonsai at a height that allows the viewer to imagine the bonsai as a full-sized tree seen from a distance, siting the bonsai neither so low that the viewer appears to be hovering in the sky above it, nor so high that the viewer appears to be looking up at the tree from beneath the ground. Peter Adams recommends that bonsai be shown as if "in an art gallery: at the right height; in isolation; against a plain background, devoid of all redundancies such as labels and vulgar little accessories."

For outdoor displays, there are few aesthetic rules. Many outdoor displays are semi-permanent, with the bonsai trees in place for weeks or months at a time. To avoid damaging the trees, therefore, an outdoor display must not impede the amount of sunlight needed for the trees on display, must support watering, and may also have to block excessive wind or precipitation. As a result of these practical constraints, outdoor displays are often rustic in style, with simple wood or stone components. A common design is the bench, sometimes with sections at different heights to suit different sizes of bonsai, along which bonsai are placed in a line. Where space allows, outdoor bonsai specimens are spaced far enough apart that the viewer can concentrate on one at a time. When the trees are too close to each other, aesthetic discord between adjacent trees of different sizes or styles can confuse the viewer, a problem addressed by exhibition displays.

Indoors, a formal bonsai display is arranged to represent a landscape, and traditionally consists of the featured bonsai tree in an appropriate pot atop a wooden stand, along with a shitakusa (companion plant) representing the foreground, and a hanging scroll representing the background. These three elements are chosen to complement each other and evoke a particular season, and are composed asymmetrically to mimic nature. When displayed inside a traditional Japanese home, a formal bonsai display will often be placed within the home's tokonoma or formal display alcove. An indoor display is usually very temporary, lasting a day or two, as most bonsai are intolerant of indoor conditions and lose vigour rapidly within the house.

Exhibition displays allow a large number of bonsai to be displayed in a temporary exhibition format, typically indoors, as would be seen in a bonsai design competition. To allow many trees to be located close together, exhibition displays often use a sequence of small alcoves, each containing one pot and its bonsai contents. The walls or dividers between the alcoves make it easier to view only one bonsai at a time. The back of the alcove is a neutral colour and pattern to avoid distracting the viewer's eye. The bonsai pot is almost always placed on a formal stand, of a size and design selected to complement the bonsai and its pot.

Containers

A variety of informal containers may house the bonsai during its development, and even trees that have been formally planted in a bonsai pot may be returned to growing boxes from time to time. A large growing box will house several bonsai and provide a great volume of soil per tree to encourage root growth. A training box will have a single tree, and a smaller volume of soil that helps condition the tree to the eventual size and shape of the formal bonsai container. There are no aesthetic guidelines for these development containers, and they may be of any material, size, and shape that suit the grower.

Formal bonsai containers are ceramic pots, which come in a variety of shapes and colours and may be glazed or unglazed. Unlike many common plant containers, bonsai pots have drainage holes in the bottom surface to allow excess water to escape the pot. The grower usually covers the holes with a piece of screen or mesh to prevent soil from falling out and hinder pests from entering the pots from below. For bonsai being shown in their completed state, pot shape, colour, and size are chosen to complement the tree as a picture frame is chosen to complement a painting. Containers with straight sides and sharp corners are generally used for formally-shaped plants, while oval or round containers are used for plants with informal designs. Many aesthetic rules guide the selection of pot finish and colour. For example, evergreen bonsai are often placed in unglazed pots, while deciduous trees usually appear in glazed pots. Pots are also distinguished by their size. The overall design of the bonsai tree, the thickness of its trunk, and its height are considered when determining the size of a suitable pot.

Some pots are highly collectible, like ancient Chinese or Japanese pots made in regions with experienced pot makers such as Tokoname, Japan or Yixing, China. Today many western potters throughout Europe and North America produce fine quality pots for bonsai.

The most common styles include formal upright, informal upright, slanting, semi-cascade, cascade, raft, literati, and group/forest. Less common forms include windswept, weeping, split-trunk, and driftwood styles.

The formal upright style, or *Chokkan*, is characterized by a straight, upright, tapering trunk. Branches progress regularly from the thickest and broadest at the bottom to the finest and shortest at the top.

The trunk and branches of the informal upright style, or *Moyogi* incorporate visible curves, but the apex of the informal upright is always located directly above the trunk's entry into the soil line. Similar to the formal upright style, branches generally progress regularly from largest at the bottom to smallest at the top, although this progression may be broken where the irregular shape of the trunk would make a branch abnormally prominent or obscure.

Slant-style, or *Shakan*, bonsai possess straight trunks like those of bonsai grown in the formal upright style. However, the slant style trunk emerges from the soil at an angle, and the apex of the bonsai will be located to the left or right of the root base.

Cascade-style, or *Kengai*, bonsai are modeled after trees which grow over water or on the sides of mountains. The apex, or tip of the tree in the Semi-cascade-style, or *Han Kengai*, bonsai extend just at or beneath the lip of the bonsai pot; the apex of a (full) cascade style falls below the base of the pot.

Raft-style, or *Netsuranari*, bonsai mimic a natural phenomenon that occurs when a tree topples onto its side, for example, from erosion or another natural force. Branches along the top side of the trunk continue to grow as a group of new trunks. Sometimes, roots will develop from buried portions of the trunk. Raft-style bonsai can have sinuous, straight-line, or slanting trunks, all giving the illusion that they are a group of separate trees—while actually being the branches of a tree planted on its side.

The literati style, or *Bunjin-gi*, bonsai is characterized by a generally bare trunk line, with branches reduced to a minimum, and typically placed the top of a long, often contorted trunk. This style derives its name from the Chinese literati who created Chinese brush paintings like those found in the ancient text, *The Mustard Seed Garden Manual of Painting*. Their minimalist landscapes often depicted trees growing in harsh conditions, with contorted trunks and reduced foliage. In Japan, the literati style is known as *bunjin-gi* . (*Bunjin* is a translation of the Chinese phrase *wenren* meaning 'scholars practiced in the arts' and *gi* is a derivative of the Japanese word, *ki*, for 'tree').

The group or forest style, or *Yose Ue*, comprises a planting of several or many trees, and typically an odd number, in a bonsai pot. The trees are usually the same species, with a variety of heights employed to add visual interest and to reflect the age differences encountered in mature forests.

The broom style, or *Hokidachi*, is employed for trees with extensive, fine branching, often with species like elms. The trunk is straight and upright. It branches out in all directions about 1/3 of the way up the entire height of the tree. The branches and leaves form a ball-shaped crown which can also be very beautiful during the winter months.

The multi-trunk style, or *Ikadabuki*, has all the trunks growing out of one spot with one root system, and it actually is one single tree. Its counterpart in nature is the tree clump formed, for example, where a single pine cone has sprouted a number of seedlings in one spot. All the trunks combine to support one crown of leaves, in which the thickest and most developed trunk forms the top.

The Shari style, or *Sharimiki*, style involves portraying a tree in its struggle to live while a significant part of its trunk is bare of bark. In nature, trees in the Sharimiki style are created by lightning or animals eating the bark.

The root-over-rock style, or *Sekijoju*, is a style in which the roots of the tree are wrapped around a rock. The rock is at the base of the trunk, with the roots exposed to varying degrees as they traverse the rock and then descend into the soil below.

The growing-in-a-rock, or *Ishizuke*, style means the roots of the tree are growing in soil contained within the cracks and holes of the rock. The rock may serve as a simple container, with the tree escaping the container and forming its own shape. Alternatively, the tree may show a definite relationship to the rock's shape, growing close to the rock and following its contours.

Not all sources agree on the exact sizes or names for these ranges, but the concept of the ranges is well-established and necessary to both the cultivation and the aesthetic understanding of the trees. In the very largest size range, a recognized Japanese practice is to name the trees 'one-handed', 'two-handed', and so on, based on the number of men required to move the tree and pot. These trees will have dozens of branches and can closely simulate a full-sized tree. At the other end of the size spectrum, there are a number of specific techniques and styles associated solely with the smallest sizes, *mame* and *shito*. These techniques take advantage of the bonsai's minute dimensions and compensate for the limited number of branches and leaves that can appear on a tree this small.

Indoor Bonsai

Indoor bonsai are bonsai which have been cultivated for the indoor environment. Traditionally, bonsai are shaped from temperate climate trees grown in containers but kept outdoors. Kept in the artificial environment of a home, these trees weaken and die. A number of tropical and sub-tropical tree species will survive and grow indoors. Some of these are suited to bonsai aesthetics and can be shaped much as traditional outdoor bonsai are.

21

English Garden

The 'English garden' or 'English landscape park' (French: *Jardin anglais,* Italian: *Giardino all'inglese,* German: *Englischer Landschaftsgarten*) is a style of landscape garden which emerged in Britain in the early 18th century, and spread across Europe, replacing the more formal, symmetrical Garden à la française of the 17th century as the principal gardening style of Europe. The English garden presented an idealized view of nature, often inspired by paintings of landscapes by Claude Lorraine and Nicolas Poussin. It usually included a lake, sweeps of gently rolling lawns set against groves of trees, and recreations of classical temples, Gothic ruins, bridges, and other picturesque architecture, designed to recreate an idyllic pastoral landscape. By the end of the eighteenth century the English garden was being imitated by the French landscape garden, and as far away as St. Petersburg, Russia, in Pavlovsk, the gardens of the future Emperor Paul. It also had a major influence on the form of the public parks and gardens which appeared around the world in the 19th century.

The predecessors of the landscape garden in England were the great parks created by Sir John Vanbrugh (1664-1726) and Nicholas Hawksmoor at Castle Howard (1699-1712); Blenheim Palace (1705-1722) and the Claremont Landscape Garden at Claremont House (1715-1727). These parks featured vast lawns, woods, and pieces of architecture, such as the classical mausoleum designed by Hawksmoor at Castle Howard. At the center of the composition was the house, behind which were formal and symmetrical gardens in the style of the Garden à la française, with ornate carpets of floral designs and walls of hedges, decorated with statues and fountains. These gardens, modeled after the gardens of Versailles, were designed to impress visitors with their size and grandeur.

William Kent and Charles Bridgeman

The new style that became known as the English garden was invented by landscape designers William Kent and Charles Bridgeman, working for wealthy patrons, including Richard Temple, 1st Viscount Cobham, Richard Boyle, 3rd Earl of Burlington, and banker Henry Hoare II; men who had large country estates, were members of the anti-royalist Whig Party, had classical educations, were patrons of the arts, and had taken the Grand tour to Italy, where they had seen the Roman ruins and Italian landscapes they reproduced in their gardens.

William Kent (1685-1738) was an architect, painter and furniture designer who introduced Palladian style architecture to England. Kent's inspiration came from Palladio's buildings in the Veneto and the landscapes and ruins around Rome - he lived in Italy from 1709 to 1719, and brought back many drawings of antique architecture and landscapes. His gardens were designed to compliment the Palladian archicture of the houses he built Charles Bridgeman (1690–1738) was the son of a gardener and an experienced horticulturist, who became the Royal Gardener for Queen Anne and Prince George of Denmark, responsible for tending and redesigning the royal gardens at Windsor, Kensington Palace, Hampton Court, St. James's Park and Hyde Park. He collaborated with Kent on several major gardens, providing the botanical expertise which allowed Kent to realize his architectural visions.

Chiswick House

Kent created one of the first true English landscape gardens at Chiswick House for Richard Boyle, 3rd Earl of Burlington. The first gardens that he laid out between 1724 and 1733 had many formal elements of a Garden à la française, including alleys forming a trident and canals, but they had something new - pictureque recreation of an Ionic temple set in a theatre of trees. Between 1733 and 1736, he redesigned the garden again, adding lawns sloping down to the edge of river, and a small cascade. For the first time the form of a garden was inspired not by architecture, but by an idealized version of nature.

Rousham in Oxfordshire is considered by some as the most accomplished and significant of William Kent's work. The patron was General Dormer, who commissioned Bridgeman to begin the garden in 1727, then brought in Kent to recreate it in 1737. Bridgeman had built a series of gardens, including a grotto of Venus, on the slope along the river Cherwell, connected by a straight alleys. Kent turned the alleys into winding paths, built a gently turning stream, used the natural landscape features and slopes, and created a series of views and tableaus decorated with allegorical statues of Apollo, a wounded gladiator, a lion attacking a horse, and other subjects. He placed 'eye-catchers', pieces of classical architecture, to decorate the landscape, and he made use of the 'ha-ha', a trench used to hide a fences so the garden seemed to go into the far distance. Finally, he added cascades modeled on those of the garden of Aldobrandini and Pratolino in Italy, to add movement and drama.

Stowe House

Stowe, in Buckinghamshire, (1730-1738), was an even more radical departure from the formal French garden. In the early 1700s, Richard Temple, 1st Viscount Cobham, had commissioned Charles Bridgeman to design a formal garden, with architectural decorations by John Vanbrugh. Bridgeman's design included an octagonal lake and a Rotondo (1720-21) designed by Vanbrugh.

Stowe, in Buckinghamshire, (1730-1738), was an even more radical departure from the formal French garden. In the early 1700s, Richard Temple, 1st Viscount Cobham, had commissioned Charles Bridgeman to design a formal garden, with architectural decorations by John Vanbrugh. Bridgeman's design included an octagonal lake and a Rotondo (1720-21) designed by Vanbrugh.

In the 1730s, William Kent and James Gibbs were appointed to work with Bridgeman, who died in 1738. Kent remade the lake in a more natural shape, and created a new kind of garden, which took visitors on a tour of picturesque landscapes. It eventually included a Palladian bridge (1738); a Temple of Venus (1731), in the form of a Palladian villa; A Temple of Ancient Virtues (1737), with statues of famous Greeks and Romans; a Temple of British Worthies (1734-1735), with statues of British heroes; and a Temple of Modern Virtues, which was deliberately left in ruins, which contained a headless statue of Robert Walpole, Cobham's political rival.

The garden attracted visitors from all over Europe, including Jean-Jacques Rousseau. It became the inspiration for landscape gardens in Britain and on the Continent.

Stourhead, in Wiltshire (1741-80), created by banker Henry Hoare II, was one of first 'picturesque' gardens, inspired to resemble the paintings of Claude Lorrain. Hoare had travelled to Italy on the Grand

Tour and had returned with a painting by Claude Lorrain. Hoare dammed a stream on his estate, created a lake, and surrounded the lake with landscapes and architectural constructions representing the different steps of the journey of Aeneas in the Aeneid by Virgil.

The most influential figure in the later development of the English landscape garden was Lancelot 'Capability' Brown (1716-1783) who began his career in 1740 as a gardener at Stowe under Charles Bridgeman, then succeeded William Kent in 1748.

Brown's contribution was to simplify the garden by eliminating geometric structures, alleys, and parterres near the house and replacing them with rolling lawns and extensive views out to isolated groups of trees, making the landscape seem even larger. 'He sought to create an ideal landscape out of the English countryside'. He created artificial lakes and used dams and canals to transform streams or springs into the illusion that a river flowed through the garden.

He compared his own role as a garden designer to that of a poet or composer. "Here I put a comma, there, when it's necessary to cut the view, I put a parenthesis; there I end it with a period and start on another theme."

Brown designed 170 gardens. The most important were:

- Petworth (West Sussex) in 1752;
- Chatsworth Derbyshire) in 1761;
- Bowood Wiltshire) in 1763;
- Blenheim Palace (Oxfordshire) in 1764.

A Chinese house was built in the garden at Stowe House as early as 1838, starting a fashion for exotic architecture in gardens. Chinese architectural features gained in popularity thanks largely to William Chambers (1723-1796), who lived in China from 1745 to 1747, and wrote a book, *The Drawings, buildings, furniture, habits, machines and untensils of the Chinese*, published in 1757. In the same year, he built a garden with a pagoda and a Chinese house in Kew, London. The garden including garden architecture symbolizing all parts of the world and all historical periods. The Anglo-Chinese Garden style became popular in the late 18th century, and Chinese pavilions appeared in English gardens all across Europe.

In the 1750s, classical architecture and Chinese architecture were joined by gothic revival ruins in English gardens. This was largely the result of poet Horace Walpole, who introduced gothic revival features into his house and garden at Strawberry Hill in Twickenham.

At Stowe, Capability Brown followed the new fashion between 1740 and 1753 by adding a new section to the park, called Hawkwelle Hill or the gothic promenade, with a gothic revival building.

The English Garden Spreads to the Continent

Descriptions of English gardens were first brought to France by the Abbé Le Blanc, who published accounts of his voyage in 1745 and 1751. A treatise on the English garden, *Observations on Modern Gardening*, written by Thomas Whately and published in London in 1770, was translated into French in 1771. After the end of the Seven Years War in 1763, French noblemen were able to voyage to England and see the gardens for themselves, and the style began to be adapted in French gardens. The new style also had the advantage of requiring fewer gardeners, and was easier to maintain, than the French garden.

One of the first English gardens on the continent was at Ermenonville, in France, built by marquis René Louis de Girardin from 1763 to 1776 and based on the ideals of Jean Jacques Rousseau, who was buried within the park. Rousseau and the garden's founder had visited Stowe a few years earlier. Other early examples were the Désert de Retz, Yvelines (1774-1782); the Gardens of the Château de Bagatelle, in the Bois de Boulogne, west of Paris (1777-1784); The Folie Saint James, in Neuilly-sur-Seine, (1777-1780); and the Château de Méréville, in the Essonne department, (1784-1786). Even at Versailles, the home of the most classical of all French gardens, a small English landscape park with a roman temple was built by the Petit Trianon and a mock village, the Hameau de la reine, Versailles (1783-1789), was created for Marie Antoinette. (See the French landscape garden).

The new style also spread to Germany. The central Wörlitzer Park, adjacent to the small town of Wörlitz, was laid out between 1769 and 1773 by the Duke Leopold III, based on the models of Claremont, Stourhead and Stowe Landscape Garden. Another notable example was The Englischer Garten in Munich, Germany, created in 1789 by Sir Benjamin Thompson (1753-1814).

The style also spread rapidly to Russia, where in 1774 Catherine the Great adapted the new style in the park of her palace at Tsarskoe Selo, complete with a mock Chinese village and a Palladian bridge, modelled after that at Wilton House.

Characteristics of the English Garden

The European 'English garden' is characteristically on a smaller scale and more filled with 'eye-catchers' than most English landscape gardens: grottoes, temples, tea-houses, belvederes, pavilions, sham ruins, bridges and statues, though the main ingredients of the English garden in England are sweeps of gently rolling ground and water, against a woodland background with clumps of trees and outlier groves. The name — not used in the United Kingdom, where 'landscape garden' serves — differentiates it from the formal baroque design of the Garden à la française. One of the best-known English gardens in Europe is the Englischer Garten in Munich.

The dominant style was revised in the early nineteenth century to include more 'gardenesque' features, including shrubberies with gravelled walks, tree plantations to satisfy botanical curiosity, and, most notably, the return of flowers, in skirts of sweeping planted beds. This is the version of the landscape garden most imitated in Europe in the nineteenth century. The outer areas of the 'home park' of English country houses retain their naturalistic shaping. English gardening since the 1840s has been on a more restricted scale, closer and more allied to the residence.

The canonical European *English park* contains a number of Romantic elements. Always present is a pond or small lake with a pier or bridge. Overlooking the pond is a round or hexagonal pavilion, often in the shape of a monopteros, a Roman temple. Sometimes the park also has a 'Chinese' pavilion. Other elements include a grotto and imitation ruins.

Notable designers of the English prototypes of the *Englischer Garten* include John Vanbrugh (1664-1726). Stephen Switzer (1682-1745), the poet Alexander Pope (1688-1744), Charles Bridgeman (1690–1738), William Kent (1685-1748).

22

Natural Landscaping

Natural landscaping, also called native gardening, is the use of native plants, including trees, shrubs, groundcover, and grasses which are indigenous to the geographic area of the garden.

Natural landscaping is adapted to the climate, geography and hydrology and should require no pesticides, fertilizers and watering to maintain, given that native plants have adapted and evolved to local conditions over thousands of years. However, these applications may be necessary for some preventative care of trees and other vegetation in areas of degraded or weedy landscapes.

Native plants suit today's interest in 'low-maintenance' gardening and landscaping, with many species vigorous and hardy and able to survive winter cold and summer heat. Once established, they can flourish without irrigation or fertilization, and are resistant to most pests and diseases.

Many municipalities have quickly recognized the benefits of natural landscaping due to municipal budget constraints and reductions and the general public is now benefiting from the implementation of natural landscaping techniques to save water and create more personal time.

Examples include:

- Building rubble used as landfill may raise soil pH (i.e. create alkaline soil), which can be problematic in regions of acidic soils (with local plants adapted to acid soils).

- Buildings cast a substantial shade, this may give rise to conditions substantially shadier than needed by local plants.
- Soil which is high in organic material and nutrients is often introduced into gardens, or many gardeners will have used fertilizers. Plants from some areas, (e.g. many Australian plants are particularly sensitive to phosphorus).
- Many native plants are adapted to, and benefit from, periodic wildfires that occurred before and during pre-modern settlement. These fires can be simulated in the garden by either 'high mowing' or a controlled burn every few years.

Many weeds in an area are usually the result of imported plants. These plants become invasive because there are no natural controls such as disease, weather, or fauna in their new environment. They take over native habitats, reducing shelter and food for local fauna. Using local provenance plants increases the biodiversity of and is important for the health of a region's overall ecology.

Much of our wild areas have been destroyed to make room for development. Housing developments have replaced native habitats with houses and vast lawns. While development won't be stopped, gardeners can keep wild areas and green spaces filled with native species on their lots and in their communities.

Despite this, there are usually plenty of indigenous plants which will grow and thrive in the area one is trying to establish a native garden.

Ecological and Habitat

Native plants provide suitable habitat for native species of butterflies, birds, and other wildlife. They provide more variety in gardens by offering myriad alternatives to the over-planted cultivars and aliens. These plants have co-evolved with animals, fungi and microbes, to form a complex network of relationships. They are the foundation of their native ecosystems, or natural communities.

Such gardens often benefit from the plants being habituated to the climate and soil conditions present and may require fewer soil amendments or pesticides/herbicides in order to present a pleasing display.

Challenges

However, while local provenance plants have adapted to local conditions (which includes climate, soil, and other native plants and animals), there will often be instances, especially in cities, where one or more of these will have been radically altered.

Types

- fully forested with leaf debris on the forest floor
- desert with arid loving plants and succulents
- grassy meadow with a variety of wildflowers and water features
- lowlands savanna with grasses and native trees
- ocean dunescape with tall, salt tolerant grasses

Wildflower Gardens

Wildflower is a term used in some countries to describe the numerous showy flowers from some drier climates, most notably southwest Western Australia, Southern Africa and North America.

Rain Gardens

Rain gardens that absorb rainwater from gutters and impervious surfaces, work much better when planted with native plants tolerant to the alternate flooding and drying cycles. Some wildflower gardens attempt to recreate a prairie landscape, including native grasses along with the flowering plants, or forbs. Such gardens benefit the local wildlife, often attracting birds, butterflies and small mammals. By carefully choosing the plants in the garden, the gardener can encourage some of these visitors to the garden. One popular type of wildflower garden specializes in attracting butterflies and is called a butterfly garden.

The native plants used in wildflower gardens often have deep root systems. This makes them good plants for absorbing runoff and allowing the water to filter back into the local water table. Wildflower gardens that focus on capturing runoff in this fashion are called rain gardens.

Advantages

- no fertilization required
- no additional water
- more water available for other uses and other people
- zero to near zero work needed for maintenance
- no lawn mowing
- erosion reduced to a minimum
- natural landscaped plants take full advantage of rainfall
- when water restrictions are implemented, natural landscaped plants will survive, while more traditional plants may not increased habitat for native flora and fauna

- where heavily forested, provides shade on homes and businesses saving energy
- native plants rarely become invasive

Disadvantages

- not good for outdoor games that require a manicured turf.
- poisonous plants such as poison ivy and/or poison oak may make the habitat home.
- increased wild animal intrusion
- in certain areas, wildfires or bushfires may be of great concern.

Effect of New Construction

In new construction, builders can either avoid clear cutting or clearing an entire property and disturbing other large flora or builders can completely clear an area of all flora to save construction time and replace the clearing with juvenile specimens once the job is complete. The downside to this is additional costs involved with purchasing replacements. The builder may also choose to plant additional native trees and other flora after construction to help the property blend with natural surroundings.

In some planned developments, natural landscaping is the requirement. Builders may not remove trees larger than a specific diameter and owners may not arbitrarily cut trees without a permit.

Land Reclamation

Throughout the world, forested areas were turned into cattle grazing or farmland. Often this land is then turned into residential or commercial use property. By returning the land back to its original state prior to human disturbance, vast amounts of energy usage and increasing pollution can be reduced. Natural landscaping costs less to install than traditional landscaping and, after the initial few years, reduces maintenance costs, combats erosion, and accommodates storm and flood waters better.

Native Plant Societies

In many parts of the world, there are societies, clubs or local groups, such as Bushcare or ASGAP in Australia or the North American Native Plant Society, which are made up of gardeners interested in growing plants local to their area, state or country. They can be the best way to find out about (and to obtain, by buying or swapping) local native plants. Many members have spent years or decades cultivating local plants or bushwalking in local areas.

23

Japanese Garden

Japanese gardens, (*nihon teien*), that is, gardens in traditional Japanese style, can be found at private homes, in neighbourhood or city parks, and at historical landmarks such as Buddhist temples, Shinto shrines and old castles.

Some of the Japanese gardens most famous in the West, and within Japan as well, are dry gardens or rock gardens, *karesansui*. The tradition of the Tea masters has produced highly refined Japanese gardens of quite another style, evoking rural simplicity. In Japanese culture, garden-making is a high art, intimately related to the linked arts of calligraphy and ink painting. Since the end of the 19th century, Japanese gardens have also been adapted to Western settings.

Japanese gardens were developed under the influences of the distinctive and stylized Chinese gardens. One of the great interest for the historical development of the Japanese garden, bonseki, bonsai and related arts is the c. 1300 Zen monk Kokan Shiren and his rhymeprose essay *Rhymeprose on a Miniature Landscape Garden*.

The tradition of Japanese gardening was historically passed down from *sensei* to apprentice. In recent decades this has been supplemented by various trade schools. The opening words of Zoen's *Illustrations for designing mountain, water and hillside field landscapes* (1466) are "If you have not received the oral transmissions, you must not make gardens" and its closing admonition is 'You must never show this writing to outsiders. You must keep it secret'.

A catalogue of features 'typical' of the Japanese garden may be drawn up without inquiring deeply into the aesthetic underlying Japanese practice. Typical Japanese gardens have at their center a home from which the garden is viewed. In addition to residential architecture, depending on the archetype, Japanese gardens often contain several of these elements:

- Water, real or symbolic;
- Rocks or stone arrangements (or settings);
- A lantern, typically of stone;
- A teahouse or pavilion;
- An enclosure device such as a hedge, fence, or wall of traditional character;
- A bridge to the island, or stepping stones.

STYLES

Karesansui Gardens

Karesansui Gardens (or 'dry landscape' gardens were influenced mainly by Zen Buddhism and can be found at Zen temples of meditation (Japan Guide). Unlike other traditional gardens, there is no water present in Karesansui gardens. However, there is raked gravel or sand that simulates the feeling of water. The rocks/gravel used are chosen for their artistic shapes, and mosses as well as small shrubs are used to further garnish the Karesansui style (Japanese Lifestyle). All in all, the rocks and moss are used to represent ponds, islands, boats, seas, rivers, and mountains in an abstract way (Japan Guide). Example: Ryoan-ji, temple in Kyoto, has a garden famous for representing this style. Daisen-in, created in 1513, is also particularly renowned.

Tsukiyama Gardens

Tsukiyama Gardens often copy famous landscapes from China or Japan, and they commonly strive to make a smaller garden appear more spacious (Japan Guide). This is accomplished by utilizing shrubs to block views of surrounding buildings, and the garden's structure usually tries to make onlookers focus on nearby mountains in the distance (Japanese Lifestyle). By doing this, it seems that the garden has the mountains as part of its grounds. Ponds, streams, hills, stones, trees, flowers, bridges, and paths are also used frequently in this style (Japan Guide).

Chaniwa Gardens

Chaniwa Gardens are built for holding tea ceremonies. There is usually a tea house where the ceremonies occur, and the styles of both the hut and garden are based on the simple concepts of the sado (Japan Guide). Usually, there are stepping stones leading to the tea house, stone lanterns, and stone basins (tsukubai) where guests purify themselves before a ceremony (Japan Guide).

Japanese gardens might also fall into one of these styles:

- Kanshoh-style gardens which are viewed from a residence;
- Pond gardens, for viewing from a boat;
- Strolling gardens (*kaiyu-shiki*), for viewing a sequence of effects from a path which circumnavigates the garden. The 17th-century Katsura garden in Kyoto is a famous exemplar.

Other gardens also use similar rocks for decoration, some of which come from distant parts of Japan. In addition, bamboos and related plants, evergreens including Japanese black pine, and such deciduous trees as maples grow above a carpet of ferns and mosses.

The Use of Stones, Water, and Plantings

Though often thought of as tranquil sanctuaries that allow individuals to escape from the stresses of daily life, Japanese gardens are designed for a variety of purposes. Some gardens invite quiet contemplation, but may have also been intended for recreation, the display of rare plant specimens, or the exhibition of unusual rocks.

Kaiyu-shiki or Strolling Gardens require the observer to walk through the garden to fully appreciate it. A premeditated path takes observers through each unique area of a Japanese garden. Uneven surfaces are placed in specific spaces to prompt people to look down at particular points. When the observer looks up, they will see an eye-catching ornamentation which is intended to enlighten and revive the spirit of the observer. This type of design is known as the Japanese landscape principle of 'hide and reveal'.

Stones are used to construct the garden's paths, bridges, and walkways. Stones can also represent a geological presence where actual mountains are not viewable or present. They are sometimes placed in odd numbers and a majority of the groupings reflect triangular shapes, which often are the mountains of China. A water source in a Japanese garden should appear to be part of the natural surroundings; this is why one will not find fountains in traditional gardens. Man-made streams are built with curves and irregularities to create a serene and natural appearance. Lanterns are often placed beside some of the most prominent water basins (either a pond or a stream) in a garden. In some gardens one will find a dry pond or stream. Dry ponds and streams have as much impact as do the ones filled with water.

Green plants are another element of Japanese gardens. Japanese traditions prefer subtle green tones, but flowering trees and shrubs are also used. Many plants in imitated Japanese gardens of the West are indigenous to Japan, though some sacrifices must be made to account for the differentiating climates. Some plants, such as sugar maple and firebush, give the garden a broader palette of seasonal colour.

During the Asuka period (538-710), gardens were supposed to express Buddhism and Taoism through replicating the mountainous regions in China (Japanese Lifestyle). Ruins of these types of gardens can be found in Fujiwara and Heijyo castle towns (Japanese Lifestyle).

During the Heian period (794-1185), gardens shifted from solely representing religious beliefs to becoming, 'a place for ceremonies, amusement, and contemplation' (Miller). Gardens began to surround mansions that had the *shinden-zukuri* style (Japanese Lifestyle). In this style, the garden was located at the front of a building, also known as the south side (Japanese Lifestyle). As part of the garden style, there was water flowing through artificial passages that eventually spilled into ponds with little islands in them (Japanese Lifestyle). Very few of these gardens have survived to this day, and thus, are certainly a rarity in modern history. Despite the lack of modern day examples, we have the book of *Sakuteiki* that describes how people of this era formulated this garden style movement (Japanese Lifestyle). Later in this period, pure-land-style gardens became popular through the Pure Land Buddhism influence, and these gardens imitated the Paradise in the Western Pureland as a result (Japanese Lifestyle). During this shift in style, the Japanese also began to model their gardens and homes after the Amitabha hall style instead of the shinden style (Japanese Lifestyle). Examples of the Amitabha style can be seen today in Mahayana Hall (Nara), Byodoin (Uji, Kyoto), the Jyoruri Temple, and Motsuji Temple (Hiraizumi, Nishi, Iwai, Iwate) (Japanese Lifestyle).

In the Kamakura and Muromachi periods (1185-1573), a great many gardens were created during these two time periods due to improved garden techniques and the development of Syoinzukuri style (Japanese Lifestyle). Zen beliefs were also flourishing at this time and had great influences over garden techniques and purposes. Another factor that allowed gardens to flourish stems from the fact that the shoguns simply enjoyed gardens. Dry landscape style also emerged during this time (Japanese Lifestyle). A notable gardener who appeared during these periods is Soseki Muso: He made Saihoji Temple (Kyoto), Tenruji Temple (Kyoto), and Zuizenji Temple (Kamakura) gardens. (Japanese Lifestyle).

After the Muromachi Period, Japanese tea ceremonies became an intricate part of Japanese culture (Japanese Lifestyle). Sen no Rikyu (1517-1591) created the traditional style of a tea house where there was usually a roji ('dewy path') leading to the house (Japanese Lifestyle). Besides the tea houses, gardens constructed in the Edo period (1603-1868) reflected the tastes and style of each individual shogun ruler. Instead of being a religious symbol, gardens shifted to being a symbol of a shogun's prestige and power (Miller). These tea house styled houses and gardens can be seen in Kenrokuen (Kanazawa), Koraku-en (Okayama), Ritsurin Park (Takamsatsu), Koishikawa Korakuen (Tokyo), and Suizenji Park (Kumamoto) (Japanese Lifestyle).Many poems were inspired and written about the different Japanese Gardens. An example of the poems written includes:

> Chiimei's haiku about a tea ceremony hut and garden: "I laid a foundation and roughly thatched roof. I fastened hinges to the joints of the beams, the easier to move elsewhere should anything displease me. ... Since first I hid my traces here in the heart of Mount Hino, I have added a lean-to on the south and a porch of bamboo. On the west I have built a shelf for holy water, and inside the hut, along the west wall, I have installed an image of Amida. ... Above the sliding door that faces north I have built a little shelf on which I keep three or four black leather baskets that contain books of poetry and music and extracts from the sacred writings. Beside them stand a folding iioto and a lute. Along the east wall I have spread long fern fronds and mats of straw, which serve as my bed for the night. I have cut open a window in the eastern wall, and beneath it have made a desk. Near my pillow is a square brazier in which I burn brushwood. To the north of the hut I have staked out a small plot of land that I have enclosed with a rough fence and made into a garden. I grow many species of herbs there."

After the tea ceremony was refined by Sen Rikyu, the tea garden, house, and utensils all served as a way to "awaken consciousness and to realize with humility our relationship with all that is around us and with the universe itself (Miller)." Also, tea ceremonies were partly designed to teach participants how to gain absolute control over body and mind. As a result, 'it emphasizes not disconnection but connection between body movement and mind'. Culturally, the Japanese followed the five Confucian virtues (loyalty, righteousness, politeness, wisdom, and trust) to ground these tea ceremony ideals off of. In short, the tea ceremonies were a cultural activity to teach Japanese/Confucian virtues that were important for life.

Noteworthy Japanese Gardens

The Minister of Education, Culture, Sports, Science and Technology of the government of Japan designates the most notable of the nation's scenic beauty as Special Places of Scenic Beauty, under the Law for the Protection of Cultural Properties. As of March 1, 2007, 29 sites are listed, more than a half of which are Japanese gardens.

In Japan

The Minister of Education, Culture, Sports, Science and Technology of the government of Japan designates the most notable of the nation's scenic beauty as Special Places of Scenic Beauty, under the Law for the Protection of Cultural Properties. As of March 1, 2007, 29 sites are listed, more than a half of which are Japanese gardens, as below:

- Boldface entries specify world heritage sites.
- Tohoku region
- Motsu-ji garden (Hiraizumi, Iwate)
- Kanto region
- Kairaku-en (Mito, Ibaraki)
- Rikugi-en (Bunkyo, Tokyo)
- Kyu Hamarikyu gardens (Chuo, Tokyo)
- Chubu region
- Kenroku-en (Kanazawa, Ishikawa)
- Kansai region
- Byodo-in garden (Uji, Kyoto)
- Jisho-ji garden (Kyoto, Kyoto)
- Nijo Castle Ninomaru garden (Kyoto, Kyoto)
- Rokuon-ji garden (Kyoto, Kyoto)
- Ryoan-ji garden (Kyoto, Kyoto)
- Tenryu-ji Garden (Kyoto, Kyoto)
- The garden of Sanboin in Daigo-ji (Kyoto, Kyoto)
- The moss garden of Saiho-ji (the 'Moss Temple') (Kyoto, Kyoto)
- Daitoku-ji garden (Kyoto, Kyoto)

- The garden of Daisen-in in Daitoku-ji (Kyoto, Kyoto)
- Isuien garden (Nara, Nara)
- Negoro-ji garden (Iwade, Wakayama)
- Chugoku region
- Adachi museum of art garden (Yasugi, Shimane)
- Koraku-en (Okayama, Okayama)
- Matsue Vogel Park (Matsue)
- Shuraku-en, (Tsuyama)
- Shikoku Region
- Ritsurin Park (Takamatsu, Kagawa)
- Kyushu Region
- Suizenji Joju-en (Kumamoto, Kumamoto)
- Ryukyu Islands
- Shikina-en (Naha, Okinawa)

However, the Education Minister is not eligible to have jurisdiction over any imperial property. These two gardens, administered by Imperial Household Agency, are also considered to be great masterpieces.

- Katsura Imperial Villa
- Shugaku-in Imperial Villa

In the English-speaking world

The aesthetic of Japanese gardens was introduced to the English-speaking community by Josiah Conder's *Landscape Gardening in Japan*. It sparked the first Japanese gardens in the West. A second edition was required in 1912. Conder's principles have sometimes proved hard to follow:

> "Robbed of its local garb and mannerisms, the Japanese method reveals aesthetic principles applicable to the gardens of any country, teaching, as it does, how to convert into a poem or picture a composition, which, with all its variety of detail, otherwise lacks unity and intent"

Samuel Newsom's *Japanese Garden Construction* (1939) offered Japanese aesthetic as a corrective in the construction of rock gardens, which owed their quite separate origins in the West to the mid-19th century desire to grow alpines in an approximation of Alpine scree.

Japanese Rock Garden

The Japanese rock gardens (*karesansui*) or 'dry landscape' gardens, often called 'Zen gardens' were influenced mainly by Zen Buddhism and can be found at Zen temples of meditation.

Japanese gardens are a living work of art in which the plants and trees are ever changing with the seasons. As they grow and mature, they are constantly sculpted to maintain and enhance the overall experience; hence, a Japanese garden is never the same and never really finished. The underlying structure of a Japanese garden is determined by the architecture; that is, the framework of enduring elements such as buildings, verandas and terraces, paths, tsukiyama (artificial hills), and stone compositions. Over time, it is only as good as the careful maintenance that it receives by those skilled in the art of training and pruning. Part of the art is to keep the garden almost static, like a painting.

Karesansui gardens can be extremely abstract and represent (miniature) landscapes also called 'mind-scapes'. This Buddhist preferred way to express cosmic beauty in worldly environments is inextricable from Zen Buddhism.

A brief definition of karesansui from the 'Bilingual dictionary of Japanese Garden Terms'

"Dry landscape (garden); dry garden. A garden style unique to Japan, which appeared in the Muromachi period (1392-1568). Using neither ponds nor streams, it makes symbolic representations of natural landscapes using stone arrangements, white sand, moss and pruned trees. In Sakuteiki (a garden book with notes on garden making: see the notes) of the Heian period (794-1185), the term indicated a stone arrangement in a part of the garden without water".

Unlike other traditional gardens, there is no water present in Karesansui gardens (or the karesansui compartment of a garden). There is gravel or sand, raked or not raked, that symbolizes sea, ocean, rivers or lakes.

Australia

- Canberra Nara park in Lennox Gardens, Canberra
- Canberra Nara Park
- Cowra Japanese Garden, Cowra, New South Wales
- Frankston High School
- Himeji Gardens, Adelaide
- Melbourne Zoo

- 'Tsuki-yama-chisen' Japanese Garden, Brisbane
- Nerima Gardens, Ipswich
- Toowomba Japanese Garden, Ju Raku En, Queensland

The act of raking the gravel into a pattern recalling waves or rippling water has an aesthetic function. Zen priests practice this raking also to help them focus their concentration. Achieving perfection of lines is not easy. Rakes are according to the patterns of ridges as desired and limited to some of the stone objects situated within the gravel area. Nonetheless often the patterns are not static. Developing variations in patterns is a creative and inspiring challenge.

Stone arrangements and other miniature elements are used to represent mountains and natural water elements and scenes, islands, rivers and waterfalls. Stone and shaped shrubs (*karikomi, hako-zukuri* topiary) are used interchangeable. In most gardens moss is used as a ground cover to create 'land' covered by forest.

Other, mostly stone, objects are sometimes used symbolically to represent mountains, islands, boats, or even people. Karesansui gardens are often, but not always, meant to be viewed from a single vantage point from a seated position.

In the garden book *Sakuteiki* 'Creating a garden' is expressed as 'setting stones', *ishi wo taten koto*; literally, the 'act of setting stones upright'. At the time the *Sakuteiki* was written, the placement of stones was perceived as the primary act of gardening. Similar expressions are also used in the text, however, to mean literally 'setting garden stones' rather than 'creating gardens'.

Make sure that all the stones, right down to the front of the arrangement, are placed with their best sides showing. If a stone has an ugly-looking top you should place it so as to give prominence to its side. Even if this means it has to lean at a considerable angle, no one will notice. There should always be more horizontal than vertical stones. If there are 'running away' stones there must be 'chasing' stones. If there are 'leaning' stones, there must be 'supporting' stones.

And note again that in many cases stone and shaped shrubs (karikomi) can be used interchangeably.

The influence of Zen on garden design was (probably) first described as such by Kuck n the early 20th century and disputed by Kuitert by the end of that century. What is not disputed is the fact that karesansui garden scenery was (and still is) inspired (or even based on) originally Chinese and later also Japanese, landscape paintings.

Though each garden is different in its composition, they mostly use rock groupings and shrubs to represent a classic scene of mountains, valleys and waterfalls taken from Chinese landscape painting. In some of them the view also incorporates existing scenery, e.g. the hills behind, as 'borrowed scenery' (using a technique called *Shakkei*).

A famous Japanese rock garden is at Ryoan-ji in northwest Kyoto, Japan.

The garden is 30 meters long from east to west and 10 meters from north to south. There are no trees, just 15 irregularly shaped rocks of varying sizes, some surrounded by moss, arranged in a bed of white gravel/sand that is raked every day.

The rocks of various sizes are arranged on small white pebbles in five groups, each comprising five, two, three, two, and three rocks. The garden contains 15 rocks arranged on the surface of white pebbles in such a manner that visitors can see only 14 of them at once, from whichever angle the garden is viewed.

The garden is not attributed to any single designer, although it is commonly believed that a leading monochrome artist named Soami (1480-1525), in association with Daisen-in, designed and laid out the garden. However Ryoan-ji's records are contradictory and indicate some other makers, and the back of one of the 15 stones is inscribed with the names of Kotaro and Hikojiro, who might have been two of the workers that did the actual construction.

There have been many attempts to explain the karesansui garden's layout. Some of these are:

- The gravel represents ocean and the rocks represent the islands of Japan;
- The rocks represent a mother tiger with her cubs, swimming to a dragon;
- The rocks form part of the kanji for *heart* or *mind;*
- See Ryoan-ji for a mathematical analysis of a rock garden.

A recent suggestion by Gert van Tonder of Kyoto University and Michael Lyons, of Ritsumeikan University, is that the rocks form the subliminal image of a tree. This image cannot be consciously perceived when looking at them; the researchers claim the subconscious mind is able to see a subtle association between the rocks. They believe this is responsible for the calming effect of the garden and is also made to have a quiet place for meditation, however their comments are speculation and not supported by Japanese traditions.

24

Persian Gardens

The tradition and style of garden design of Persian gardens (Persian influenced the design of gardens from Andalusia to India. The Taj Mahal is one of the largest Persian gardens of the world, but the gardens of the Alhambra equally show the influence of Persian garden style on a more intimate scale.

From the time of the Achaemenid dynasty the idea of an earthly paradise spread through Persian literature and example to other cultures, both the Hellenistic gardens of the Seleucids and the Ptolemies in Alexandria. The Avestan word *pairidaêza*, Old Persian *paridaida*, Median *paridaiza* (walled-around, i.e., a walled garden), was transliterated into Greek *paradeisoi*, then rendered into the Latin *paradisus*, and from there entered into European languages, e.g., French *paradis*, German *Paradies*, and English *paradise*. The word entered Semitic languages as well: Akkadian *pardesu*, Hebrew *pardes*, and Arabic *firdaws*.

As the word expresses, such gardens would have been enclosed. The garden's purpose was, and is, to provide a place for protected relaxation in a variety of manners: spiritual, and leisurely (such as meetings with friends), essentially a *paradise on earth*. The Persian word for 'enclosed space' was *pairi-daeza*, a term that was adopted by Christian mythology to describe the garden of Eden or Paradise on earth.

The manner in which the garden is constructed may be formal (with an emphasis on structure) or casual (with an emphasis on nature), following several simple rules governing the design. This is said to allow a maximisation, in terms of function and emotion, of what may be done in the garden.

The origin of Persian gardens may date back as far as 4000 BCE; the decorated pottery of that time displays the typical cross plan of the Persian garden. The outline of Cyrus the Great's garden, built around 500 BCE, is still viewable today.

During the reign of the Sassanids (third to seventh century CE), and under the influence of Zoroastrianism, the presence of water in art grew increasingly important. This trend manifested itself in garden design with greater emphasis placed on fountains and ponds in gardens.

During the Arab occupation the aesthetic aspect of the garden increased in importance, overtaking the utility of the garden. During this time the aesthetic rules by which the garden is governed grew in importance. An example of this is the *chahar bagh* ( ), a form of garden which attempts to emulate Eden, having four rivers and four quadrants, representing the world. The design sometimes extends one axis longer than the cross-axis and creaters water channels running through each of the four gardens to connect to a central pool.

The invasion of Persia by the Mongols in the thirteenth century saw a new emphasis on highly ornate structure within the garden, examples of which include tree peonies and chrysanthemums. The Mongol empire then carried a Persian garden tradition to other parts of their empire (notably India).

Babur introduced the Persian garden to India; the now unkempt Aram Bagh garden in Agra was the first of many Persian gardens he created. The Persian concept of an ideal, paradise-like garden is perfectly embodied in the Taj Mahal.

The Safavid Dynasty (seventeenth to eighteenth century) built and developed grand and epic layouts that went beyond being a simple extension to a palace and became an integral aesthetic and functional part of it. In the following centuries European garden design began to influence Persia, particularly the design of France and secondarily that of Russia and the United Kingdom. Western influences led to changes in the use of water and the species used in bedding.

The traditional forms and style are still used among the population of Iran. They are also be found in historic sites, museums and affixed to the houses of the rich.

Sunlight and its effects were an important factor of structural design in Persian gardens. Textures and shapes were specifically chosen by architects to harness the light.

Due to the dry heat of Iran, shade is also very important in the garden, without which it could not be usable. Trees and trellises largely feature as biotic shade; pavilions and walls are also structurally prominent in blocking the sun.

Also related to the heat is the importance of water in the gardens. A form of underground tunnel, below the water table, called a qanat is used to irrigate the garden and its environs. Well-like structures then connect to the qanat, enabling the drawing of water.

Alternatively, an animal driven Persian well would be used to draw water to the surface. Such wheel systems could also be used to move water around surface water systems, such as those which exist in the *chahar bagh* style. Trees were often planted in a ditch called a *jub*, which prevented water evaporation and allowed the water quick access to the tree roots.

The Persian style often attempts to integrate indoors with outdoors through the connection of a surrounding garden with an inner courtyard. Designers often place architectural elements such as vaulted arches between the outer and interior areas to open up the divide between them.

The oldest representational descriptions and illustrations of Persian gardens come from travelers who reached Iran from lands to the west. These accounts include Ibn Battuta in the fourteenth century, Ruy Gonzáles de Clavijo in the fifteenth century and Engelbert Kaempfer in the seventeenth century. Battuta and Clavijo make only passing references to gardens and do not describe their design.

Kaempfer made careful drawings and converted them into detailed engravings after his return to Europe. They show chahar bagh type gardens with the following features: an enclosing wall, rectangular pools, an internal network of canals, garden pavilions and lush planting. There are surviving examples of this garden type at Yazd (Dowlatabad) and at Kashan (Bagh-e Fin). The location of the gardens Kaempfer illustrated in Isfahan (city) can be identified.

The six primary styles of the Persian garden may be seen in the following table, which puts them in the context of their function and style. Gardens are not limited to a particular style, but often integrate different styles, or have areas with different functions and styles.

Hayat

Publicly, it is a classical Persian layout with heavy emphasis on aesthetics over function. Man-made structures in the garden are particularly important, with arches and pools (which may be used to bathe). The ground is often covered in gravel flagged with stone. Plantings are typically very simple — such as a line of trees, which also provide shade.

Privately, these gardens are often pool-centred and again structural. The pool serves as a focus and source of humidity for the surrounding atmosphere. Again, there are few plants - this is often due to the limited water available in urban areas.

Meidan

This is a public, formal garden that puts more emphasis on the biotic element than the *hayat* and that minimises structure. Plants range from trees, to shrubs, to bedding plants, to grasses. Again, there are elements such as a pool and gravel pathways which divide the lawn. When structures are used, they are often built, as in the case of pavilions, to provide shade.

Chahar Bagh

These gardens are private and formal - the basic structure consists of four quadrants divided by waterways or pathways. Traditionally, such gardens would be used in work-related functions for the rich (such as entertaining ambassadors). These gardens balance structure with greenery, with the plants often around the periphery of a pool and path based structure.

Park

Much like many other parks, the Persian park serves a casual public function with emphasis on plant life. They provide pathways and seating, but are otherwise usually limited in terms of structural elements. The purpose of such places is relaxation and socialisation.

Like the other casual garden, the park, *bagh* emphasizes the natural and green aspect of the garden. Unlike the park it is a private area often affixed to houses and often consisting of lawns, trees, and ground plants. The waterways and pathways stand out less than in the more formal counterparts and are largely functional. The primary function of such areas is familial relaxation.

25

Greek Gardens

A distinction is made between Greek gardens, made in ancient Greece, and Hellenistic gardens, made under the influence of Greek culture in late classical times. Little is known about either.

Before the coming of proto-Greeks into the Aegean, Minoan culture represented gardens, in the form of subtly tamed wild-seeming landscapes, shown in frescoes, notably in a stylised floral sacred landscape with some Egyptianising features represented in fragments of a Middle Minoan fresco at Amnisos, northeast of Knossos. In the east wing of the palace at Phaistos, Maria Shaw believes, fissures and tool-trimmed holes may once have been planted. In the post-Minoan world, Mycenaean art concentrates on human interactions, where the natural world takes a lessened role, and following the collapse of Mycenaean palace-culture and the loss of the literacy connected with it, pleasure gardens are unlikely to have been a feature of the 'Greek Dark Age'.

In the eighth century BCE the works of Homer contain one reference to gardens, in the Neverland of Alcinous in the purely mythic Phaeacia, which stood as much apart from the known world of Homer's hearers as it did from the heroic world of Achaeans he was recreating, with much poetic licence:

> 'We live far off', said Nausicaa, 'surrounded by the stormy sea, the outermost of men, and no other mortals have dealing with us'.

"Now, you'll find a splendid grove along the road — poplars, sacred to Pallas — a bubbling spring's inside and meadows run around it. There lies my father's estate,his blossoming orchard too, as far from town as a man's strong shout can carry. Take a seat there"

The gardens of the palace were of an unearthly lushness, in the fenced orchard outside the courtyard, fronting the high gates.

"Here luxuriant trees are always in their prime pomegranates and pears, and apples glowing red, succulent figs and olives swelling sleek and dark. And the yield of all these trees will never flag or die, neither in winter nor in summer, a harvest all year round."

The description is beloved of writers on gardens, nevertheless. No such gardens were known to Homer's contemporaries, as far as archaeologists can discern, any more than palaces like Alcinous', whose very doors were of bronze. The gardens of Greek myth were *untended* gardens, maintained in orderly fashion simply because order, *themis*, was in the nature of things, as in the garden of the Hesperides, which was an orchard.

Archaeologists have not identified planted courtyards within the palaces of Mycenean culture nor in Greek houses of the Classical period. Public places were planted with trees, as Plato directed in his *Laws*, "The fountains of water, whether of rivers or springs, shall be ornamented with plantings and buildings for beauty", though he does not offer details.

In 1936 the surroundings of the Temple of Hephaestus at Athens were excavated to bare rock, in which rectangular planting pits were identified, which ran round three sides of the temple but not across its front and were lined up with the columns of the temple. In their bases were the shattered remains of flower pots in which layered stems had been rooted; however, associated coins show that the first of these plantings had been made not before the third century BCE. By that time, in mainland Greece and Ionia, the influence of Achaemenid Persia was paramount in humanly-tended gardens, but in the previous century, of Alexander the Great, Plutarch observed that as a boy he would inquire of Persian visitors to his father's court in Macedon, about Persian roads and military organization, but never of the Hanging Gardens of Babylon; Herodotus, who probably visited Babylon in the mid-fifth century, does not mention the hanging gardens. Xenophon, under Achaemenid Persian influence, planted a grove upon his return to Athens. The myth, set in Macedon, of Silenus discovered drunken by Midas can be dated to the Hellenistic period simply from its setting, a rose garden.

In Athens, the first private pleasure gardens appear in literary sources in the fourth century. The Academy had its site in an ancient grove of plane trees sacred to an obscure archaic hero, Akademos. Sacred groves were never actively planted, but simply existed from time immemorial and were *recognized* as sacred: hey have no place in the history of gardens, save as a resort for contemplation and, at Plato's Academy, for intellectual discourse. By contrast, the olive trees in the Academy, watered by the river Cephissus, were planted, grown, it was said, from slips taken of the sacred olive at the Erechtheum. The *temenos*, or sacred ground, of the Academy was walled round, for ritual reasons, as pleasure gardens would be, for practical ones; within its precincts were buildings: small temples, shrines and tombs, in addition to that of the presiding hero. In 322 BCE Theophrastus, the father of botany, inherited Aristotles garden, along with his scholars and his library; of the garden we know only that it had a walk, and that Theophrastus lectured there: it may have been in some respects a botanical garden with a scientific rather than recreational purpose. On his return to Athens in 306 BCE, the philosopher Epicurus founded The Garden, a school named for the garden he owned about halfway between the Stoa and the Academy that served as the school's meeting place; little is actually known of the ascetic philosopher's garden, though in cultural history it grew retrospectively in delight: of his garden at Geneva, *Les Délices*, Voltaire could exclaim, with more enthusiasm than history, "It is the palace of a philosopher with the gardens of Epicurus — it is a delicious retreat". Gardens of Adonis, under Syrian influence, were simple plantings of herbal seedlings grown in saucers and pots, which, when they collapsed in the heat of summer, were the signal for mourning for Adonis among his female adherents: these were not gardens in any general sense.

Though Harpalus, Alexander's successor at Babylon, grew some Greek plants in the royal palace and walks, mainland Greece, mother of democracy and Western cultural traditions, was not the mother of European gardens: the great Hellenistic garden was that of the Ptolemaic dynasty in Alexandria, a grand, walled paradise landscape that included the famous Library, part of the Musaeum. Water-powered automata and water organs featured in Hellenistic gardens, playthings devised by technicians such as Hero of Alexandria, who, not incidentally, also devised machinery for the stage. In late classical times the peristyle form became dominant in grand private houses. This was a paved courtyard, which came to be outfitted with potted plants, a Persian and Egyptian idea, surrounded by a roofed colonnade. It was used for palaces and gymnasia.

Index